THE
JEWS
OF
DETROIT

THE JEWS OF DETROIT

From the Beginning, 1762-1914

ROBERT A. ROCKAWAY

WAYNE STATE UNIVERSITY PRESS   DETROIT   1986

Copyright © 1986 by Wayne State University Press,
Detroit, Michigan 48202. All rights are reserved.
No part of this book may be reproduced without formal permission.

ISBN 0-8143-1808-8

Library of Congress Cataloging-in-Publication Data

Rockaway, Robert A., 1939-
    The Jews of Detroit.

    (Great Lakes books)
    Bibliography: p.
    Includes index.
    1. Jews—Michigan—Detroit—History.   2. Detroit
(Mich.)—History.   I. Title.   II. Series.
F574.D49J567   1986   977.4′34004924   86-15866
ISBN 0-8143-1808-8

TO MY PARENTS AND THE MEMORY OF MY GRANDPARENTS

CONTENTS

ILLUSTRATIONS AND MAPS

ILLUSTRATIONS

MAPS

PREFACE

THIS VOLUME IS A HISTORY of the Detroit Jewish community from 1762 to the onset of World War I. Although this period preceded my own life, it was also a personal journey through the past. My grandparents came to Detroit from Russia before the First World War, and in writing this book I not only learned more about them but about myself as well.

The purpose of this study, which is a revised and expanded version of my doctoral dissertation, is to acquaint the Detroit Jewish community of today with its "roots." I am indebted to the late Irving I. Katz for opening the archives of Temple Beth El to me, to Aid and Miriam Kushner, the present curators, and to the staffs of the American Jewish Archives, the American Jewish Historical Society, and the Burton Historical Collection for their assistance over the years. An unexpected source of information, nostalgia, and inspiration came from the "Hannah Schloss Old Timers," and the residents of the Detroit Jewish Home for the Aged, whose reminiscences enriched my knowledge of the early community. I am grateful to friends and colleagues—Philip Slomovitz, Leonard Simons, Bernard Goldman, Lloyd Gartner, Sidney Fine, Sam Warner, William Toll, Raymond Mohl, and others—for their input, comments, and suggestions. My gratitude goes as well to Anne Adamus, whose skillful editing greatly improved these pages.

I would also like to thank the Jewish Welfare Federation of Detroit, which sponsored the publication of this volume as part of its sixtieth anniversary.

Finally, a most special thanks goes to my wife, Batya, for her patience, understanding, and endless cups of tea.

Robert A. Rockaway
Tel Aviv University
January 1986

THE
JEWS
OF
DETROIT

A 1764 map of French Detroit. (Courtesy of the William L. Clements Library, University of Michigan.)

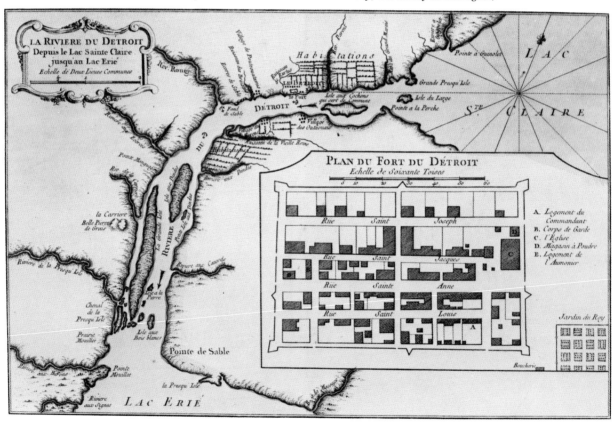

1. FRONTIER TOWN
Jews in Early Detroit

ON THE BANKS OF THE DETROIT RIVER, in an area as "richly set with islands as is a queen's necklace with jewels," Detroit in its early years failed to reflect the promise of its surroundings. The growth of the settlement, founded in 1701 by Antoine Laumet de la Mothe Cadillac as a trading outpost and French fort, was stunted by a series of events. The French and Indian Wars, in which the fort fell into British hands, the American Revolution, and hostile Indians prevented Detroit's population from exceeding twenty-two hundred inhabitants in its first century. The sleepy settlement primarily served as a trading post and stopover on the trade route from Montreal. Trappers and traders regularly visited Detroit, and among them were a few Jewish traders.

Detroit's first known Jewish settler was Chapman Abraham. The German-born trader arrived in Detroit from Montreal, Canada, in 1762 and remained intermittently until his death in 1783. He traded in wine and brandy, supplied muskets, gunpowder, ball and shot to the British, and bought and sold land. A year after his arrival in the settlement, the Indians of the Ohio Valley rose up against the British under the leadership of the Ottawa chief, Pontiac. In the

struggle, Pontiac's Conspiracy of 1763, the Indians captured every western fort except Detroit and Pittsburgh. Abraham, apparently unaware of the start of the hostilities, was transporting five boats of salable goods from Niagara to Detroit when the Indians captured him. They tied him to a stake and prepared to torture him first and then burn him. As was their custom, they allowed him a last drink before setting him ablaze. Unbeknownst to Abraham, the beverage was boiling hot. He raised the brew to his lips, drank, and, scalded, screamed in pain and threw the bowl and its contents into the face of the Indian who brought it. Believing this to be the act of a mad man, the Indians set him free. Whether true or not, this incident was used by the American poet and short-story writer Stephen Vincent Benet as the basis for his story "Jacob and the Indians." Abraham retained his membership in the Jewish congregation of Montreal and died in that city shortly after the birth of his son.[1]

Another German-born trader, Ezekiel Solomon, came to Fort Michilimackinac (Mackinaw City) in 1761, becoming the first Jewish settler in Michigan. Like Chapman Abraham, Solomon experienced the horrors of the Indian uprising. According to Pontiac's

A 1794 drawing of Detroit. Artist unknown. (Courtesy of the Burton Historical Collection.)

plan, the Indians were to simultaneously attack all the British forts and annihilate their garrisons at one stroke. At Michilimackinac (Mackinac), the Indians, in a planned action, began a game of lacrosse and, at an exciting moment, "accidently" threw the ball close to the fort's open gate. Pretending to chase after the ball, the players dropped their crosses, snatched weapons which their squaws had hidden under their blankets, and dashed into the fort. Once inside the stockade, they surprised and slaughtered the inhabitants. Solomon fell into the hands of the Ottawa Indians and was one of the few Englishmen, military or civilian, to survive. The Ottawas later took him to Montreal and ransomed him. In 1769, Solomon married Louise Dubois, a French Canadian woman, in

that city. Despite his marriage to a Christian, Solomon remained an active member of Montreal's Sephardic congregation, Shearith Israel, and served on its board of directors. Shearith Israel, founded in Montreal in 1768, was Canada's first Jewish congregation.

Using Mackinac as the base of his operations, Solomon traded in a wide variety of dry goods, cotton and linens, as well as flour, tobacco, iron ware, guns, gunpowder, shot and ball, rum, brandy, wine, and furs. When the revolutionary war broke out, the British encouraged the creation of a cooperative, centralized enterprise or "general store" at Mackinac. It was easier for the British to watch one company than twenty-five or thirty, and it would cut down on the smuggling

4

of much needed supplies into the United States, where there was a ready market for English manufactured and consumer goods. Under the terms of this plan, the traders created a single store, forebore to trade privately, and agreed to split the profits in proportion to the stock each put into the common pot. Solomon became a member of this company, believed to be the first department store operation in North America. In 1789 Solomon shifted to Detroit, living there for some years and engaging in business with John Askin, one of the area's most important merchants. Solomon later moved back to Mackinac and died there sometime between 1805 and 1808.[2]

British-born Levi Solomons, also known as Solomon ben Isaac Halevi, a cousin and business partner of Ezekiel Solomon, was also captured by the Ottawa Indians during Pontiac's uprising. However, unlike Ezekiel, who supported the British in their war

Levi Solomons. (Courtesy of the American Jewish Archives.)

An 1818 drawing of Detroit. (Courtesy of the Burton Historical Collection.)

An 1820 lithograph of the Detroit River, when the first steamer, *Walk-in-the-Water*, arrived in Detroit. (Courtesy of the Burton Historical Collection.)

with the Americans, Levi provided food and hospital facilities to the American forces who occupied Montreal for a brief period during the Revolution. He first came to Montreal from Albany, New York, in 1760, helped found Congregation Shearith Israel and served as its *parnas* (president) in 1778. Because he had supported the Americans, he was branded a traitor after the British recaptured Montreal and, together with his family, was evicted from his home on July 4, 1776.

Subsequently hounded out of Montreal, he removed for a time to Detroit, where he is listed as a resident in 1783. The American government never compensated Solomons for the losses he sustained or the help he rendered the revolutionary army. He later returned to Montreal, where he died in 1792.[3]

A number of other solitary Jews, of whom little is known, appeared in Detroit at the end of the eighteenth and early decades of the nineteenth centuries.

6

In 1798, two years after the Americans occupied Detroit, the name of Isaac Moses appears in the records of the Zion Lodge, Detroit's first Masonic lodge. Moses was likely the city's first Jewish mason. Ezekiel Peltier, born in 1799, the son of Sophia Solomon (one of Ezekiel Solomon's daughters) and Isidore Peltier, lived in Detroit for many years before moving to Monroe, Michigan, in 1846. According to the journal of the Common Council of Detroit, one Alex Cohen received payment for grading a street in 1835. Thereafter, Jewish names vanish from city records until 1845, when the *Detroit City Directory* lists the names of Solomon Bendit, Moses Rendskopf (later Rindskoff), and Solomon Freedman. The following year the *City Directory* contained three additional names, those of Adam Hersch, Jacob Silverman, and Frederick Cohen.

British-born Frederick Cohen came to Detroit from Woodstock, Canada, in 1837 and established himself as a prominent portrait painter, Michigan's first Jewish artist. Handsome, genial, and witty,

View of Detroit in 1836, painted in 1836 by American artist William James Bennett (1787–1844). Paint on canvas, 17.5″ by 25″, accession no. 34.24. (Courtesy of the Detroit Institute of Arts. Gift of the Fred Sanders Company in memory of its founder, Fred Sanders.)

Cohen billed himself as a "portrait, miniature, historical and scriptural painter," and enjoyed promenading about town in a brass-buttoned, blue swallow-tailed coat, a buff waistcoat, and a high, white beaver hat. Although considered something of a dandy, Cohen was nobody's fool. Once, a prominent Detroit mason contractor and his daughter, dissatisfied with Cohen's portraits of them, returned the paintings and refused to pay. Cohen thereupon painted asses' ears on the man's head and a beard on the daughter's face and hung the portraits in the post office. Shortly thereafter the contractor paid his bill. Apart from portraits, Cohen decorated panels for lake passenger steamers, an art form much appreciated by the traveling public of that day. In addition to his own work, Cohen taught painting, numbering Detroit marine artist Robert Hopkin and Lewis T. Ives, a well-known Michigan portrait painter, among his pupils. Cohen married in 1855 and moved to Oberlin, Ohio. He died during a hunting trip in 1858.[4]

Although they are not mentioned in the *City Directory*, it is known that Edward Kanter and Charles Bresler arrived in Detroit in the 1840s. Edward Kanter, a native of Breslau, Germany, came from a prominent Jewish family. His father was a prosperous linen merchant and his mother a relative of the German parliamentarian Edward Lasker. Kanter graduated from the Breslau Gymnasium equipped, among other things, with a knowledge of Greek, Latin, German, French, English, and Hebrew. A spirit of adventure seized him early in life and he ran away from home, first to Paris and then, as a stowaway, to New Orleans. He disembarked in New Orleans literally without a penny in his pocket and shortly thereafter contracted yellow fever. A relief committee of New Orleans Jewish residents cared for him until he recovered. One of the members of this committee, Isaac Hart, later moved to Detroit. Once well, Kanter peddled cigars, clerked in a drug store and, feeling restless again, worked his way north, passing through St. Louis, Missouri, Pekin, Illinois, and Chicago. He arrived in Detroit in 1844 at the age of twenty but soon moved on to Mackinac Island, Michigan, working as a

Frederick Cohen, portrait painter. (Courtesy of the Rabbi Leo M. Franklin Archives of Temple Beth El.)

Edward Kanter, friend to the Indians, Detroit's first Jewish banker, founder of the German American Bank, and state legislator. (Courtesy of the Rabbi Leo M. Franklin Archives of Temple Beth El.)

clerk and interpreter for the American Fur Company, the successor to John Jacob Astor's venture. Kanter's facility for languages showed itself in the rapidity with which he learned Indian dialects. In a short time, he mastered the Huron, Chippewa, and Pottawatomie tongues.

Kanter remained on Mackinac for eight years, returning to Detroit in 1852. He became Detroit's first Jewish banker when he helped to organize the Ameri-can National Bank in 1865 and founded the German American Bank in 1871. It was his unique friendship with the area's Indians, however, that conferred a special status on Kanter and made him something of a folk hero. Because of his bustling ways, the Indians dubbed Kanter "Bosh-bish-gay-bish-gon-sen," meaning "Firecracker," and never missed an opportunity to call on him in Detroit or to send him greetings. One summer day in 1860 passersby were startled to see

The Kanter block and the German American Bank, circa 1880. (Courtesy of the Burton Historical Collection.)

Kanter squatting solemnly and silently smoking with a group of Indians in front of his store. A delegation of chiefs on their way to see the Great Father in Washington would not pass through Detroit without first visiting and smoking a pipe of peace with their good friend "Firecracker." Detroit officialdom, mindful of Kanter's many contributions to the city, named a street after him in 1884.[5]

Charles Bresler, born in Germany in 1817, came to New York as a young man and started his business career peddling "Yankee notions," often going as far west as Detroit. He came to Michigan sometime in the 1840s, headquartering in Ypsilanti, where he bought horses for shipment back east. After residing in New York, Cincinnati, and Cleveland, he moved to Detroit and opened a fur business. This proved so successful that he opened branch offices in Europe. In the course of his long business career, he crossed the ocean more than 190 times. Bresler also made a fortune importing steel pens and retired as one of Detroit's first millionaires.[6]

In spite of its location on the Detroit River, which connects Lake St. Clair with Lake Erie and the upper Great Lakes with the lower Great Lakes, Detroit continued to be a small trading center through the early decades of the nineteenth century. Beginning in the 1830s, however, with the completion of the Erie Canal and improvements in the navigation of the Great Lakes and the expansion of the railroads, Detroit finally capitalized on its site. As a consequence, more and more immigrants came to the city for jobs, and by 1850 Detroit held enough Jews to form a community.[7]

NOTES

1. Irving I. Katz, *The Beth El Story* (Detroit: Wayne State University Press, 1955), pp. 22–34.

2. Katz, *Beth El*, pp. 13–22.

3. Katz, *Beth El*, pp. 34–36.

4. David E. Heineman, "Jewish Beginnings in Michigan before 1850," *Publications of the American Jewish Historical Society* 13 (1905), pp. 64–66; Katz, *Beth El*, pp. 47–49; *Detroit City Directory*, 1846, p. 169. Recent investigation has thrown doubt on whether Frederick Cohen was himself a Jew. The evidence indicates that while he somewhere had a male Jewish ancestor, he was not Jewish.

5. Silas Farmer, *History of Detroit and Wayne County and Early Michigan* (Detroit: Silas Farmer and Co., 1890; Gale Research Company, 1969), pp. 867–69, 942; Katz, *Beth El*, pp. 54–56; Heineman, "Jewish Beginnings," pp. 59–63.

6. Heineman, "Jewish Beginnings," p. 63; *Detroit Free Press,* December 13, 1898, p. 12.

7. Katz, *Beth El*, pp. 42, 47.

2. MAKING A HOME
Early Settlers and Settlement

FEW DETROITERS IN 1850 had ever seen a Jew. If they had any notion about Jews, it derived from ancient stereotypes, prejudices, and superstitions. The *Detroit Free Press* reflected this general ignorance by printing stories which characterized Jews as "mysterious," "cursed," and wanderers. As the Jewish population grew, so too did the public's awareness of them. The press mirrored this change in articles describing the lives of Detroit Jews and Jewish activities. The earliest of these were simple notices announcing the closing of Jewish businesses on Yom Kippur. By the end of the decade, however, the *Free Press* and *Detroit Daily Advertiser* featured lengthy pieces about Jewish holidays, such as Passover, and the manner of their celebration by Detroit's Jews.[1]

As in many other American cities between 1830 and 1860, the first Jews who arrived in Detroit were men, and they came from Germany, primarily Bavaria and Prussia. Although German in language, education, and general culture, Jews abandoned Germany because of the innumerable disabilities imposed on them. Restricted in their right to marry (so the government could prevent the Jewish population from increasing), handicapped in acquiring legal residence,

prohibited from practicing the trades they had learned, subjected to special taxes, and humiliated daily, many young Jewish men saw little future for themselves in Germany. While some fought for emancipation, others opted to emigrate to a free country.[2]

As a consequence of this emigration, the Jewish population of the United States increased from 4,000 in 1820 to 50,000 in 1850 to more than 250,000 by 1880. The immigrants were generally young, unmarried males, who sent for the rest of their families once they had established themselves. They arrived at a time of great economic and territorial growth in the United States, and the fact that they were single allowed them to easily move and change occupations, a distinct advantage in America's expanding economy. Large numbers of Jewish immigrants fanned out across the continent to Chicago, St. Louis, Cincinnati, and Milwaukee, as well as to smaller cities in the South and Far West. Most of those who traveled west began their careers as peddlers because a peddler needed little or no capital to start (merchants proved willing to extend them credit) and because peddling filled a vital economic role by bringing the city's goods to the countryside. With hard work and luck, the basket, trunk, and pack peddler might accumulate enough money to buy a horse and wagon and, later, a store. German Jewish peddlers supplied goods to German farmers, whose language and tastes they knew, in Michigan, Ohio, and Illinois.[3]

By mid-century, Detroit, with a population of 20,019, was Michigan's largest city and most important center for the traffic and trade in foodstuffs. Detroit retained its commercial character for the next twenty years, but situated near abundant natural resources such as timber, copper, iron, and lead, the city started to become an industrial center as well. In 1880, Detroit's population reached 116,340 persons, 39 percent of whom were foreign-born. Amongst the foreign-born, the Germans comprised the largest ethnic group.[4]

Detroit's economic potential and sizeable German community attracted German Jews, and by 1850 the city contained fifty-one Jews, twenty-nine males and twenty-two females. Of the twenty-nine adults (those eighteen and over), twenty-five had been born in Germany, two in the United States, one in England, and one in Poland. Occupationally, they included ten merchants, two cigar makers, a peddler, blacksmith, grocer, physician, and portrait painter. Most of the settlers came to Detroit from somewhere else in the United States. Isaac and Sarah Cozens arrived with their five children after more than ten years in New York; Leopold and Rachel Poppenheimer and their three children after more than eight years in New York; and Marcus and Betsy Cohen lived in New York and Ohio before settling in Detroit

Lithograph of Detroit, circa 1855. (Courtesy of the Burton Historical Collection.)

Campus Martius in 1860. (Courtesy of the Burton Historical Collection.)

with their four children. This pattern continued over the next sixty-five years: Detroit was the second, third, or even fourth stop of Jewish immigrants, but rarely the first.[5]

ECONOMIC LIFE

A great deal has been written about the economic mobility of the nineteenth-century German Jewish immigrants in America. Starting from peddler, so the legend goes, many rose to become merchant princes and bankers. Needless to say, this "rags to riches" myth is an exaggeration. While a number of German Jews did amass fortunes that rivaled those of America's post-Civil War entrepreneurs and fabled robber barons, the vast majority did not. It is true, however, that by the third quarter of the nineteenth century a majority of America's Jews had achieved solid middle- and upper-middle-class economic status. To what extent was this true for the Jews who settled in Detroit?[6]

By the 1870s Detroit's Jewish community contained a small group of men who rose from modest be-

Samuel Heavenrich, clothing manufacturer and business leader. (Courtesy of the Rabbi Leo M. Franklin Archives of Temple Beth El.)

Samuel Sykes's advertisement in D. W. Umberline's *City Directory* in 1860. (Courtesy of the Detroit Historical Museum.)

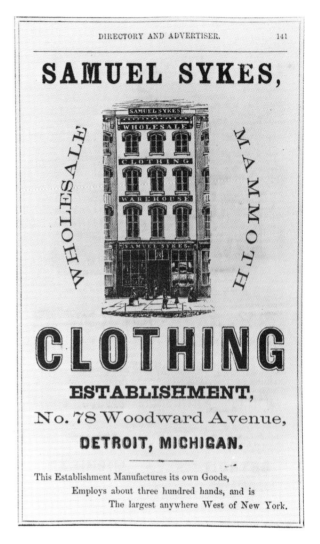

DIRECTORY AND ADVERTISER. 141

SAMUEL SYKES,

WHOLESALE   MAMMOTH

CLOTHING

ESTABLISHMENT,

No. 78 Woodward Avenue,

DETROIT, MICHIGAN.

This Establishment Manufactures its own Goods,
Employs about three hundred hands, and is
The largest anywhere West of New York.

ginnings to positions of wealth and prominence. Samuel Heavenrich came directly from Bavaria to Detroit in 1853, when he was fourteen years old. He began working for his brother-in-law, Samuel Sykes, an importer of "French and Belgian Broad Clothes, Cassimeres and Vestings." Heavenrich became Sykes's partner in 1860, and when the Civil War broke out they contracted to manufacture uniforms for Michigan's soldiers. This proved so profitable that Sykes retired in 1862, going to Europe with his family and leaving Heavenrich as sole proprietor of the business. Heavenrich's brother Simon joined him in 1863, and together they formed the Heavenrich Brothers Clothing firm. Giving up the retail end of the business in 1865, they devoted themselves to manufacturing clothing, and their factory was the first in the country to use steam-driven machinery for cutting several layers of cloth to a pattern at one time. By 1871 they owned a large building, employed over 350 people, and grossed more than $500,000 per year.[7]

14

Simon Heavenrich, clothing manufacturer and business leader. (Courtesy of the Rabbi Leo M. Franklin Archives of Temple Beth El.)

Heavenrich Brothers Clothing store in 1880. (Courtesy of the Detroit Historical Museum.)

After the failure of the Revolution of 1848, Simon Freedman, then twenty-three years old, left Germany to start a new life in America. Coming to Detroit in 1852, he and his brother Herman opened a dry goods business. Their enterprise prospered, and by 1870 each brother claimed more than $40,000 in real estate and $50,000 in personal property. Magnus and Martin Butzel arrived in Detroit in 1861 and joined their brother-in-law Emil Heineman, who had come ten years earlier, in the wholesale clothing trade. In 1862 they opened the firm of Heineman, Butzel and Company and supplied uniforms to the Union army. After the war, they manufactured ready-made clothing

Simon Freedman, clothing merchant and communal leader. (Courtesy of the Rabbi Leo M. Franklin Archives of Temple Beth El.)

Freedman and Brothers advertisement (*bottom, right*) in the Detroit *General Directory* in 1853. (Courtesy of the Rabbi Leo M. Franklin Archives of Temple Beth El.)

Heavenrich Brothers' advertisement in Clark's *City Directory*, 1862. (Courtesy of the Detroit Historical Museum.)

HEAVENRICH BRO'S
(SUCCESSORS TO S. SYKES & CO.,)
78 Woodward Avenue,
DETROIT, - MICHIGAN,

Would respectfully invite their friends and the public at large to the splendid and

WELL SELECTED STOCK
—OF—
READY-MADE
CLOTHING!

CLOTHS, CASSIMERES, VESTINGS,
TAILORS' TRIMMINGS AND
GENTS' FURNISHING GOODS,

Which they at all times keep on hand, in such large quantities and at such astonishing low prices as to defy competition. All they ask of the public is to give them a call, and everybody will be pleased, as well as satisfied that they can buy goods cheaper at the MAMMOTH CLOTHING HALL than in any other establishment in the Western country.

HEAVENRICH BROTHERS,
78 Woodward Avenue, Detroit,
and 29 Delaware Street, Leavenworth, Kansas.

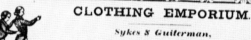

CLOTHING EMPORIUM.
Sykes S Guiterman,
south side of Jefferson Avenue, between Bates and Randolph Streets
IMPORTERS OF
French & Belgian Broad-Cloths, Cassimeres
AND VESTINGS.
MERCHANT TAILORS.
Wholesale and Retail Dealers in READY MADE CLOTHING, keep constantly on hand a general assortment of Gentlemen's Furnishing Goods.
SAM'L SYKES   SIMON GUITERMAN

I. KAUFFMANN,
Wholesale and Retail
CLOTHING EMPORIUM,
KEARSLEY BLOCK, JEFFERSON AVENUE,
DETROIT.
CLOTHING MADE TO ORDER   GOOD FIT WARRANTED

FREEDMAN & BROTHERS,
Dealers in Fancy, Staple, and Millinery Goods.
Wholesale and Retail,
No. 133, Jefferson Avenue, Detroit, Michigan.
Silks, Dress Goods and Shawls, of every description, Cloaks, Visites, Bonnets, Ribbons, Flowers, Fringes, Gimps, Trimmings, Silk and Thread Lace, Needlework, &c. &c.   The Trade and Milliners supplied on the most liberal terms.
JOSEPH FREEDMAN, Detroit, Mich.   SOLOMON FREEDMAN, N. York.
WILLIAM FREEDMAN, Cleveland, Ohio.

Martin Butzel, clothing manufacturer and civic leader. (Courtesy of the Rabbi Leo M. Franklin Archives of Temple Beth El.)

Emil S. Heineman's advertisement in D. W. Umberline's *City Directory* in 1861. (Courtesy of the Detroit Historical Museum.)

and men's furnishings. By 1880 their company had grown into one of the largest clothing manufacturing concerns in Michigan, employing 425 workers. The brothers Seligman and Emmanual Schloss were Bavarians who came to Detroit in 1851. They immediately entered the retail trade and, in 1853, branched out into the wholesale dry goods business. By 1880 their firm employed 320 people. The firms of Heineman and Butzel, the Heavenrich brothers, and the Schloss brothers were among the nineteen largest commercial establishments in Detroit in 1880.[8]

Not all of Detroit's successful Jews made their fortune in the clothing business. Morris Fechheimer, born in Bavaria in 1823, arrived in Detroit in 1851. He did begin his business career as a clothier, but was wiped out in the Panic of 1857. He started over by selling liquor, and in 1861 he entered into partnership with David Workum, opening the firm of Fechheimer

17

Morris Fechheimer, wine merchant and distiller. (Courtesy of the Rabbi Leo M. Franklin Archives of Temple Beth El.)

The wholesale clothing store of Heineman, Butzel and Company in 1880. (Courtesy of the Detroit Historical Museum.)

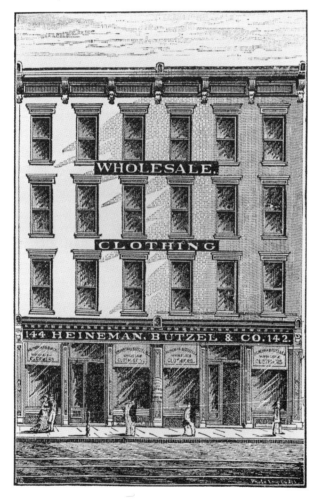

and Workum, Dealers in Wine and Liquors. When Workum left Detroit in 1877, Fechheimer and his brother Henry established a company that distilled bourbon and rye whiskies and imported wines and liquors. Occupying a five-story building on Larned Street, Morris C. Fechheimer and Company became one of Detroit's largest liquor wholesalers. Hungarian-born Julius Freud came with his parents and other members of his family to Eagle Harbor in northern Michigan's mining and timber country. Before he was twenty, he had opened a mining company store and a lumber business with his brother Leopold and operated a lumber mill in Saginaw, Michigan, and a flour mill in East Tawas, Michigan. In 1858, Freud moved to Detroit and sold real estate. Twenty years later, at age forty, he was a millionaire.[9]

These men's successes resulted from a combination of factors: their own astuteness and enterprise; the push the Civil War gave to Detroit's economy, especially to those engaged in manufacturing and selling ready-made clothing; and the fact that they came to

Morris C. Fechheimer and Company, importers of wine and
liquors. (Courtesy of the Rabbi Leo M. Franklin Archives of
Temple Beth El.)

Julius Freud, real estate dealer and civic leader (Courtesy of
the Rabbi Leo M. Franklin Archives of Temple Beth El.)

the city unmarried, which allowed them the freedom to experiment and take risks. In addition, all of the most successful individuals created family firms, which provided initial advantages in manpower and resources.

Samuel Heavenrich left a diary which shows that his own success resulted from his drive, hard work, luck, and family connections. Although he came to the United States alone, as a lad of fourteen, he was never left to his own resources. A family friend looked after him on board ship, secured him lodgings in New York, and arranged for his trip to Detroit. Once in Detroit, he did not have to search for work: he started immediately in his brother-in-law's business. As soon as Heavenrich entered the firm, he began learning English "so as to make myself useful in business." He had "no time for boys' sports or play, but [only for] business from morning till night," which meant from 7:00 A.M. to 9:00 P.M. After work, Heavenrich went to night school "to learn English and bookkeeping." And he and his family counted a banker, shipowner, and wealthy businessmen among their relatives and close friends.[10]

While not every Jew reaching Detroit during the 1850s and 1860s attained the financial pinnacle of these businessmen, many achieved some degree of economic mobility and improved their financial status by 1870. Isaac Wertheimer, who began as a peddler in 1858, became a clothing merchant and owned $1,000 in personal property by 1870; salesman Ludwig Levi became a clothier and by 1870, owned $4,000 in personal property and maintained a servant; and grocer Isaac Warshauer became a hat dealer and in 1870 owned $1,000 in personal property. Even those who remained in the same low-status occupation for some time achieved a degree of economic success in terms of increased wealth. By 1870 laborer Mauritz Mendelsohn, who arrived in Detroit in 1860, had amassed $3,000 in real estate and $500 in personal property; peddler Jacob Burnstine owned $500 in real estate and $300 in personal property; and peddler Levi Moses was worth more than $1,000 in 1870.[11]

An increasing number of Eastern European Jews, mostly Polish, began to settle in Detroit begin-ning in the 1860s. These immigrants differed from their German Jewish predecessors in that they were older, averaging thirty-seven years of age, married, and accompanied by their families. Most, like forty-seven-year-old Moses Edloff, thirty-two-year-old Harris Jacobs, and thirty-five-year-old Isaac Levi, had come with their wives and children from other places in the United States. A few, such as forty-year-old Nathan Zelliger, thirty-eight-year-old Solomon Esbonstine, and thirty-year-old Moses Levi and their families, immigrated to Detroit directly from Europe. And for some, Detroit was merely the latest stop in an ongoing odyssey. Abraham Joseph, forty-seven years old and with a wife and nine children in 1870, lived in England, New York, and Canada before coming to Detroit in 1869; forty-eight-year-old Abraham Kohn had already lived in New York, Pennsylvania, Illinois, and Wisconsin when he arrived in Detroit with his wife and five children; and fifty-four-year-old Albert Rosenfield dwelled in Maryland, Ohio, Illinois, and Kansas before settling in Detroit with his wife and seven children in 1865. Rosenfield stayed long enough in each place, however, for at least one of his children to be born there. Despite this influx of Eastern Europeans, the Germans remained the major ethnic group among Detroit's Jews through the 1870s, when the Jewish population grew to about one thousand.[12]

Peddling was a primary occupation among the Eastern European Jewish immigrants, as it had been for the earlier German Jewish settlers. Upon their arrival, over two-thirds of the Eastern European newcomers began working as peddlers because of the small amount of capital necessary to start and because of the relative speed with which one could commence earning a living—a crucial factor for men with families to support. Peddling also attracted Orthodox Jews, who were prohibited from working on the Sabbath, since peddlers could control the hours and days they worked. With money borrowed from friends, relatives, or Jewish loan associations, the peddler bought himself notions, dry goods, fruit, junk, and rags, which he hawked on Detroit's streets. Since most of Detroit's Eastern European Jews had been in the United States for varying periods of time, they knew some

English. This enabled them to roam all over the city, bargaining and selling their wares in other immigrant enclaves and in native American neighborhoods. Some of the more adventurous souls traveled to outlying communities to do business.

Although peddling offered independence and the opportunity to earn enough money to eventually open a shop or store, it was a difficult life. The long hours, hard work, and constant exposure to the elements took their toll on a peddler's health. Nevertheless, those who continued in the trade got a basic business training and learned how to deal with all kinds of people. Owing to the unfavorable economic conditions in the 1870s, resulting from the Panic of 1873, and the depression which followed, a number of the Eastern Europeans left Detroit to try their luck elsewhere. However, many of those who started as peddlers and chose to remain in the city continued in this occupation throughout the decade.[13]

In spite of the economic slump, Detroit's Jewish community attained solid middle class status by 1880. More than half of the city's employed Jewish males were proprietors or managers, compared to only 2 percent for the general male labor force, and over two-thirds of the Jewish males worked in white-collar occupations, as opposed to 25 percent for the city as a whole (see Tables 1, 2, and 3; Appendix A at the end of this volume contains all tables cited). Jews also had

A view of Woodward Avenue, looking north from the corner of Clifford Street, circa 1875. The group of trees is Grand Circus Park. (Courtesy of the Detroit Historical Museum.)

Map 1. German and Eastern European Residential Patterns, 1880

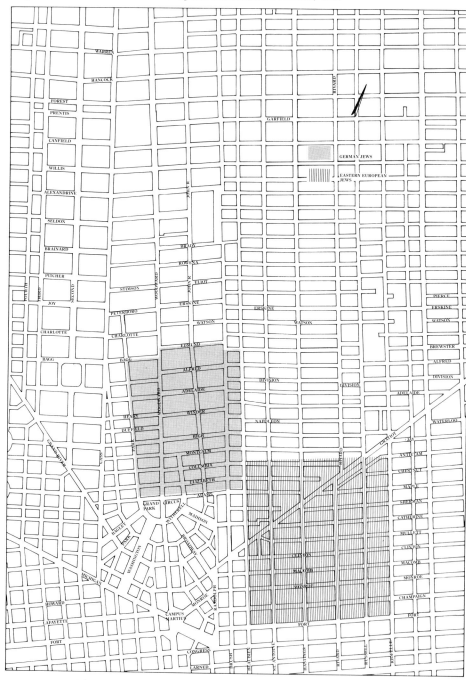

a higher proportion of white-collar workers than any other ethnic groups in the city; only native white Americans had a lower percentage of semiskilled and unskilled workers (Table 4). Overall, 70 percent of the Jews were in trade (business and commerce) and 17 percent in manufacturing versus 20 percent in trade and 46 percent in manufacturing for the general population (Table 5).

Contrasting the occupational distribution of Detroit's Jews with Jews in other American cities, we find that Detroit Jewry had a lower proportion of white-collar workers (69 percent) than Los Angeles (80 percent), Columbus, Ohio (83 percent), and Atlanta, Georgia (94 percent). However, the Detroit Jewish community contained a higher percentage of proprietors, managers, and officials (56 percent) than Los Angeles (44 percent) and Columbus (42 percent). Approximately 34 percent of the Jews in Los Angeles held clerical and sales positions; in Columbus it was 37.5 percent and in Detroit only 9 percent. In all of these communities, Jewish occupational mobility was greater than that of the general population.[14]

Once in Detroit, the early German Jewish immigrants tended to remain. More than 60 percent of the German Jewish heads of households in 1860 were still in Detroit twenty years later. This geographic stability is related to economic status: persons of high occupational status, such as proprietors, stayed in the community; those of low status did not. Within the Detroit Jewish community, however, the immigrants frequently changed residences. Those same heads of households in 1860 moved at least once by 1870.[15] On the other hand, more than 60 percent of the Eastern European Jews listed in the 1870 census and *Detroit City Directory* were no longer in the city by 1880.

Throughout the period between 1850 and 1880, Detroit still had an abundance of unused space within the city limits and even in the city's center. Detroit was also a city of single family homes: more than 92 percent of the city's homes in 1880 contained only one family. This sparse development and wealth of single family dwellings allowed Detroit to absorb a large number of immigrants without encountering the overcrowding already existing in cities like New York. The availability of space also gave people some freedom to choose where they would live. Depending on the quality and price of available housing and the accessibility to places of employment, these new Detroiters' choices of residence more often than not reflected their desire to associate with members of their own ethnic group or socioeconomic class.[16]

By 1880 the older German Jewish settlers lived alongside Germans and native white Americans employed in white-collar jobs in an area defined by Brewster on the north, Adams Street on the south, Park on the west, and Beaubien on the east. The Eastern Europeans dispersed amongst Germans of lower occupational status in an area circumscribed by Columbia on the north, Fort Street on the south, Riopelle on the east, and Beaubien on the west. Nothing even remotely resembling a Jewish ghetto as yet existed (see Map 1).

CIVIC AND POLITICAL LIFE

During the 1850s, Detroit's Jews were too busy earning a living and establishing themselves to spend much time in politics. Two exceptions were Edward Kanter and Liebman Adler. Kanter, a Democrat, was elected to one term in the state legislature in 1856, twice ran for the office of state treasurer, and acted as secretary of the Democratic State Central Committee in the 1860s. In the bitterly fought election of 1856, in which the nativistic Know-Nothing movement endeavored to keep foreign-born immigrants from holding elective office, the Know-Nothing party's candidate for mayor received 2,026 votes, as compared to the 2,798 for the Democratic winner, and the Know-Nothings won half of the seats on the city council. Kanter's legislative victory was a personal tribute in that the local Protestant churches supported him, and he received more votes than any of the native-born candidates also elected to the legislature from Detroit. Liebman Adler, rabbi of Congregation Beth El, never ran for elective office, but actively campaigned for the abolitionist cause during his stay in Detroit from 1854

23

Picture of First Michigan Volunteer Infantry on Campus Martius in 1861. (Courtesy of the Burton Historical Collection.)

to 1861. Never equivocal in his antislavery senti-ments, Adler openly declared for the Republican Party because of its stance on this issue.[17]

Detroit's native-born population expressed lit-tle overt antagonism toward Kanter's political activ-ity, but during the 1856 campaign segments of the city's German community attacked his Jewishness. Commenting on this in the German Jewish news-paper, *Die Deborah*, Liebman Adler noted that a few days before the election the local German Republican newspaper warned German voters to "keep an eye on the Jewish population," and on election day even edu-cated Germans sought to influence voters by remind-ing them that Kanter was a Jew. Adler castigated the newspaper for its "stupid and dangerous incitement to naked power and infringement of the free right to vote," and the German people for their propensity to "fanaticism." He suggested that the German in the

24

United States "should learn moderation from his kindred neighbor, the Anglo-Saxon American."[18]

Detroit was not the only city whose German newspaper attacked Jews. The German press in Baltimore, for example, was similarly inclined. One of the reasons for this animosity was that many of the German residents of these cities, themselves recent immigrants, carried to America some of the anti-Jewish sentiments and stereotypes popular in their homeland. Germany had a long and virulent history of anti-Semitism stretching back to the Crusades. Throughout the nineteenth century even enlightened and educated Germans expressed serious reservations about granting citizenship and equal rights to the Jews, whom they saw as a distinct people who posed a threat to German values and civilization. These attitudes gained currency among the masses as well. Thus, German Americans were more prone to view

Simon Wertheimer's discharge papers from the Union army. (Courtesy of the Rabbi Leo M. Franklin Archives of Temple Beth El.)

the presence of Jews as a threat than were native Americans, who had no such lengthy tradition of hatred.[19]

The Civil War provided Jewish Detroiters with opportunities to display their patriotism and become more active in civic life. Simon and Herman Freedman contributed five hundred dollars to the state's emergency war fund, while Edward Kanter helped recruit soldiers for Michigan's regiments. Military service drew 181 Michigan Jews into the Union army, approximately half of them from Detroit. At the time, there were about 151 Jewish families in the entire state, which meant that an average of more than one man enlisted from each family. On the home front, fur dealer Mark Sloman joined the city's civilian police force and assisted fugitive slaves in escaping to Canada. The wives of Isaac Altman, Isidore Frankel, and Simon Freedman helped to organize the Ladies' Soldiers Aid Society, the first such organization formed in the United States during the war.[20]

During the hate-filled period of the war, the United States experienced a significant rise in anti-Semitism, with Jews in the Union, the Confederacy, and the territories accused of disloyalty. Despite the fact that Detroit's Jews were overwhelmingly Unionist, they did not escape unscathed. In 1863 the *Detroit Commercial Advertiser* published an anti-Semitic diatribe which claimed that "the tribe of gold speculators, who are doing their best to create distrust of the government," were "of foreign birth and exclusively of the people who look up to Abraham as their father." These "hooked nose wretches speculate on disasters and a battle lost to our army is chuckled over by them, as it puts money in their purse."[21] After this outburst, no other attack against Jews appeared in the city's press for the remainder of the war, and the agitation subsided nationally once the hostilities ended. Visiting Detroit in 1867, Rabbi Isaac Mayer Wise reported that the city's Jews "live in the best understanding and harmony with their neighbors and are esteemed as men, citizens and merchants."[22]

This peace was shattered one month later in what came to be known as Detroit's Yom Kippur Day riot. A group of Polish Jews, needing a place to pray

Mark Sloman, fur dealer and civic leader. (Courtesy of the Rabbi Leo M. Franklin Archives of Temple Beth El.)

on the High Holy Days, contracted to lease a building on Rivard Street, which once served as a Methodist Episcopal church and afterward as the home of Congregation Beth El. The building was being converted into a theater, but the owner agreed to suspend work and allow the Jews to use the premises for their New Year services. Everything went along smoothly until the lease expired—on Yom Kippur. The congregation was in a panic because they could not pray while the carpenters worked. They solved the problem by agreeing to pay the carpenters' wages provided they stopped working during the services. The owner consented and both parties signed an agreement to that effect. They further agreed that the painters could work behind a curtain provided they made no noise.[23]

Services progressed without incident until the afternoon, when some congregants, feeling that the painters made too much noise, asked them to stop work. Contending that they worked as quietly as could be expected under the circumstances, the painters refused. One word led to another; someone pushed; someone else threw paint; and a general free-for-all ensued, punctuated by shouts, screams, and curses. Both sides threw pieces of lumber, sticks, and bricks, and the painters, being in the minority, beat a hasty retreat. Three painters escaped. Two others, less fortunate, were thrown out of the window. The noise and

David J. Workum, wine merchant
and school inspector (1875–76).
(Courtesy of the Rabbi Leo M.
Franklin Archives of Temple
Beth El.)

tumult attracted a crowd, which was followed by a lone policeman. After trying, unsuccessfully, to restore calm, the officer called for reinforcements. Police hastily converged on the scene and separated the combatants. The owner of the building sued the congregation for malicious trespass; the painters sued them for assault and battery. The congregation, in turn, sued the painters for assault, battery, and disturbing public worship. When it appeared that a trial might drag on, all parties agreed that they could do without the adverse publicity and settled out of court.[24]

The political and civic undertakings of Detroit's German Jews continued after the Civil War. By 1880 Mrs. Herman Freedman and Mrs. Albert Landsberg had served on the board of trustees of the city's Protestant Orphan Asylum, and Edward Kanter, Moses Cohen, Simon Heavenrich, and Magnus Butzel served as vice presidents of the Democratic Central Association of Detroit. Recognizing the growing influence and importance of the city's Jewish community, Detroit's political leaders appointed Jews to a variety of patronage posts and civic offices. Edward Kanter served as inspector of the Detroit House of Correction from 1872 to 1876 and as president of the Board of Poor Commissioners in 1880 and 1881. Adam E.

Bloom, a lawyer, served on the Board of Education from 1878 to 1880; David J. Workum was a school inspector for the Sixth Ward in 1875 and 1876; Louis Rosenthal served as a constable in this same ward in 1880 and 1881; and Frederick Feldman collected taxes for the Thirteenth Ward in 1877.[25]

The increasing visibility of Jews in politics did not always meet with the approbation of the rank and file. Louis Gruenthal, a grocer and member of Detroit's Reform congregation, Temple Beth El, was a candidate for delegate to the Democratic legislative convention in 1876. When he and his Jewish supporters appeared at the city's Democratic caucus, they were sneered at and jeered with cries of "vote for the Jew" and "see the Jews" and were manhandled by the crowd. Incidents of this nature remained rare, however, and Jews continued participating in partisan politics.[26]

Although economic security and increased leisure help to explain the increased Jewish activity in civic and political affairs, another factor merits equal consideration. Never completely comfortable in their roles as American citizens, many of Detroit's first-generation Jews perceived civic and political activism as a direct and public way to demonstrate their fidelity to the United States and as a means of gaining respect among non-Jews. They did succeed in gaining acceptance in the formal and religious sectors of city life. By 1880 pulpit exchanges had been instituted, and city officials and clergymen regularly attended synagogue dedications. In the social sphere, however, Jews suffered total exclusion: not a single Jewish name appeared on the rosters of the city's elite social clubs. This ostracism, established in the 1870s, persisted in Detroit until after World War II.[27]

While it is true that many Jews of this generation preferred socializing amongst themselves, thus partially accounting for their absence in non-Jewish social clubs, it is also true that successful German Jews sought a social recognition commensurate with their hard-won economic status. Their exclusion from these clubs resulted from other factors. After the Civil War, significant numbers of middle-class Americans found themselves rich and desired a higher social status. So many successful people clamored for admission into the more prestigious circles that social climbing stopped being a simple expectation and became a bona fide social problem.

To protect their gains against newcomers, the old wealth and successful social climbers sought to tighten the loose, indistinct lines of class. They did this by establishing nonmonetary standards for social acceptance: candidates had to display knowledge of formalized etiquette, be listed in social registers and blue books, and be members of elite social clubs. Economically successful Jews entered more prominently than other ethnic groups into the struggle for status. To Americans of the upper crust, these Jews displayed all the vices of the nouveau riche—tasteless ostentation, lack of manners, and lack of culture—and ex-

cluding them from elite clubs became a means of stabilizing the social order.[28]

Despite a foreign-born population of almost 40 percent by 1880, late-nineteenth-century Detroit remained an Anglo-Saxon Protestant stronghold with ethnic penetration of the city's social elite kept to a minimum. This resulted in the development of parallel elite social structures among Detroit's non-Anglo Saxon groups. The exclusion of German Jews from Detroit's elite clubs led them to create the Phoenix Social Club in 1872 and the Independence Social Club in 1873. This reinforced their sense of Jewish identity, an identity which many of them sought to maintain and perpetuate even while they integrated into American life.[29]

NOTES

1. *Detroit Free Press*, February 19, 1850, p. 1, July 27, 1850, p. 2, October 13, 1853, p. 3, September 13, 1855, p. 1, April 21, 1859, p. 1; *Detroit Daily Advertiser*, April 21, 1859, p. 1.

2. Rudolf Glanz, "The Immigration of German Jews Up to 1880," in *Studies in Judaica Americana*, ed. Glanz (New York: Ktav Publishing Co., 1970), pp. 89, 91-93; Marc Lee Raphael, *Jews and Judaism in a Midwestern Community: Columbus, Ohio, 1840-1975* (Columbus, Ohio: Ohio Historical Society, 1979), pp. 10-15; Lloyd P. Gartner, *History of the Jews of Cleveland* (Cleveland: Western Reserve Historical Society, 1978), p. 8. Approximately 60 percent of the Jewish foreign-born residents of Detroit up to the 1870s were German in origin. The others came from Hungary, Poland, and Russia. See the Woodmere Cemetery Records of Burials, 1871-1913, Temple Beth El Archives, Birmingham, Michigan; Burton Historical Collection, Detroit Public Library, Detroit, Michigan; and the U.S. Manuscript Census Schedules, Wayne County, City of Detroit, and Michigan, of 1850, 1860, 1870, and 1880.

3. Arthur Goren, *The American Jews* (Cambridge, Mass.: Belknap Press, 1982), pp. 1-2, 21-25; Glanz, "Immigration of German Jews," p. 96.

4. From 1860 to 1870, manufacturing jobs jumped form 1,363 to 10,612, more than triple the rate of population growth; capital invested in manufacturing increased from $1.5 million to $24.6 million, and the value of the finished products from $2.1 million to $21.5 million. Ten years later the number of persons employed in manufactur-

ing increased to 16,111, and the value of finished products to more than $30 million. See Olivier Zunz, *The Changing Face of Inequality: Urbanization, Industrial Development, and Immigrants in Detroit, 1880-1920* (Chicago: University of Chicago Press, 1982), pp. 2-3; Melvin G. Holli, ed., *Detroit* (New York: New Viewpoints, 1976), p. 54; *Tenth Census of the United States, 1880: Social Statistics of Cities* 2 (Washington, D.C.: Government Printing Office, 1887), pp. 598-616; John Andrew Russell, *The Germanic Influence in the Making of Michigan* (Detroit: University of Detroit, 1927), pp. 219-29, 328-35. There were 2,855 immigrants from the German Empire in Detroit in 1850 (Jo Ellen Vinyard, "The Irish on the Urban Frontier: Detroit, 1850-1880" [Ph.D. diss., University of Michigan, 1974], p. 284). By 1860, the Germans had become the largest foreign-born group in Detroit and remained so till 1900. In 1890, they comprised 43 percent of the city's foreign-born population (Holli, *Detroit*, p. 62).

5. Allen A. Warsen, "An Important Discovery," *Michigan Jewish History* (January, 1970), pp. 4-7; Warsen, "Analysis of a Discovery," *Michigan Jewish History* (June, 1970), pp. 14-16; Warsen, *Addenda to Autobiographical Episodes* (Oak Park, Mich., 1974), pp. 4-6; U.S. Manuscript Census Schedules, Wayne County, and the City of Detroit, 1850. The 1853-54 *City Directory* lists 113 Jews living in Detroit.

6. On the economic status of late nineteenth-century American Jewry, see John S. Billings, *Vital Statistics of the Jews in the*

United States (Washington, D.C., 1890); Steven Hertzberg, *Strangers within the Gate City: The Jews of Atlanta, 1845-1915* (Philadelphia: Jewish Publication Society of America, 1978), pp. 38-43, 139-54; Raphael, *Jews and Judaism*, pp. 35-49; Peter R. Decker, "Jewish Merchants in San Francisco: Social Mobility on the Urban Frontier," *American Jewish History* 67 (June, 1979), pp. 396-407; and Mitchell Gelfand, "Progress and Prosperity: Jewish Social Mobility in Los Angeles in the Booming Eighties," *American Jewish History* 67 (June, 1979), pp. 408-33.

7. Samuel Heavenrich, "Memories" (Detroit, 1929), in the Heavenrich File, Temple Beth El Archives, Temple Beth El, Birmingham, Michigan; *Detroit Free Press*, March 25, 1871, p. 1; Phyllis Lederer, "A Study of Jewish Influences in Detroit" (M.A. thesis, Wayne State University, 1947), pp. 78-79.

8. Freedman File, Temple Beth El Archives; U.S. Manuscript Census Schedules, City of Detroit, 1870, pp. 77, 118; Butzel File, Temple Beth El Archives; Lederer, "Jewish Influences," pp. 73-77; Zunz, *Changing Face*, p. 18; Russell, *Germanic Influence*, pp. 328-35.

9. Fechheimer File, Workum File, Freud File, Temple Beth El Archives; U.S. Manuscript Census Schedules, Wayne County and City of Detroit, 1880.

10. Heavenrich, "Memories," pp. 4-8.

11. U.S. Manuscript Census Schedules, City of Detroit, 1870; *Detroit City Directory*, 1860.

12. The data on the Eastern Europeans was collected from the U.S. Manuscript Census Schedules, City of Detroit, 1870, Ward 1 and Ward 3. The ethnic composition of Detroit's Jewish community is derived from the Federal Census Schedules of 1870 and 1880, and the Woodmere Cemetery Records of Burials. Detroit's Jewish population is estimated from the synagogue and organizational membership lists and the U.S. Manuscript Census Schedules, City of Detroit, 1880 (Wards 1, 3, and 5).

13. Out of a sample of twenty-four Eastern European newcomers, taken from the 1870 Federal Census, seventeen were peddlers. Ten of them could not be located in 1880, neither in the *City Directory*, the 1880 Census Schedule for Detroit, nor on any synagogue or organizational list. Of the fourteen who could be found, seven remained peddlers.

14. Hertzberg, *Strangers*, p. 39; Raphael, *Jews and Judaism*, p. 48; Gelfand, "Progress," pp. 419-20.

15. The German Jewish heads of households in 1860 were taken from the membership lists of Congregation Beth El and compared with the membership list of 1877 and the City Directory of 1880. The Congregation Beth El materials are located in two depositories: the Congregation's archives at the Temple Beth El and at the Burton Historical Collection.

16. Zunz, *Changing Face*, pp. 32-33, 46, 52-57, 78-79.

17. *Detroit Free Press*, September 25, 1856, p. 1; Simon Wolf, *The American Jew as Patriot, Soldier and Citizen* (Philadelphia, 1895), p. 425; *Die Deborah*, December 19, 1856, p. 140. Know-Nothingism was an anti-Catholic, anti-immigrant secret political party organized in the 1850s by native-born Protestants to keep out of public office anyone not a native-born American. Officially called the American Party, it was popularly known as the Know-Nothing party because, when questioned by outsiders, members answered, "I know nothing."

18. *Die Deborah*, December 19, 1856, p. 140.

19. Isaac M. Fein, *The Making of an American Jewish Community: The History of Baltimore Jewry from 1773 to 1920* (Philadelphia: Jewish Publication Society of America, 1971), p. 203.

20. *Detroit Free Press*, November 7, 1861, p. 1; Irving I. Katz, *The Jewish Soldier from Michigan in the Civil War* (Detroit: Wayne State University Press, 1962), pp. 7-9, 15-16; Lederer, "Jewish Influences," pp. 75-77; Silas Farmer, *History of Detroit and Wayne County and Early Michigan* (Detroit: Silas Farmer and Co., 1890; Gale Research Company, 1969), p. 310.

21. *Israelite*, March 6, 1863, p. 277.

22. *Israelite*, September 6, 1867, p. 6.

23. *Detroit Advertiser and Tribune*, October 10, 1867, p. 1.

24. *Detroit Advertiser and Tribune*, October 10, 1867, p. 1, October 25, 1867, p. 1.

25. See the *Detroit, Michigan, Annual Reports* for 1871-81; Farmer, *History of Detroit*, pp. 212, 646, 757-58; and the *Thirty-fifth Annual Report of the Board of Education of the City of Detroit for the Year 1877* (Detroit: Post and Tribune Book and Job Printing Establishment, 1878); *Detroit City Directory*, 1871-72, p. 38. The Board of Poor Commissioners was a city charity whose members were appointed by the Common Council on the nomination of the mayor; nominees served in an advisory capacity without pay. The mission of the Board was "to supply provisions, fuel and medical aid to the needy worthy poor of Detroit at their homes, and make contacts with hospitals for the care of the sick; to provide for the burial of the poor and to give transportation to poor desiring to leave the city" (see Zunz, *Changing Face*, p. 268).

26. *Detroit Advertiser and Tribune*, September 9, 1876, p. 4.

27. The elite social clubs examined were the Detroit Club, the Yondotega Club, and the Detroit Athletic Club. See also Martin Marger, "The Force of Ethnicity: A Study of Urban Elites," *Journal of University Studies* 10 (Winter, 1974), pp. 82-91.

28. John Higham, "Social Discrimination Against Jews, 1830-1930," in *Send These to Me: Jews and Other Immigrants in Urban America*, ed. Higham (New York: Atheneum, 1975), pp. 144-51.

29. Marger, "Force of Ethnicity," pp. 1-108; Zunz, *Changing Face*, pp. 204-6, 217.

Plaque on the Blue Cross-Blue Shield Building in Detroit.
(Courtesy of the Archives of Congregation Shaarey Zedek.)

3. NOT BY BREAD ALONE
Establishing a Jewish Community

ON SEPTEMBER 22, 1850, in time for the holidays of Rosh Hashanah and Yom Kippur, twelve German Jews met and organized an Orthodox congregation called the Bet El (House of God) Society—the first Jewish congregation in Michigan (soon afterwards the name was changed to Beth El). The founders held services in the home of Isaac Cozens and engaged Rabbi Samuel Marcus of New York as their first spiritual leader. Marcus served as *hazzan* (cantor), teacher, *shohet* (ritual slaughterer), and *mohel* (circumcizer) at an annual salary of two hundred dollars. This was not an insignificant amount when one considers that the finest seven-course dinner in town cost twenty-five cents.[1]

Like congregations elsewhere in the United States, Beth El sought its religious leadership not from the old-style rabbinic scholar and judge, but from a new-style rabbinic preacher and teacher. Not all rabbinic teachers and preachers were actually rabbis, such as Marcus, and there was confusion concerning their status. In his reminiscences, Isaac Mayer Wise, one of the founders of Reform Judaism in America, described the *hazzan* of the late 1840s as a "reader, cantor, . . . teacher, butcher, circumcizer, blower,

gravedigger, secretary." He "read *shiur* [a lesson from the Talmud] for the departed sinners, and played cards or dominoes with the living; in short, he was a kol-bo, an encyclopedia, accepted bread, turnips, cabbage, potatoes as a gift, and peddled in case his salary was not sufficient."[2]

After hiring Marcus, the congregation purchased one half acre of land on Champlain (now Lafayette) Street for a cemetery. They paid $150, half in cash and half in interest-bearing notes due in six and twelve months. The congregation also opened a Hebrew-German-English Day School, where the children of congregants received secular and religious instruction, and organized a "Hebrah Bikur Cholim" society to visit and attend to the sick, with Charles Bresler as its first president. In 1852 the congregation rented and furnished a room above the store of Silberman and Hersch, "dealers in all kinds of cigars, tobacco and snuff," at 220 Jefferson Avenue, for a place of worship.[3]

Rabbi Marcus died during Detroit's cholera epidemic, which raged through the summer of 1854, killing an average of three persons a day. To replace him, Beth El hired Dr. Liebman Adler, recently arrived

The home of Isaac and Sarah Cozens at Congress and St. Antoine Streets. (Courtesy of the Rabbi Leo M. Franklin Archives of Temple Beth El.)

from Germany and recommended by Dr. Wise. Beth El's transition from Orthodox Judaism to Reform began with Adler's arrival in Detroit.[4]

REFORM

Beginning in early nineteenth-century Germany, the Reform movement was a conscious attempt by enlightened, educated Jews to modernize Judaism in order to improve the image of the Jew in the eyes of enlightened gentiles. They also wished to stem the conversion to Christianity by Jews estranged from the traditional ritual and frustrated by legal and social discrimination against them. They altered the Jewish mode of worship to bring it more into conformity with contemporary aesthetic standards. In the traditional German or Polish synagogue, the service was chanted entirely in Hebrew in an un-Western, un-Germanic style, with the worshipper—dressed in hat and prayer shawl—sitting, standing, or swaying to and fro while responding in his own way to the cantor or prayer leader. To the acculturated German Jews, such a spontaneous, informal religious ceremony appeared undignified and oriental.

Some of the modifications they introduced included maintaining greater decorum in the synagogue, unison in prayer, a mixed choir, hymns and musical responses in the modern style, family pews, and prayers and sermons in the vernacular. Reform theoreticians distinguished between what they claimed were the laws and customs rooted in historical circumstances and the more universal precepts of religion and morality that were found in Mosaic monotheism and prophetic idealism. Defining Judaism as a universal faith that emphasized the ethical tradition and morality, they argued that to fulfill its destiny Judaism must be free to adjust to changing circumstances without being bound by centuries of rabbinic traditions.[5]

Reform Judaism rarely achieved an independent radical program in German communities because of the powerful and conservative Jewish communal bodies in each city. These organizations appointed rabbis for the community synagogues and their primacy was recognized by the government. Reform achieved greater success in the United States because of the voluntaristic character of American life, America's tradition of congregational autonomy and separation of church and state, and the absence of recognized Jewish communal authority or strong communal leadership.[6]

In the United States, American Reform rabbis generally divided into two camps: the moderates, led by Isaac Mayer Wise of Cincinnati, and the radicals, led by David Einhorn of Baltimore and later New York. Wise cared less for ideas and theories and more about the modernization of the service and the institutionalization of American Judaism. Einhorn, less pragmatic than Wise, sought to establish a sound theoretical foundation for Reform. After his death, his followers, led by his son-in-law, Kaufmann Kohler, articulated the main tenets of American Reform Judaism in the Pittsburgh Platform of 1885. This statement asserted that Judaism was a "progressive religion, ever striving to be in accord with the postulates of reason," and dedicated to social justice. It rejected all Mosaic laws which "are not adopted to the views and habits of modern civilization" and rejected any national aim or character for Judaism. "We consider ourselves no longer a nation, but a religious community, and therefore expect neither a return to Palestine, nor sacrificial worship under the sons of Aaron, nor the restoration of any of the laws concerning the Jewish state."[7]

From the outset, Beth El engaged a series of highly educated and enlightened rabbis who were well versed in the tenets and philosophy of German Reform and subscribed to the aims of Isaac Mayer Wise. A group of Beth El's more wealthy, active, and influential members, such as Simon Heavenrich, Magnus and Martin Butzel, Marcus Cohen, and Simon Freedman, supported them in their efforts. These men had their own reasons for wanting Reform. As they swiftly became Americans in citizenship and business, they wanted their lives as Jews to acquire the forms and decorum of other American religions. Isaac M. Wise's term "American Judaism" suggests what they sought. Although sentiment and custom tied most Beth El members to traditional Judaism and some conservative laymen resisted the change, by the end of the 1860s the battle for Reform had been won.

Liebman Adler (1812–92) was born in Lengsfeld, Germany, and there received his early biblical and rabbinic training. He continued his Hebrew studies in rabbinic academies in Gelnhausen and Frankfort and pedagogical studies at a teachers' seminary in Weimar. Upon graduating, Adler accepted a teaching post in the city of his birth, remaining there till called to Detroit. In Detroit, he performed the duties of a rabbi, *hazzan, shohet,* teacher, and *mohel,* became an active abolitionist, helped to organize the city's first Jewish women's society, "Ahabas Achjuous" [*sic*] (Sisterly Love), and fostered moderate

Sarah Cozens, founding member of Temple Beth El. (Courtesy of the Rabbi Leo M. Franklin Archives of Temple Beth El.)

Portrait of Isaac Cozens. (Courtesy of the Rabbi Leo M. Franklin Archives of Temple Beth El.)

reforms at Beth El. He instituted the preaching of sermons and influenced the congregation to adopt a new constitution and bylaws that incorporated Isaac M. Wise's ideas. The constitution explicitly stated that Beth El "shall, in all its religious institutions, pay due attention to the progress of the age, and maintain the respect due to customs or laws handed down to us by our pious fathers." In cases of innovation and change, the document provides that "this congregation shall attempt to remain in unity with the majority, at least, of the American congregations, and shall always attempt to produce uniformity in the American synagogue." Following this, Adler introduced some alterations in the liturgy and added prayers in the German language.[8]

Adler's initial success stemmed in part from the prestige he enjoyed among his congregants and colleagues, for spiritual leaders of his intellectual stature were still a rarity within the American Jewish community. Wise acknowledged this state of affairs when he wrote that in the course of his travels in 1856, outside of Liebman Adler of Detroit, he did not find "one teacher, *chazan*, reader, or congregational official who had enjoyed even a common school education."[9]

The adoption of the constitution and various innovations embittered and angered Beth El's more traditional members, and they never fully accepted or accommodated to the changes. The Reverend Isaac Leeser of Philadelphia, the first national leader in American Jewish life, perceived this tension and resentment on his first visit to Detroit in 1857. He cautioned the congregation's leaders against instituting additional reforms: "We trust that for the sake of the

Second site of Temple Beth El (the white building, *second from right*) at 172 Jefferson above the store of Silberman and Hersch. (Courtesy of the Rabbi Leo M. Franklin Archives of Temple Beth El.)

Liebman Adler, rabbi of Temple Beth El (1854–61) and an abolitionist. (Courtesy of the Rabbi Leo M. Franklin Archives of Temple Beth El.)

Marcus Cohen conducted the first religious services in Detroit before Beth El engaged its first rabbi. (Courtesy of the Rabbi Leo M. Franklin Archives of Temple Beth El.)

public peace, no more alterations will be attempted; for it is one thing to have order, but quite another to force measures on a part of the community which would necessarily provoke resistance."[10] Ignoring this advice, Adler and his supporters pressed for a choir and Isaac Wise's newly issued *Minhag America* prayer book. This time, however, they encountered defeat. Undaunted, Adler invited Wise to Detroit in hopes that the latter's presence would promote his campaign. Alarmed at what they saw as a conspiracy against them, Beth El's Orthodox members resolved to block all new innovations.[11]

At a particularly rancorous congregational meeting in 1860, the traditionalists challenged the legality of the 1856 constitution and bylaws and demanded a new vote. During the debate that followed, the reformers called their Orthodox co-congregants "reactionary fanatics" who held back the forces of progress and enlightenment, while the traditionalists accused the reformers of being "radical opportunists" who endangered the future of Judaism. By a small majority, the congregation voted to confirm the 1856 constitution. The dispirited traditionalists realized they no longer could win, and so in 1861, after an attempt was made to introduce music and a mixed choir, seventeen of them withdrew from the congregation and organized the Shaarey Zedek (Gates of Righteousness) Society.[12]

Because of its small size and limited resources, Beth El's goal of acquiring a synagogue building by 1855 remained unfulfilled. Four years later, despite an increase in membership and funds, little had changed. Frustrated by this lack of progress, Adler submitted his resignation. The congregation's executive board induced him to stay by promising that a synagogue building would be purchased forthwith. Nothing was done, however, for another four months. When Adler again threatened to resign, the congregation formed a Synagogue Building Association, with Edward Kanter as president. In the interim, Beth El leased a hall "to be used as a meeting house and schoolroom" over John C. Sherer's Drug Store at 39 Michigan Grand Avenue (now Cadillac Square), for a yearly fee of $140. Apprised of this situation by Adler, Isaac Wise wrote

The Rivard Street synagogue (1861-67). (Courtesy of the Rabbi Leo M. Franklin Archives of Temple Beth El.)

that "our brethren of Detroit have no synagogue of their own and no expectation to get one very soon. There is not that enterprise and energy in congregational affairs among our brethren of Detroit as among the rest of our western congregations." Prodded into action by such criticism, Beth El purchased the French Methodist Episcopal Church and adjoining parsonage on Rivard Street between Croghan (now Monroe) and Chaplain (now Lafayette) in 1860 for $3,500.[13]

At this juncture, Adler accepted a call to become the rabbi of Chicago's Kehilath Anshe Ma'arab (Congregation of the Men of the West). His successor was Rabbi Abraham Laser, who remained Beth El's spiritual leader for three years. The dedication of the new synagogue, with Rabbi Laser conducting the ceremonies and Isaac M. Wise preaching the inaugural

Abraham Laser, rabbi of Temple Beth El from 1861 to 1864. (Courtesy of the Rabbi Leo M. Franklin Archives of Temple Beth El.)

congregant, and moved decisively toward institutionalizing Reform. Not all Orthodox members left at the time of the schism, and those who stayed, while continuing Orthodox in their personal religious behavior, acquiesced in the innovations. Beth El's membership grew from twenty-three after the split to seventy by 1870, with the congregation's financial position improving accordingly.[15]

Under Laser Beth El passed a new constitution and bylaws, replaced their Orthodox *Minhag Ashkenaz* with Wise's *Minhag America*, introduced a three-year cycle of reading from the *Torah* in place of the Orthodox yearly cycle, abolished *aliyot* (calling up to the *Torah*) and the wearing of the *talit* (prayer shawl) at services, permitted men and women to sit together at services, retained the choir and instrumental music, and introduced the confirmation of boys and girls on Shavuot (Feast of Weeks). In addition to his rabbinical duties, Laser organized the Ladies' Society for the Support of Hebrew Widows and Orphans in the State of Michigan, later popularly known as the "Frauen Verein." Although reelected for another term at an increased salary, Laser resigned in 1864, much to the congregation's regret.[16]

During the next twelve years, Beth El had five rabbis, none of whom served for more than three years: Isidore Kalisch (1864-66), Elias Eppstein

sermon, took place in the afternoon on Friday, August 30, 1861. I. J. Benjamin, celebrated world traveler and author of *Eight Years in Asia and Africa*, arrived in Detroit overland from California and participated in the ceremonies. He later described his Detroit stopover in the book *Three Years in America*. A melodeon and a mixed choir, led by Abraham J. Franklin, accompanied the dedication exercises as well as the Friday evening and Saturday morning services. From then on, music and a choir became part of Beth El's ritual. The *Detroit Free Press*, the *Detroit Tribune and Advertiser*, and the *Israelite* of Cincinnati all carried accounts of the dedication.[14]

After the Orthodox secession, Beth El enjoyed a period of "peace and good will," according to one

Kaufmann Kohler, rabbi of Temple Beth El (1869-71), distinguished leader of American Reform Judaism. (Courtesy of the Rabbi Leo M. Franklin Archives of Temple Beth El.)

36

Congregation Beth El on Washington Boulevard and Clifford Street (1867–1902). (Courtesy of the Rabbi Leo M. Franklin Archives of Temple Beth El.)

(1866–69), Kaufmann Kohler (1869–71), Emanuel Gerechter (1871–73), and Leopold Wintner (1873–76). Additional reforms introduced during these years included the establishment of Friday evening services (1867) and the abolition of the second day of festivals and wearing of the talit by the rabbi (1870).[17]

In 1867 Beth El purchased the Tabernacle Baptist Church, on Washington Avenue and Clifford Street, for $17,000 and, at an additional cost of $10,000, converted it to a synagogue. The dedication, with Isaac M. Wise delivering the dedicatory prayer and sermon, took place on Friday, August 30, 1867. Rabbi Eppstein, in his opening address, called the new synagogue a temple, referring to the Reform movement's identification of the Jewish house of worship with the original temple of Solomon in Jerusalem. From then on, Beth El designated its synagogue as "Temple Beth El."[18]

During Leopold Wintner's term, Beth El officially affiliated with the Union of American Hebrew

Congregations and helped to establish the Hebrew Union College in Cincinnati. Wintner also has the distinction of being the first Detroit rabbi invited to preach in a Christian church, the Universalist Church of Our Father, in May 1876. These achievements notwithstanding, Wintner repeatedly clashed with the Temple's executive board over modifications in the service. The issue was not so much the alterations as who had the final word in authorizing them. Since the rabbi was a paid employee, dependent upon the congregation for his livelihood, the outcome was rarely in doubt. At a stormy meeting in 1875, the executive board informed Wintner that only "members of the congregation" could authorize changes in the services and "ordered" him "to preach in the German language only" on the High Holy Days. The board also passed a motion empowering the trustees "to procure a suitable rabbi who can preach in the English and German languages." Wintner thereupon notified the board that he declined to be "a candidate after the expiration of the term of my office as I wish to go to Europe."[19]

Hoping to avoid another such confrontation, president Martin Butzel sent Wintner's successor, Dr. Heinrich (Henry) Zirndorf, a letter spelling out in great detail exactly what the congregation expected of him. Zirndorf accepted the conditions and was elected for a term of three years at a salary of $2,400 per year. After informing Zirndorf of his selection, Butzel suggested he "sell furniture and all bulky articles, but retain all linens, wearing apparels, bedding and such articles which are easily packed." He also cautioned Zirndorf about immediatley taking sides in the controversy raging within the Reform movement between the easterners, led by Einhorn, and the westerners, led by Wise. "Both parties claim to be reformers and the true champions of enlightenment and knowledge—but these pen and ink warriors indulge in personalities to a great extent,—not always creditable to themselves nor to the laymen. . . . You will have ample opportunities in future to judge for yourself upon the true merits of the pretensions or reality of their claims."[20]

Zirndorf (1829–93), poet, playwright, and scholar, was born in Furth, Bavaria, and educated privately. Between the ages of nineteen and twenty-six, he lived and studied in Munich, moving to Vienna in 1855. While in Vienna, Zirndorf wrote verse and published a play. In 1859 he accepted the post of rabbi in Lipto-Szent-Miklos, Hungary, but resigned after a short time. He then took a position as a private tutor in London, living, writing, and teaching there for thirteen years. Zirndorf returned to Germany as rector of the Hebrew Teacher's Institute in Munster in 1873 and remained there until called to Beth El in 1876. He left Detroit in 1884 to become professor of history at the Hebrew Union College and associate editor of *Die Deborah*. Congregation Ahabas Achim of Cincinnati chose Zirndorf to be their rabbi in 1889, a post he held till his death.[21]

Religious apathy and non-attendance at services became particularly worrisome to Beth El's leaders during Zirndorf's ministry. Fewer members kept *kashrut*, many worked on Saturday, and more and more of them dispensed with traditional Friday evenings at home with their families, preferring instead to go out. Hoping to attract members who worked on Saturday, the executive board inaugurated a Friday evening lecture series in 1876. Attendance at these also remained low, partly because they conflicted with social gatherings held about town on the same evening. In an effort to involve the younger, native-born generation in the Temple's religious life, Zirndorf introduced the reading of the *haftorah* (selections from the Prophets) by young men of the congregation. None of these measures, however, generated the hoped-for religious revival. Ironically, at the very time Beth El's services became more acceptable to the congregation, fewer and fewer members bothered attending.[22]

EDUCATION

When the first Jewish families organized Congregation Beth El, primary education in Detroit was in its infancy, having first opened in 1842. Wanting to provide their children with a strong general and specifically Jewish education, they established an all-day

Heinrich Zirndorf, rabbi of Temple Beth El (1876–84) and a poet, playwright, and scholar. (Courtesy of the Rabbi Leo M. Franklin Archives of Temple Beth El.)

Hebrew-German-English School, which met six days a week. The Beth El rabbi directed the German and Hebrew departments with another director, usually a non-Jew, responsible for the English portion of the curriculum. The rabbi and hired teachers and volunteers from the congregation taught classes in German, Hebrew, and English composition and the Jewish religion.[23]

The founding of Jewish day schools in America did not necessarily result from a zeal for Jewish education. The underlying reasons were the absence or inadequacy of public schools or the Protestant sectarian tone of those which did exist. The eventual establishment of public schools without such features as prayers, Bible and especially New Testament readings and moralizing, and strongly Christian holiday observance, signaled the demise of the Jewish schools. A new ideology regarded the tax supported, religiously neutral, universal public school as the essential training ground for good American citizens. American Jews enthusiastically adopted this outlook, and they believed that Jewish children could best become loyal and fully accepted Americans by mingling freely in public school with children of all religions and social classes. Sectarian Jewish education suggested undesirable, even dangerous, separation.[24]

The idea of the non-sectarian public school also complimented Reform Judaism's conception of the Jews as fully integrated citizens of the modern secular state, differentiated only by religion. Consequently, Reform Jews perceived these schools as a blessing and a necessity, since they were a microcosm of the society in which Jewish children would find their place as adults. For more than one hundred years, Jews continued to view the public school as the symbol and guarantee of Jewish equality and full opportunity in America.[25]

A few opponents did question whether Jewish children should be enrolled in the new public schools. Isaac Leeser stressed the inevitable Christian influence of public schools where virtually all the teachers and most of the pupils were Christians, and Bernard Felsenthal, a Chicago Reformed rabbi, urged the need for Jewish schools to raise an American Jewish intellectual class comparable to that of European Jewry. Few people paid attention to their views, however, and after 1860 scarcely any private Jewish day schools remained in the United States.[26]

Detroit reflected this trend. By the 1860s Detroit's public schools had become more non-sectarian, and Beth El members felt fewer inhibitions in enrolling their children. They also concluded that as citizens and taxpayers it was unnecessary for them to support a private school and employ teachers for secular instruction so long as their children could receive this training in the public schools. For these reasons, Beth El discontinued its day school in 1869 and opened a part-time religious school in its stead. Beth El children henceforth received their religious education in sessions held on Saturday afternoon, Sunday morning, and twice weekly after public school hours.[27]

The religious school's subjects consisted of Hebrew, Bible, history, and religion and Bar Mitzvah instruction for boys; textbooks included Isaac M. Wise's *Minhag America* prayer book and *Essence of Judaism* and Samuel Adler's *Biblical History*. The children of non-members and of persons unable to pay could be admitted by special permission of the school's board of trustees. Every June the rabbi of Beth El conducted a public examination of the pupils in the presence of the school board and parents.[28]

The change to a part-time religious school led to a loss of interest by parents and a drastic decline in pupil attendance. In his president's report of 1876, Magnus Butzel reminded the congregation how ungrateful they would be "toward *Him* who preserved us if we suffered our good, good cause to die out by being indifferent in the main point, which alone can perpetuate a love for our holy religion. The instruction

David Marx, founding member of Congregation Shaarey Zedek and Detroit's first kosher butcher, with his family in 1860. (Courtesy of the Archives of Congregation Shaarey Zedek.)

of Jewish children in the moral faith and sacred history of their ancestors." Two years later, Seligman Schloss tried to induce enrollment by assuring parents that children sent to the religious school would become "good members of lodges with higher aims in view than more insurance money after death." Nothing Beth El's rabbis or presidents could say or do, however, noticeably improved the congregation's interest in religious education for their young.[29]

THE ORTHODOX COMMUNITY

The seventeen men who withdrew from Beth El formed the Orthodox congregation Shaarey Zedek on September 27, 1861, with Hiram Kraushaar, formerly a trustee at Beth El, as its first president. Within its first few months, Shaarey Zedek attracted a number of other Orthodox Jews, upping its membership to thirty-six, and hired the Reverend M. Sapper as its spiritual leader. The congregation rented a hall at 39 Michigan Grand Avenue (the same place Beth El worshiped at from 1859 to 1861) for services and adopted the *Minhag Polin* (Polish Ritual) as its ritual. For $450 the congregation purchased, in 1862, one and a half acres of land near the D & M Railroad junction for a cemetery. This subsequently became known as the Smith Street or Beth Olam cemetery.[30]

By 1864 the congregation had grown to sixty-four members and felt sufficiently affluent to purchase as its synagogue the former St. Mathews Colored Episcopal Church, on the corner of Congress and St. Antoine Streets, at a cost of $4,500. The dedication took place on September 23, 1864, with Dr. Isidore Kalisch of Beth El delivering the introductory prayer and sermon in English. He probably spoke in English because Detroit's acting mayor, Judge Wilkins, and most of the city's aldermen attended the ceremony.[31]

Three years later the congregation had grown to eighty members, mostly of Polish, German, and Hungarian origin, had established an afternoon religious school, and had organized a Bikkur Cholim and Chevra Kadisha Society for the relief of the sick and

The first building owned by Shaarey Zedek, at Congress and St. Antoine Streets. (Courtesy of the Archives of Congregation Shaarey Zedek.)

for service to the families of deceased members. In the event of illness, the Society provided the member with a doctor, medicine, and an allocation of five to six dollars per week for living expenses. Members of the Society also attended to the sick person until he recovered sufficiently to care for himself.[32]

None of the men who served as Shaarey Zedek's spiritual leaders during the first twenty-five years of its existence had rabbinic ordination. This changed in 1877, when the congregation hired Rabbi E. Rosenzweig of Boston, Massachusetts, who ministered from 1877 to 1881. The same year Rosenzweig arrived, Shaarey Zedek laid the cornerstone for a new synagogue, the first to be built by Detroit Jews and the first building in Michigan built specifically as a synagogue.[33]

Plans for the synagogue began in 1876, when the congregation addressed a circular to the Jews of Detroit, appealing to their "paternal generosity for assistance in behalf of our undertaking in the way of improvements about to be made on our property." The bulletin explained that Shaarey Zedek's present

40

"wooden structure, well neigh 30 years old," was "altogether unworthy of the sacred purpose of worship" and had to be replaced. Although the congregation was "taxing themselves to the utmost," they fell short of the estimated twelve thousand dollars needed to erect a building. Therefore, the circular continued, "we earnestly and hopefully invoke your sympathy and assistance and shall expect, when occasion offers, to reciprocate in a similar manner to such of our brethren as may be found in like circumstances."[34] This tactic must have worked, for construction of the building began the following year.

At the cornerstone laying ceremonies on Friday, July 4, 1877, noted the *Detroit Free Press*, "the streets were crowded with spectators, while on the

Congregation Shaarey Zedek in 1877, the first synagogue to be built by Detroit Jews. (Courtesy of the Archives of Congregation Shaarey Zedek.)

platform were between 300 and 400 persons among them Mayor Lewis and members of the city council." Rabbi Rosenzweig recited a prayer, Dr. Max Lilienthal of Cincinnati delivered the address, and Dr. Zirndorf of Temple Beth El offered a prayer. A tin box deposited in the cornerstone contained the constitution, bylaws, and membership roll of Shaarey Zedek; a list of Beth El members together with Temple's constitution and bylaws; the constitutions of the United States and the State of Michigan; copies of all the Jewish newspapers in the country and of the Detroit papers of July 3, 1877; a silver Jewish coin and an American coin each dated 1877; and the constitution of the order of B'nai B'rith. The mayor received the honor of laying the cornerstone.[35]

The Panic of 1873 severely shook Detroit's business community, and, although the economy regained some of its strength by 1877, funds remained scarce and contributions, for any cause, difficult to obtain. Mounting construction costs, exceeding the original estimates, proved a drain on Shaarey Zedek and caused considerable strain and dissension among its members. Congregational meetings turned into shouting matches with members hurling accusations of waste, extravagance, and selfishness at each other. Unable to resolve their differences peaceably, the congregation split into three factions, with the main Shaarey Zedek group meeting in Kittelberger's Hall on Randolph Street, another group at the home of Mr. Kinsell on Gratiot Avenue, and the third in Funke's Hall on Macomb Street. One faction later joined Congregation B'nai Israel; the other formed Congregation Beth Jacob in 1878. Left with only thirty-five members, Shaarey Zedek was unable to make the final payments on the construction and could not take possession upon completion of the building. The builders took a deed for the building, and the brick supplier held a mechanics' lien.[36]

On the night of July 12, 1880, a tremendous explosion gutted the structure from the basement to the roof, causing four thousand dollars in damage. Every stained glass window shattered, sash and casings buckled and broke, whole sections of the gallery and ceiling collapsed, and the roof and main wall split and cracked. Police investigators discovered an open gas pipe in the basement and suspected vandals to be the perpetrators of the blast.[37]

The edifice was not repaired and suffered further, according to the *Detroit Free Press*, from "depradations committed by boys and tramps." It was sold at auction in 1881 for $6,775. At this juncture, David W. Simons, Reuben Mendelsohn, then president of the congregation, and a small group of Shaarey Zedek members succeeded in renting the newly renovated building from the buyer, and the congregation began holding services there. With a resurgence in its membership, which reached seventy by 1884, Shaarey Zedek repurchased the structure for $10,500. At the formal reopening of the synagogue, on January 17, 1886, Samuel Ginsburg recounted the trials and tribulations of the past nine years and congratulated the president and those members whose efforts made possible "the rededication of this, our old 'shule' to be held by us forever and forever."[38]

The influx of Eastern European Jews into Detroit during the 1870s led to the founding of the Orthodox congregations of B'nai Israel (1871) and B'nai Jacob (1875). Disaffected congregants from Shaarey Zedek and B'nai Israel organized Beth Jacob in 1878. Consisting of Polish and Russian Jews, all three congregations used the Polish ritual in their services.[39]

One of these congregations, B'nai Israel, had a particularly stormy existence. From the outset the congregation suffered from sporadic attendance at daily and Sabbath services and a conspicuous decline in personal religiosity amongst its members. The congregation's leaders tried reversing this trend through a series of fines and penalties but only succeeded in antagonizing the members and weakening their own authority. As a consequence, congregational meetings became little more than open forums for venting personal grievances and trading insults. Matters continued in this vein until the congregational election of 1878, when a sizeable contingent of members, accusing B'nai Israel's leaders of fraud and corruption, withdrew to form congregation Beth Jacob. One year later the remnants of B'nai Israel voted to merge with Shaarey Zedek.[40]

By the 1870s elements of class and status, in addition to differing religious attitudes, separated Detroit's Orthodox Jewish congregations from the Reformed Temple Beth El. Beth El members lived on the city's finest residential streets, belonged to the most exclusive Jewish social club, the Phoenix, and enjoyed a higher economic status than members of the Orthodox congregations (see Tables 6 and 7 and Maps 2 and 3). Although Beth El cooperated with Shaarey Zedek and B'nai Israel in charity work and synagogue dedications, its congregants consciously viewed themselves as Detroit's Jewish high society and elite and refused to mingle with the other synagogues' members on terms of social equality.[41] The history of the Phoenix Social Club serves as a case in point. Founded by Beth El members in 1872, the Phoenix limited its membership to a very small, select group and, until its disappearance in the 1930s, remained Detroit's most important and exclusive Jewish city club. Membership in the Phoenix symbolized the attainment of the apex of the Jewish status hierarchy; Temple Beth El congregants constituted over 90 percent of the club's membership.[42]

WELFARE

Early Jewish philanthropy in Detroit, as elsewhere in the United States, centered in the synagogue. Beth El's first constitution provided that "on application for charitable purposes the president shall have a right to grant a sum not exceeding $5.00." For larger sums, he consulted with his board of trustees. Generally, the congregation assisted three types of cases: the poor, local Jew who, because of incapacity or misfortune, needed aid; immigrants who often arrived penniless and had to be helped until able to establish themselves; and transients who remained in Detroit until they could be sent to another town. In addition to money, Beth El provided free seats in the synagogue on the High Holy Days, *matzoth* for Passover, wood during the winter months, and free burial service.[43]

Residence of Emil S. Heineman, at 428 Woodward Avenue, built in 1859. (Courtesy of the Detroit Historical Museum.)

Although the congregations—Beth El, Shaarey Zedek, and B'nai Israel, as well as the later ones— maintained *Bikkur Cholim* and *Chevra Kadisha* societies to visit and care for sick congregants and assist families of departed members, the growth of the community combined with the deep-rooted Jewish tradition of aid to the distressed resulted in the establishment of other charitable societies. A Young Men's Hebrew Benevolent Society, with an enrollment of thirty members, was established in 1861.

43

Residence of Samuel Heavenrich at 468 Woodward Avenue, circa 1880. (Courtesy of the Detroit Historical Museum.)

Residence of Simon Heavenrich, at 43 Winder Street, was built in 1875. (Courtesy of the Detroit Historical Museum.)

Eight years later Beth El founded with Shaarey Zedek the Gentlemen's Hebrew Relief Society (later called the Beth El Hebrew Relief Society), Detroit's first centralized Jewish philanthropic agency under congregational auspices, "for the purpose of relieving all deserving Jewish applicants, who may be considered by its officers to be worthy of the society's bounty."[44]

In 1863 Isaac Mayer Wise appealed to a number of rabbis to organize women's societies in their communities in order to raise funds for a widows' and orphans' home to be established under the auspices of B'nai B'rith. Responding to Wise's appeal, Rabbi Laser called a meeting of Beth El women to create such a society. Because a large number of the participants objected to sending widows and orphans from all parts of the country to one home, the group decided to form a women's society for the support of Jewish widows and orphans within the state of Michigan only. This Ladies' Society for the Support of Hebrew Widows and Orphans in the state of Michigan aimed "to support needy widows and orphans of the Jewish faith and eventually to erect an orphan asylum in the city of Detroit so as to give these orphans a proper Jewish and general education." A male congregant, Louis Hirschman, served as the organization's first president.[45]

A number of controversies threatened to split the Ladies' Society during the first decade of its existence. One involved a number of Beth El's male congregants, who questioned the women's (any woman's) ability to manage the charity and its finances according to "sound business principles." An early compromise was reached in which the women would be the elected officers and the men would comprise the society's board and advisory committee.

Another dispute arose in 1868 when the local B'nai B'rith Pisgah Lodge solicited funds for the Jewish Orphan Asylum in Cleveland. Mrs. Louis Hirschman, then president of the Ladies' Society, refused to make a contribution on the grounds that this violated the Society's constitution, which specified that the Society was organized to take care of local needs only. At a special meeting, a majority voted in favor of making the contribution, whereupon Mrs. Hirschman re-

Map 2. Residential Distribution of Temple Beth El Members, 1877

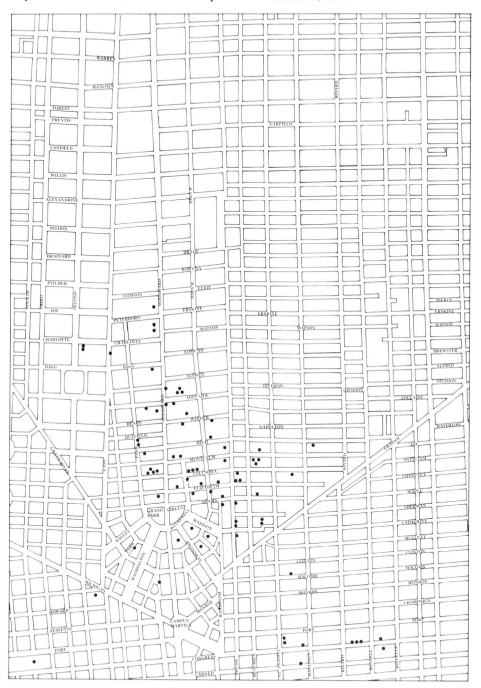

signed, taking her husband with her. Subsequently, a group of members secured a court injunction to prevent the withdrawal of Society funds for any but local purposes. Bitterness and friction between members continued until a coterie of Beth El ladies, led by Mrs. Emil Heineman, organized the Subsidiary Society for the Cleveland Orphan Asylum to raise money for that institution. Their work merited special praise from Isaac M. Wise at the Asylum's inaugural ceremony in 1868.[46]

Temple Beth El women played a significant role in Jewish philanthropy in Detroit. Economically secure, their children grown and able to care for themselves, these women devoted an enormous amount of their leisure time to charity. While their husbands frequently lent a helping hand in raising funds, the women traveled about the city, visiting the poor, comforting the sick, and making the arrangements necessary for the well-being of pensioners. The men determined how much of the Temple's resources could be allocated to charity; the women decided where and how the money was spent.

Reflecting the Jewish community's increasing diversity, a number of other charitable societies, some short-lived, sprang up by 1880. The ladies of Congregation Shaarey Zedek organized their own women's auxiliary for the support of local widows and orphans in 1863. A Purim Association, dedicated to assisting the poor, formed in 1871, and members of Shaarey Zedek and B'nai Israel established the Chevra Bikkur Cholim Society of Detroit, Michigan in 1874. Also created were the Shomrey Sabbath Society, an organization that provided assistance, loans, and sick relief to "Israelites who regularly keep the Sabbath" and a Ladies Hebrew Benevolent Society, both incorporated in 1880.[47]

Each of these charities raised money through membership dues and fund raising affairs, the most popular being *Simchat Torah* (Rejoicing in the Law) and Purim dances. One Purim masquerade ball, held in 1864 under the auspices of the Ladies' Society for the Support of Hebrew Widows and Orphans, charged fifty cents admission (children at half price) and sold coffee, cake, and sandwiches for ten cents each. The

Ladies' Society discontinued their Purim balls in 1877 because so many other Jewish organizations held them that their social value and material benefits no longer justified the expense and effort.[48]

Detroit Jews expressed commitment to the Jewish people by assisting not only local Jews but also needy Jews in other parts of the nation and the world. Detroiter Simon Heavenrich was one of the directors of the Cleveland Orphan Asylum, while the local Subsidiary Society continued raising funds on its behalf. Temple Beth El assisted Jews in Hamilton, Ohio, erect a synagogue and responded to an urgent appeal from Adolphe Cremieux, of the Alliance Israelite Universelle, by sending five hundred francs to aid Jewish victims of the Russo-Turkish war. In 1878 Congregation B'nai Israel and some dozen other Jewish Detroiters contributed from one to ten dollars each to help the Jewish community in Palestine. Members of Beth El extended their largess to include local non-Jewish philanthropies, contributing to Detroit's Protestant Orphan Asylum, House of Providence and Home of the Friendless, and Women's Hospital.[49]

ACCULTURATION

Americanization and cultural assimilation proceeded rapidly within the older German Jewish community. English supplanted German as Beth El's "official" language in 1876, and American and secular themes and motifs began to predominate the celebration of Jewish holidays. Hanukkah (Festival of Lights) parties for children concentrated more on "Red Riding Hood's Rescue," magic lantern shows, pantomimes, and "Negro whimsicalities and singing, with the usual bones and tamborine" and less on the festival's religious or historical significance. Passover became an occasion for sermons about George Washington, Abraham Lincoln, and the Declaration of Independence; Purim and *Simchat Torah* served as little more than excuses for dances and balls. At the same time, the congregation displayed its patriotism on American national holidays by holding large prayer meetings,

Map 3. Residential Distribution of Shaarey Zedek, B'nai Israel, and B'nai Jacob Members, 1877

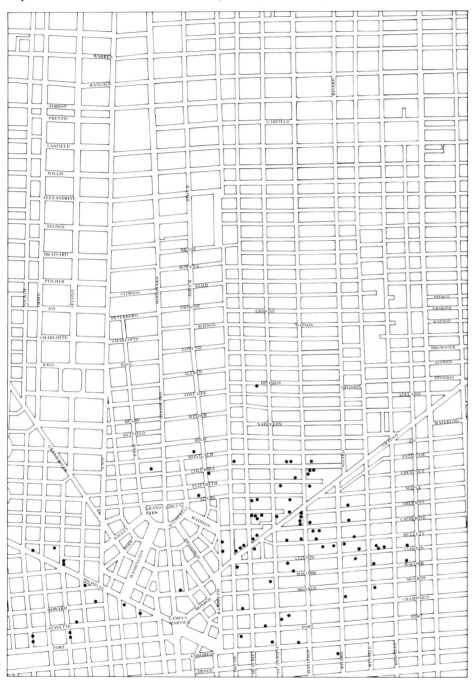

featuring a special talk by the rabbi, and sponsoring commemorative socials with names like "Washington Tea Party."[50]

Despite their increasing secularization, many Jewish Detroiters wished to maintain their Jewish identity. Philanthropy provided one way of doing so; belonging to a Jewish organization offered another. Pisgah Lodge No. 34, of the International Order of B'nai B'rith, America's oldest Jewish fraternal and service organization, was established in 1857 by twelve members of Congregation Beth El. For many years the lodge remained an adjunct of the Temple, with the leaders of one being officers of the other. Twenty years after Pisgah's founding, a second B'nai B'rith lodge, Peninsular Lodge No. 272, arose with a broader-based membership than the older lodge. A branch of the Free Sons of Israel, the nation's second oldest Jewish fraternal organization, Montefiore Lodge No. 12, came into existence in 1864. The lodge's articles of incorporation stated that "candidates for admission must be of unreproachable character, sound mind and body; not have any visible or invisible disease and must have some occupation whereby he gains an honest livelihood." Primarily interested in mutual aid, Montefiore Lodge, was Detroit's first Jewish organization, other than a synagogue, to purchase a cemetery for its members and their families. A rival of Montefiore Lodge was organized in 1867 under the name of "Charity Lodge no. 14 of the Improved Order Free Sons of Israel."

In 1867 seven members of Congregation Shaarey Zedek established King David Lodge No. 8 of the Order Kesher Shel Barzel (Iron Knot). Within ten years, Detroit contained three additional branches of the order—Bethel Lodge (1969), Nathan Lodge (1876), and Detroit Lodge (1875). Fraternal organizations proved popular because they offered fellowship, mutual aid, life insurance, and death benefits. They also broke down some of the feelings of isolation local Jews may have felt by presenting opportunities, through district and regional conventions, for association with Jews from other parts of the United States. Membership in a national Jewish fraternal order assumed increasing communal importance, as it often furnished the only link with Jews and Judaism that religiously unaffiliated Jews had.[51]

NOTES

1. Irving I. Katz, *The Beth El Story* (Detroit: Wayne State University Press, 1955), pp. 65-67; 174-75; *Occident*, April, 1852, p. 58. The charter members of Beth El were Jacob Silberman, Solomon Bendit, Joseph Freedman, Max Cohen, Adam Hersch, Alex Hein, Jacob Lang, Aron Joel Friedlander, Leo Bresler, Charles E. Bresler, and Louis Bresler.

2. Isaac M. Wise, *Reminiscences* (Cincinnati: Leo Wise and Company, 1901), p. 45.

3. Katz, *Beth El*, pp. 66-67; Irving I. Edgar, "The Early Sites and Beginnings of Congregation Beth El," *Michigan Jewish History* (November, 1970), pp. 5-11.

4. Katz, *Beth El*, p. 70; *Israelite*, September 8, 1854, p. 70.

5. Nathan Glazer, *American Judaism* (Chicago; University of Chicago Press, 1972), pp. 27-34.

6. *Ibid.*

7. *Ibid.*, pp. 36-42.

8. *The Jewish Encyclopedia 1* (New York, 1905), p. 197; Simon Wolf, *The American Jew as Patriot, Soldier and Citizen* (Philadelphia, 1895), p. 425; *Die Deborah*, December 19, 1856, p. 140; Irving I. Katz,"Sisterly Love Society Existed in Detroit in 1859," *Michigan Jewish History* (January, 1972), pp. 16-18; *Israelite*, December 26, 1856, p. 196.

9. Wise, *Reminiscences*, p. 303.

10. *Occident*, September, 1857, pp. 306-7. Isaac Leeser (1806-68) was the spokesman for traditional Judaism. German born, he served as the minister of Congregation Mikveh Israel in Philadelphia and founded the first American Jewish periodical, *Occident*, in 1843.

11. *Israelite*, December 3, 1858, p. 174, August 26, 1859, p. 63.

12. Leo M. Franklin, "The Jewish Reform Movement in Detroit," *The Reform Advocate*, March 2, 1912, p. 4; Eli Grad, "Congregation Shaarey Zedek, Detroit, Michigan: A Centennial History,

1861-1961" (typescript), pp. 9-12, Shaarey Zedek File, Temple Beth El Archives.

13. *Israelite*, August 26, 1859, pp. 62-63, October 12, 1860, p. 118.

14. *Israelite*, March 29, 1861, p. 310, September 13, 1861, p. 86; Katz, *Beth El*, pp. 74-75; *Detroit Free Press*, August 31, 1861, p. 1; *Detroit Tribune and Advertiser*, August 31, 1861, p. 1.

15. *Israelite*, December 20, 1861, p. 198, July 17, 1863, p. 18; "A Call to Detroit—1869," *American Jewish Archives* 19 (April, 1967), pp. 34-40.

16. Katz, *Beth El*, pp. 76-78.

17. See Appendix B for the biographies of these rabbis.

18. *Detroit Free Press*, August 31, 1867, p. 1; *Israelite*, September 6, 1867, p. 6.

19. "Beth El Executive Board Minutes, 1874-89," October 3, 1875, February 13, 1876, Burton Historical Collection, Detroit, Michigan.

20. Butzel to Zirndorf, March 22, 1876, Butzel to Zirndorf, June 9, 1876, Heinrich Zirndorf Collection, American Jewish Archives, Cincinnati, Ohio.

21. *The Jewish Encyclopedia* 12 (New York, 1905), p. 687.

22. Beth El Executive Board Minutes, 1874-89, September 16, 1877, October 6, 1878, February 2, 1879, Burton Historical Collection; *Israelite*, November 9, 1880, p. 166.

23. Irving I. Katz, "Jewish Education at Temple Beth El, 1850-1871)," *Michigan Jewish History* (June, 1968), pp. 24-29; *Detroit Free Press*, April 9, 1862, p. 1.

24. The material on Jewish education in the United States is taken from two works by Lloyd P. Gartner: *Jewish Education in the United States: A Documentary History* (New York: Teachers College Press, 1969), pp. 7-9, and "Temples of Liberty Unpolluted: American Jews and the Public Schools, 1840-1875," in *A Bicentennial Festschrift for Jacob Rader Marcus*, Bertram W. Korn, ed. (New York: Ktav, 1976), pp. 157-89.

25. Gartner, *Jewish Education*, pp. 7-9.

26. *Ibid.*, p. 8.

27. Katz, "Jewish Education at Beth El," pp. 29-31; Beth El School Board Minutes, 1871-98, p. 5, Burton Historical Collection.

28. Beth El School Board Minutes, August 17, 1872, pp. 7, 26-27; Katz, "Jewish Education at Beth El," pp. 29-31.

29. Beth El Annual Reports, June 14, 1874, April 21, 1872, June 13, 1872; Report of Magnus Butzel, September 24, 1876; Report of S. Schloss, October 16, 1878; Beth El School Board Minutes, pp. 53-64, Burton Historical Collection.

30. Grad, "Congregation Shaarey Zedek," p. 15; *Hamagid*, August 28, 1867, p. 268. The seventeen founders of Shaarey Zedek were Isaac and Raphael Epstein, Leopold Fink, Marcus and Jacob Freud, Samuel Fleischman, Hiram Kraushaar, Morris and Ludwig Levy, David Marx, George Morris, Louis Myers, Samuel Newman, Jacob Robinson, Harris Solomon, Isaac Warshauer, and Isaac Wertheimer. See Eli Grad and Bette Roth, *Congregation Shaarey Zedek* (Southfield, Mich.: Congregation Shaarey Zedek, 1982), p. 22.

31. *Israelite*, October 7, 1864, p. 117; *Detroit Free Press*, September 24, 1864, p. 1; Grad and Roth, *Shaarey Zedek*, p. 23.

32. *Hamagid*, August 28, 1867, p. 268; Grad and Roth, *Shaarey Zedek*, p. 23.

33. *Israelite*, November 3, 1876, p. 7; Shaarey Zedek File, Temple Beth El Archives. Shaarey Zedek's spiritual leaders from 1861 to

1877 were M. Sapper (1861-63), A. Shappera (1863-65), Laser Kontrovich (1865-67), A. Goldsmith (1867-70), and B. Moskowitz (1870-77). See Grad and Roth, *Shaarey Zedek*, p. 155, for a complete list of Shaarey Zedek's rabbis, as well as for a full history of that congregation.

34. *Israelite*, November 3, 1876, p. 6.

35. *Detroit Free Press*, July 6, 1877, p. 1.

36. Grad, "Congregation Shaarey Zedek," pp. 23-24; *Detroit Free Press*, September 3, 1879, p. 1.

37. *Detroit Evening News*, July 13, 1880, p. 4.

38. *Detroit Tribune*, January 18, 1886, p. 1.

39. *Detroit Free Press*, January 27, 1876, p. 1, September 4, 1879, p. 1.

40. See the Constitution of Congregation Beinei Israel, 1874, Temple Beth El Archives; *Detroit Free Press*, October 4, 1878, p. 1, October 6, 1878, p. 1, October 9, 1878, p. 1, September 4, 1879, p. 1.

41. Beth El and Phoenix Social Club members referred to themselves as the "elite" and "better sort" and restricted their social affairs to those announced by formal invitation. See the *Israelite*, September 13, 1872, p. 6, October 4, 1872, p. 10, March 8, 1878, p. 6; Katz, *Beth El*, p. 183.

42. Martin Marger, "The Force of Ethnicity: A Study of Urban Elites," *Journal of University Studies* 10 (Winter, 1974), pp. 88-89. See also the Phoenix Social Club registers of 1877, 1900, and 1912; *Detroit Blue Book, 1896-97* (Detroit: Blue Book Publishing Co., 1896), p. 332; and *Israelite*, September 13, 1872, p. 6. Paul Leake in 1912 included the Phoenix Social Club among the five most prominent Detroit Clubs (Paul Leake *History of Detroit* [Chicago: Lewis Publishing Co., 1912], p. 250).

43. Constitution of Congregation Beth El, 1851; Articles of Incorporation of Congregation Beth El, 1851, Temple Beth El Archives; *Occident*, August, 1852, pp. 265-66; *Detroit Jewish News*, September 2, 1949, p. 3.

44. Grad "Congregation Shaarey Zedek," p. 18; Constitution Beinei Israel, 1874, Temple Beth El Archives; *Israelite*, February 8, 1861, p. 254; *Detroit Jewish News*, September 2, 1949, p. 13. In 1872-73, the Gentlemen's Hebrew Relief Society granted 209 requests for relief to fifty-two persons, twenty-nine of whom were residents of Detroit, twelve regular pensioners, and twenty-three strangers passing through the city (*Detroit Jewish News*, September 2, 1949, p. 13).

45. Constitution of the Ladies' Society for the Support of Hebrew Widows and Orphans, 1865, pp. 3-8, Temple Beth El Archives; *Detroit Jewish News*, September 9, 1949, p. 6. A clause in the Ladies' Society's constitution made it possible for a person "to have the kaddish prayer recited by orphans on the anniversary of their death [*Yahrzeit*], at each service of the synagogue, by contributing to the society during their lifetime a sum of not less than $50."

46. Minute Book, Ladies Society for the Support of Hebrew Widows and Orphans, pp. 10-12; *Detroit Jewish News*, September 23, 1949, p. 61; *Inaugural Book, Cleveland Orphan Asylum, 1868* (Cleveland, 1869), pp. 3, 21, Temple Beth El Archives.

47. *Hamagid*, August 28, 1867, p. 268; *Israelite*, February 3, 1871, p. 7, July 2, 1880, p. 7, March 26, 1880, p. 6.

48. *Detroit Jewish News*, September 23, 1949, p. 61; Minutes, Ladies Society for the Support of Hebrew Widows and Orphans, p. 5, Temple Beth El Archives; *Detroit Free Press*, February 16, 1873, p. 1; *Jewish Messenger*, March 15, 1878, p. 2.

49. Beth El Executive Board Minutes, 1874-89, September 23, 1877, p. 104, April 7, 1878, p. 112, April 21, 1878, p. 114, Temple Beth El Archives; *Israelite*, March 31, 1871, p. 7, December 28, 1877, p. 5; Salo Baron, "Palestinian Messengers in America, 1849-79: A Record of Four Journeys," in *Steeled by Adversity*, ed. Baron (Philadelphia: Jewish Publication Society of America, 1971), p. 255.

50. *Detroit Daily Post*, July 21, 1869, p. 5; Katz, *Beth El*, p. 87; Beth El Executive Board Minutes, 1874-89, October 3, 1875, p. 35,

Temple Beth El Archives; Beth El School Board Minute Book, 1871-78, November 6, 1871, p. 2, Temple Beth El Archives; *Israelite*, May 7, 1875, p. 6, December 29, 1876, p. 5, December 10, 1880, p. 191.

51. See the Jewish fraternal orders and organizations files in the Temple Beth El Archives; *Detroit Daily Post*, July 21, 1868, p. 2; *Israelite*, August 19, 1859, p. 55, February 5, 1875, p. 6; *Detroit Free Press*, February 14, 1875, p. 1.

4. NEW IMMIGRANTS
The Eastern European Community

THE MASS MIGRATION of Eastern European Jews to the United States unofficially began in September 1881, when the first party of pogrom victims landed in New York. Three months later Detroit received its first group of such immigrants. They proved to be the vanguard of an Eastern European immigration, mostly from Russia, that continued unchecked till World War I and that had an enormous impact on Detroit's established Jewish community.[1]

Poverty and oppression were the major causes of this migration. The assassination of Czar Alexander II in 1881 and the accession of Alexander III spelled disaster for Russia's Jews. A few sporadic pogroms (organized massacres of Jews) occurred prior to Alexander III, but beginning with his regime the pogrom became a feature of czarist rule. Although not directly engineered by the central government, these attacks on Jews were tolerated by Russian officialdom, despite an occasional face-saving protest to the contrary. Undoubtedly, no serious excesses could have occurred without the tacit consent of the authorities, for experience demonstrated that the least show of force by the police checked the violence of the mob. In the 1880s, the intent of the pogrom was to destroy and plunder Jewish property. Once set loose, however, the frenzied mobs often committed acts of mutilation, rape, and murder.[2]

Numerous restrictive laws also contributed to Jewish anguish in Russia. The most severe of these, the May Laws of 1882, prohibited the Jews from living anywhere but in the towns and villages within the Pale of Settlement, those territories of western Russia where Jews were permitted to reside legally. The Pale encompassed an area of approximately 386,000 square miles. By 1897 almost 4,900,000 Jews lived there, constituting about 94 percent of the Jewish population of Russia and 12 percent of the population of the area. The May Laws also forbade Jews from owning or managing real estate or farms outside the cities of the Pale and prohibited them from engaging in any business activity on Sundays and Christian holidays. These laws, together with the Russian government's harsh limits on the number of Jews allowed to enter secondary schools, universities, and the professions, created intolerable economic hardship for the Jewish population. These restrictions set the Jews apart in ways other than physical; Jews appeared to be citizens of a special class to which the general laws and protections did not apply. Thus, the peasants in the mobs which destroyed Jewish lives and property frequently believed that they acted under an order of the czar.[3]

Mob excesses reached their highest pitch of frenzy during the reign of Nicholas II (1894–1917), who employed the pogrom as a means of diverting the growing disaffection of his people and of curbing the growing revolutionary activity. By blaming the misery of the masses on the Jews, the Russian government hoped to cover its own corruption and inefficiency— the real causes of the suffering. The killing, pillaging, and raping, which characterized the pogroms of 1903 and 1905 and which were tolerated by the government, convinced even the most optimistic and "Russified" among the Jews that Russia offered them little hope, security, or safety. Some of them emigrated to Palestine or joined one of the burgeoning revolutionary parties; the vast majority of the disaffected emigrated to America.[4]

At the same time, a large number of Jews began coming to the United States from Rumania and Galicia because of the discrimination and hardship prevalent in those countries. The Rumanian government treated its Jews as "foreigners" in terms of rights and as "natives" in terms of duties, such as army service and payment of taxes, and rarely granted them citizenship despite numerous treaties guaranteeing them this right. Between 1878 and 1903 the Rumanian government gave only two hundred Jews citizenship. The Rumanians also restricted Jews economically. At one time or another they prohibited them from selling liquor, from acting as money brokers or commission merchants, from entering the professions of law, medicine, chemistry, and pharmacy, and barred them from the tobacco trade. By 1903, through a series of acts and decrees, the government excluded Jews from more than two hundred occupations and trades. Pogroms, which began in 1866 and erupted intermittently throughout the remainder of the nineteenth century, added to the misery of Rumania's Jews.[5]

Galicia, economically the most backward province in Austria-Hungary, became the third great source of migrating Jews. Although emancipated in 1867 and unaffected by pogroms or residential restrictions, Galician Jewry endured a terrible and grinding poverty. Most of Galicia's Jews lived as *luftmenschen,* subsisting on petty trade, pawnbroking, "casual" occupations, and handicrafts, with few of them enjoying any sort of economic security. After 1866, their lot worsened. Rising nationalism led to boycotts of Jewish merchants and the removal of Jews from their jobs. In addition, Jewish traders competed unsuccessfully with cheap factory products that flooded the eastern provinces of the empire; the expansion of the railways adversely affected Jewish teamsters and truckers; and the competition from Viennese clothing firms, which opened branches in the large cities of the province, put many Jewish tailors out of business. According to the 1897 census, Jews, comprising 11 percent of the population, made up 52 percent of the "independents of no vocation." Even among the poverty-stricken Eastern European Jews, Galicians had the reputation of being the poorest of the poor.[6]

While many Jews fled home and country to escape violence, terror, and deprivation, others came to America because of its lure. This pull factor is amply illustrated in the hundreds of immigrant letters published in the European Hebrew and Yiddish press which spoke of America as a land of freedom, equality, and opportunity, *di goldene medine,* "the golden land," the magic land, the promised land. Mary Antin reminisced that at the end of one Passover seder some of those around the table said not "'May we be next year in Jerusalem,' but 'Next year—in America!'"[7]

Whether pushed or pulled, from 1881 to 1914, close to two million Jews entered the United States, over 75 percent of them from Russia. Jews comprised 9 percent of the nearly twenty million immigrants who came to America during this period. They increased the country's Jewish population from an estimated 400,000 in 1888 to 3.3 million by 1917. Detroit's Jewish population reflected this change, growing from 1,000 in 1880 to 10,000 in 1900 to about 34,000 by 1914, with Russian Jews constituting over 75 percent of the total.[8]

The Russians coming to Detroit were young: 16 percent were under the age of twenty, more than 40

Jefferson Avenue in the 1880s. (Courtesy of the Detroit Historical Museum.)

percent were in their twenties, and about 30 percent were in their thirties. Of those sent to Detroit by the Industrial Removal Office (IRO)—an immigrant removal agency headquartered in New York—15 percent were between the ages of fifteen and twenty, 60 percent were in their twenties, and 22 percent were in their thirties. The Russian Jewish emigration was a family movement; almost 70 percent of the Russians in Detroit and over half of the three thousand men sent by the IRO were married. Most of the married men sent by the IRO came without their wives; two thirds of them still had their families in Europe. Practically all the Russians coming to Detroit had lived in

the United States for varying lengths of time. A majority of the IRO men had been in the country less than six months, while the majority of the non-IRO immigrants had lived in the United States for more than a year.[9]

The city these immigrants encountered was undergoing a change from a modest manufacturing center to one of the world's major industrial metropolises. Based on the value of all its manufactured goods, Detroit ranked nineteenth among American cities in 1880, seventeenth in 1890, and sixteenth in 1900—moving only three notches in twenty years. Detroit's population also grew slowly, ranking eighteenth in

Jefferson Avenue, circa 1910. (Courtesy of the Burton Historical Collection.)

1880, fifteenth in 1890, and thirteenth in 1900, with 285,704 people. Under the influence of automobile manufacturing, however, Detroit changed dramatically.[10]

Automobile assembly began about 1900, when Ransom Olds moved from East Lansing, Michigan, to Detroit and created the Oldsmobile, the first commercially built car in the United States. Henry Ford opened his plant the following year, and three years later Henry Leland created the Cadillac Company. The total number of factory employees in Detroit was 60,554 when Leland started his firm. Of these workers, the automobile industry employed only 2,232 or 3.8 percent. At that time, the city had a diversified manufacturing economy with foundry and machine shop products, pharmaceuticals, and stoves and fur-

naces leading its list of goods produced. Motor vehicles ranked only fourth in the total value of manufactured products.

By 1909 the number of persons employed in manufacturing had doubled, while in automobile factories it had increased eightfold. In 1914 workers in automobile manufacturing comprised 40 percent of the total number of manufacturing employees. Detroit employed 17 percent of the nation's auto workers in 1904 and 47 percent of them in 1914. Between 1909 and 1914, almost 85 percent of America's growth in the automobile industry occurred in Detroit. In 1900 Detroit produced only 4,192 passenger cars; fifteen years later the figure stood at 895,930. During this same period, Detroit moved from sixteenth place as an industrial center, as measured by the value of its product, to fourth. Auto manufacturing transformed Detroit from a diversified trade and manufacturing city into a one-industry town.[11]

The spectacular growth of the automobile industry naturally attracted migrants. Detroit, with 465,766 residents, rose to ninth place in population among American cities in 1910. A decade later, Detroit had climbed to fourth place with 993,678 people. Of the 528,000 people added to Detroit's population between 1910 and 1920, more than 420,000 came from American farms, lumber camps, and mines and foreign lands.[12]

The Eastern European Jews came to the city for a variety of reasons. Detroit's reputation as a growing industrial center and a pleasant place to live attracted immigrants who had experienced economic hardships and difficult living conditions elsewhere. One newcomer, Louis Friedman, wrote enthusiasti-

Central Marketplace in Cadillac Square in 1890. Behind it is the area of Eastern Market. (Courtesy of the Burton Historical Collection.)

Michigan and Woodward Avenues in 1890. (Courtesy of the Burton Historical Collection.)

A traffic jam at Woodward Avenue and Grand Boulevard, circa 1912. (Courtesy of the Burton Historical Collection.)

cally that in Detroit "if only one wants to work, there is no shortage of work" and "the working class does not live in foul, airless rooms, as in New York, because the rent is cheaper here. Detroit is to be marveled at for her freedom and her clean air, which is like that found in a park full of beautiful trees." Louis Polansky advised his friends to come because "there is plenty of work in this town." Other immigrants came because relatives or *landsman* (fellow countrymen) had already settled in the city and could help them get established. Nathan Kaluzny reminisced how he originally left Galveston, Texas, his port of entry, for New York because he had relatives there. After a long period of unemployment and of sleeping at night in Central Park, he moved to Detroit because a cousin in the city promised him work. Other immigrants came because Jewish relief agencies in other communities, feeling Detroit offered better employment opportunities, sent them.[13]

Immigrants to Detroit usually arrived at one of three railroad depots: the Michigan Central, the Union, and the Grand Trunk. At each of these places, police officers and representatives from private agencies were on hand to assist and direct the arrivals. As soon as the immigrants disembarked, railroad officials grouped them together so the police could collect their medical inspection certificates and register their local addresses. Two of the depots provided special rooms for the immigrants, and railroad officials, the police, and the organizational representatives cooperated in the processing. The immigrants who had friends or relatives waiting for them received first priority, and as soon as they were positively identified, they were

City Hall in 1910. (Courtesy of the Detroit Historical Museum.)

sent on their way. Those immigrants who wanted a taxi paid a flat rate (one dollar in 1914) to be taken to any part of the city. The remainder were directed to their destinations by the intercity secretary of the YMCA, an agent of the local traveler's aid society, or the police officer on the spot.[14]

During the early stages of the Russian emigration, Detroiters expressed sympathy for the pogrom victims and anger and outrage at the government that persecuted them. Feelings of apprehension surfaced, however, as the migration showed little sign of abating. By the early 1890s, the city's press began referring to the immigration as an "incursion" and "threatening tide." One blatantly nativist piece in the *Detroit News* accused the newcomers of posing a health hazard because "they came from cholera infested cities of Europe and carried the plague with them." Although not likely to infect Detroit's "better classes of American citizens," the cholera would certainly run rampant among the "foreigners whose houses and clothing are absolutely filthy, and who go down into garbage heaps and jerk out the choicest bits of old meat and decaying fruit for food." This element lived, among other places, "along the upper section of Hastings street, where many Polish Jews have settled."

These charges received a boost at a public forum a few weeks later when Detroit alderman J. Christopher Jacob claimed to possess information proving that Russian Jews brought cholera to the United States. Despite a prompt, factual rebuttal by Temple Beth El's respected rabbi Louis Grossmann, Detroiters' fear of the plague approached hysteria. The Reverend J. R. Johnson, a local minister, added fuel to the fire by contending that the immigrants threatened more than just the nation's physical health, but its very soul. Since these Jews were "a pauper and lawless class," he said, they would undoubtedly "combine with our own worst elements to break down the American Sunday," which would destroy America's "grand Christian civilization." Some time later, a visiting clergyman, the Reverend Isaac Lansing of Scranton, Pennsylvania, delivered a racist sermon in Detroit's Fort Street Presbyterian Church alleging that the Russian Jewish immigration posed a

greater menace to the United States than the "yellow peril."[15]

The reactions of Detroiters reflected the national mood. Until the 1880s, most immigrants to the United States came from England, Scotland, Ireland, Germany, and the Scandinavian countries. Beginning in the 1880s and extending to World War I, the immigrants came chiefly from Southern and Eastern Europe. This "New Immigration," as it came to be called, triggered anxiety and prejudice amongst native Americans and others, such as the Irish, who themselves had once been the victims of similar fears, because it appeared so unlike the earlier immigrations. The newcomers, whom the economist and reformer Henry George once referred to as "human garbage," were primarily Catholic, swarthy, "undersized," and landless peasants. Most were illiterate and lacked trades and marketable skills.

The Eastern Europeans, coming from countries such as Russia and Austria-Hungary, which were breeding grounds for revolutions and revolutionaries, created panic among American patricians who feared a loss of influence on their nation's destiny. Henry Adams dramatically called for a *Götterdämmerung* in which "men of our kind might have some chance of being honorably killed in battle" so as to avoid being enslaved by Jews. When an anarchist bomb killed seven policemen and wounded seventy in Chicago's Haymarket Square in 1886, it confirmed American phobias about radical foreigners fomenting strikes and labor unrest. The stereotype of the foreigner as anarchist was further reinforced when a psychotic Polish anarchist, Leon Czolgosz, assassinated President McKinley in 1901.[16]

Two significant events in the 1890s, the official announcement of the disappearance of the frontier and the panic that occurred in 1893 and the resultant depression that lasted until 1897, sapped American optimism and confidence in the ability of the United States to absorb the new immigrants. At the same time, social Darwinism and European racial theories exerted an influence upon Americans already panicky about what they regarded as an alien invasion. Believing that the newcomers would produce social degeneration and destroy everything America stood for—freedom, democracy, and capitalism—many old-line Americans clamored for immigration restriction as a means of preserving American values and culture. From 1882, Congress passed acts excluding paupers, convicts, those likely to become public charges, idiots, the insane, polygamists, prostitutes, persons suffering from contagious diseases, anarchists, alcoholics, advocates of the violent overthrow of the United States government, and the Chinese (1904). Attempts to bar immigrants illiterate in their own language failed until 1917, when Congress overrode President Woodrow Wilson's veto. Finally, in 1924, the Johnson Quota Law effectively ended immigration from Southern and Eastern Europe.[17]

THE JEWISH QUARTER

Notwithstanding protests and warnings of doom, the immigrants continued to come, crowding into the old German area on Detroit's east side. In the 1890s, the east side was the most colorful and economically diversified area of Detroit. "It has the churches, the synagogues, the breweries and the beer gardens that for elegance and desirability cannot be excelled in any other portion of the city," wrote the *Detroit News-Tribune* in 1896. "But while this is true, the fact remains that there are also on the east side certain sections with environments especially their own as to make them striking examples of foreign customs transported to American soil."[18]

One of these sections was the Jewish quarter located in a rectangle formed by Monroe, Watson, Brush, and Orleans Streets, with Hastings Street the major business thoroughfare. This remained the Jewish district, housing primarily Eastern European Jews, for the next two decades (Map 4). Although Russian Jews predominated in the quarter, it contained an intermingling of other ethnics as well. A sample of five houses on Napoleon Street in 1892 showed the occupants to be five Russian Jewish families, totaling 24 people, one English couple, and a

Pictures from "Springtime in Detroit's Ghetto," *Detroit Free Press*, May 9, 1909, showing the Eastern European Jewish district. (Courtesy of the Burton Historical Collection.)

Map 4. The Jewish Quarter

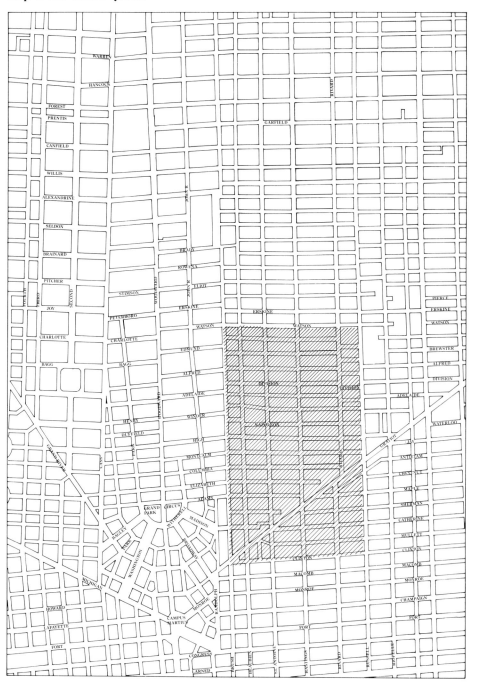

Single homes on Second Avenue in 1910. (Courtesy of the Burton Historical Collection.)

black family of four. Another sample of an area in the heart of the Jewish district, bounded by Hastings, St. Antoine, High, and Montcalm Streets, contained 299 people in 1900. They included 58 persons born in Russia, 38 born in the United States of Russian parents, 37 born in Germany, 48 born in the United States of German parents, 46 white Americans, 14 blacks, and some people of mixed parentage. Ten years later, Jews comprised over 60 percent of the adults living in this same region.[19]

Detroit's Russian Jewish quarter differed significantly from the classic ghetto and tenement districts of New York's lower east side. Throughout the pre-World War I period, Detroit remained basically a city of single family dwellings. In their classic study of the tenement house problem, Robert DeForest and Lawrence Veiller described turn-of-the-century Detroit as a city with no housing problem and no tenements. "The homes of the majority of the working-men and poorer people of the city are for the most part thoroughly comfortable, and most of the people live in separate houses, there being very few houses throughout the city where there are so many as three families in one building, and only a small number of cases where there are two families living in the same house."

While Detroit's immigrant districts became more congested over time, the only area to approach the squalor and overcrowding of Manhattan's slums was Detroit's black ghetto. The Russian Jews lived in

Rebecca Hertzberg in her home on east Elizabeth in 1895. (Courtesy of the Archives of Congregation Shaarey Zedek.)

small, relatively newly built (many were about fifteen years old in 1900) houses and not in dilapidated homes abandoned by previous occupants. Most of these homes had been built by German architects, builders, contractors, and carpenters who invested in the area and rented the structures to the Jews. Only in a few sections in the downtown area and near the city center were old tenements rented to the poor by absentee landlords.[20]

In terms of amenities, the east side was one of the least desirable areas of the city in which to live. The region continually lagged behind the west side in the number of water pipes laid, sewers installed, streets paved, and railway lines extended. Residential areas in most of Detroit were generally separate from industrial regions, but on the east side factories often dotted the neighborhoods, creating a pattern of intensive land use. The district was also more crowded, had

62

higher rents, and higher disease and death rates than other parts of the city.[21]

Nonetheless, the east side attracted Russian Jews because it was close to their places of work and contained all the elements necessary to give them a feeling of security and to cushion their adjustment to the city and, in some cases, to America. Variously dubbed "New Jerusalem," "Little Jerusalem," and "the Ghetto" by the city's press, the Jewish district abounded with "Hebrew stores of every description: butchers, grocers, bakers, clothiers, shoemakers, printing shops and restaurants," practically everything Detroit's Jews needed for a self-contained existence. "A Hebrew might live his lifetime in the quarter and never leave its confines," marveled one observer. In his 1907 report, the president of Detroit's United Jewish Charities observed of the Jewish immigrants that "though we suggest to them that we can find better and more spacious quarters in districts not so close to the center of the city, they prefer to suffer deprivation and discomfort in order to be in close contact with those who are closest to them, either because of birthplace or because of religious inclinations."[22]

Due to the continuous influx of newcomers and as a consequence of their having to share accommodations in order to pay the rent, the district eventually suffered from severe overcrowding and congestion. The *Jewish American,* the city's Anglo-Jewish weekly, ruefully concluded in 1911 that the Jewish quarter contained "tenement houses that are actually unfit to live in; old, decrepit, polluted and infected hovels, where human beings endeavor to exist and where a young generation is reared." Worse, the area became one of the city's prime breeding grounds for illness and disease, especially the dreaded tuberculosis.[23]

These conditions took their toll, and the community experienced a rise in family desertion and juvenile delinquency. However, criminal activity remained low during the prewar period. Russian Jews engaged in practically no crimes of violence but occasionally did get arrested for receiving stolen goods and larceny. Mostly, they were arrested for "acting in a suspicious manner," disturbing the peace, and ped-

Picture from "Detroit's Ghetto and Its People," *Detroit Free Press*, April 2, 1911, showing the Eastern European Jewish district. (Courtesy of the Burton Historical Collection.)

dling without a license. This resulted more from the immigrants' ignorance of the law and unfamiliarity with American conventions than from deliberately unlawful behavior. The majority of those arrested were released, and the number of Jewish prisoners in the Detroit House of Correction remained consistently low. Out of 2,407 prisoners in 1885 only six were Jews; in 1896 the figure was six Jews out of 1,339 prisoners; for 1900 it was four Jews out of 1,751 prisoners; and in 1910 there were nine Jews out of 2,808 prisoners.[24]

Although immigrant Jews flocked to the east side, they rarely stayed at one address for long. Examination of two randomly selected streets in the Jewish quarter over a span of fifteen years confirms what contemporary observers recognized: that the community was in constant flux. Of the eighteen Jews living on High Street between St. Antoine and Hastings in 1900, only one was still there ten years later. And of the twenty-two Jews on the street in 1910, only six remained in 1914. Of the seventeen Jews residing on Winder Street between Hastings and St. Antoine in 1905, four remained in 1910 and two in 1914. The Jews were not unique in this regard: only two of the non-Jews living on Winder Street in 1910 remained in 1914 (Table 8).[25]

This high rate of mobility can be attributed to the residents' desire for larger and better quarters as their economic status improved or, conversely, to their need for less expensive rooms as their fortunes fell. Other reasons could be their wish to relocate to a block with a higher Jewish density; a need to be closer to their place of work; or their leaving the city en-

tirely. This latter reason was especially true of single people or those who came to Detroit without their families. In addition, despite all its ethnic color and vibrancy, the east side, in terms of city services, health, sanitation, and crime rate, was not the most pleasant place in which to live or raise a family. Hence, many Russian Jews shifted to more suitable locations as soon as they could, which was why most of them rented their homes. A study of Detroit housing in 1900 reveals that 55 percent of the Germans and 44 percent of the Poles owned their own homes but only 14 percent of the Russian Jews owned theirs. Twenty years later, 41 percent of the Germans and 52

A jewelry store on Grand River and Oregon Streets, circa 1910. (Courtesy of the Archives of Congregation Shaarey Zedek.)

The United News Company, a novelty wholesale and retail store on Jefferson Avenue, circa 1910. (Courtesy of the Archives of Congregation Shaarey Zedek.)

percent of the Poles but only 30 percent of the Russian Jews owned their homes. This indirectly spurred Jewish economic mobility. Whereas German and Polish workingmen tied up their assets in their homes, Russian Jews invested their capital in business or their children's education.[26]

EARNING A LIVING

Contemporary accounts give the impression that Detroit's Russian Jews engaged in one of two occupations: business or peddling. "The first thing which impresses you," began one typical description of the Jewish district, "is the unmistakable evidence of commercial activity. The last thing of which you are reminded on leaving the district is that its people are all

business." Another account explained that the Russian Jew's economic "start is usually modest—a pack, perhaps, containing a few dollars worth of goods with which he goes from door to door, possibly a rickety old pushcart discarded by a more prosperous countryman and purchasable for its full value, together with a battered tin horn, which he blows lustily as he makes his way through the alleys in quest of rags or paper or old iron rubbers." If penniless on arrival, the newcomer could usually borrow money "from another, for most of these people had a life struggle getting started. Besides, the loan is amply secured, and the money will net something in the way of interest."[27]

Closer scrutiny of the early twentieth-century community shows Jews working at a wide variety of jobs in factories, offices, crafts, and trades (Table 9). Contrary to the stereotype of the Jew as peddler, less than 20 percent of Detroit's Jewish labor force ped-

The Detroit Yiddish Directory of 1907. Title page and advertisements. (Courtesy of the College of Jewish Studies Library.)

GOOD NEWS!

We wish to inform the Detroit Jewish public that we have built a gorgeous Russian and Turkish Steambath with all the latest improvements, newest machines, and steam from heated stones.

Hot and cold baths at any time, and a kosher Mikveh (ritual bath) for all the daughters of Israel, which is always open.

186 Alfred St. corner Antoine
Louis Schlussel, Proprietor

dled for a living. One study, based on a sample from the 1900 Census, compared selected ethnic groups in Detroit and found 30 percent of the Russian Jews in white-collar occupations, 17 percent of the German immigrants, 20 percent of the Irish, and 6 percent of the Poles (Table 10).[28]

A Detroit Yiddish directory, published in 1907, gives the names, addresses, and occupations of more than 2,300 Jews. After excluding the German Jewish members of Temple Beth El and women, we gain a picture of the Eastern European Jews' occupational structure at that time (Table 11). Comparing these figures with the entire city's male working population as delineated in the 1910 United States Census, we find 47 percent of the Jews employed as proprietors, managers, officials, and white-collar workers, as opposed to 21 percent of the general population (Table 12). At the same time, 74 percent of the Jewish working women were engaged in white-collar jobs as compared to 28 percent of the total female work force (Table 13).[29] Only one sector of Detroit's economy, the waste industry, can be said to have been dominated by Jews. By 1890 four times as many Jews as non-Jews dealt in rags, paper, junk, and scrap; a generation later Jewish waste dealers outnumbered non-Jewish dealers by 196 to 10.[30]

With minor variations, Jewish economic mobility in Detroit approximated that of Jews in other cities around the United States. In Los Angeles, New York, Atlanta, Columbus, and Portland, to name a few, Russian Jews enjoyed a higher occupational status than the general population. This success is usually attributed to several socio-historical factors, such as a centuries-old Jewish tradition of focusing on commerce, trade, industry, and scholarship; prior experience in urban environments; and the possession of the middle-class values of literacy, thrift, preparing for the future, and moderation. All of these well prepared Jews to deal with the economic opportunities and vicissitudes encountered in the American city.

The Eastern European Jewish family was child-centered and fostered a strong sense of family obligation. Consequently, successful relatives were willing to assist the younger generation to stay in school. The most successful Eastern Europeans are also found to be those who entered their family's business or started a business with their relatives. Another element to be considered in explaining Jewish success relates to the Jews' self-image as a special people. Excelling in their chosen fields is a means by which Jews can prove to themselves and to others that they are indeed a unique group. It is also a way of gaining approval from the host society. Accordingly, Jews were

THE GRADUATE RUSSIAN MIDWIFE

Miss Fanny Tchernoff is well known to everyone in Detroit for her noble care of rich and poor alike. Any woman may consult with her free of charge. Office: 284 Alfred St.

דיא גראדואירדטע

רוססישע

אַקושערין

מים פעני טשערנאָו

איז גוט בעקאַנט צו אלעמען
אין דעטראָים מים איהר
נאָבעלע בעהאַנדלונג
אַרעמע און רייכע.

יעדע פרוי קען זיך אן עוצה האַל־
טען נאָנין פרייא.

אָפֿים:
284 אלפרעד סטרים

BREAD PHILOSOPHY

Bread is strength. Bread is life. But depends on eating the right kind of bread. Such bread you can get at I. Feigenson, 498 Antoine St. My bread is thoroughly sifted and well-mixed and baked. My bakery is well lighted and clean. My pumpernickles, bagel, buns and cakes are tastiest. The Sabbath 'Chalehs' (breads) are unusual.

ברוים פֿילאָאָפֿיע'

ברוים איז קראַפֿם, ברוים איז לעבען.
אַבער דאָם דעהאַנגם זיך אַריב איהר עסם דעם ריכטיגען ברוים
אזא ריכטיגען ברוים קרים איהר ביי

י. פֿיינענסאָן

498 ענמואיין סמרים.

ביי ברוים איז אן נום חיכענגליאם, נום אויסגעקנאָטען,
אן נום אויסגעבאַקען.
סיין בעקערי איז ליכטיג און ריינליך, און רייו
סיינע פּאָמפּערניקעל, בייגעל, בולקעם און קייקעם
דיא נעשמאַקסטע.
דיא שבת'דינע חלהת איז א אויסנאַהם.

TEA AND COFFEE

The only right place to get tea and coffee is at S. Rabinowitz. Any grocer, even a push cart vender, can sell coffee and tea. The important thing is to know quality and that special yiddish flavor.

S. Rabinowitz,
392 Hastings St.

Horseshoing can be done by any blacksmith. But not any blacksmith can really satisfy. Only Sol Wolfson is long known as the best horseshoer in Detroit and doesn't have to praise his own work.

When your horse injures his foot and develops blood-poisoning, don't take it to a doctor, but bring it to me and the horse will be cured.

New wagons made to order. All work guaranteed.
402 St. Antoine St., cor. High

טהעע און קאָפֿפֿע

דער איינציגער ריכטיגער פּלאַטץ
פיר אמתע גוטע טהעע אונד
קאָפֿפֿע איז נור
ביי
ס. ראבינאָוויץ

392 הייסטינגס סטרים

דארט קרינם איהר עס.

S. RABINOWITZ
392 Hastings Street

פֿערד סמידען

קען יעדער סמי, אבער ניט יעדער סמי קען אייך
צופֿרידען שטעלען.

דארום דארף איהר צו סמידען אייער פֿערד אין א
זיכער און רוליענעל פֿלייס.

סאָל וואָלפֿסאָן

402 ענמואיין סם. קאָרנער האַי סם.

Abe Hertzberg and his taxicab company on Broadway
Avenue, circa 1912. (Courtesy of the Archives of
Congregation Shaarey Zedek.)

willing to make the investments and sacrifices necessary to insure success. And centuries of experience as an often-maligned minority taught Jews that in order to succeed, they had to be better than their non-Jewish neighbors and competitors. This led them to expect and demand more of themselves and their children.[31]

Although a high percentage of Detroit's Russian Jews classified as working class, only a fraction of them enrolled in the labor movement. This paralleled the local trend, for throughout the late nineteenth century and into the 1930s, Detroit was a non-union town, the least organized major city in the country. The great inpouring of Eastern Europeans, most of them with agricultural backgrounds and no union experience, together with the major technological changes in automobile manufacturing had a debilitating effect on the older crafts and skills. During the first great spurt of manufacturing growth between 1905 and 1910, the craft unions experienced difficulty in organizing and their strikes failed. Meanwhile, the number of unorganized workers grew. A powerful clique of industrialists, gathered together in the Employers Association of Detroit, won a key strike in 1907, dealing a severe blow to organized labor. One historian has gone so far as to call this event the "Waterloo of organized labor" in Detroit. From then on, until 1937, when the United Auto Workers (UAW) won its historic sit-down strike against General Motors, Detroit maintained a reputation as the "graveyard of organizers."[32]

The lack of unity of purpose among Detroit workers is illustrated by the fate of one all-Jewish union, Local 4 of the United Cloth, Hat and Capmakers of North America. At the end of 1904, Local 4 struck against the Detroit Cap Company, which sought to impose piece work in place of work by the week, as well as other demands. However, the local cutters' union and the Detroit branch of the Syndicalist Industrial Workers of the World (IWW), both led by one Lazarus Goldberg, refused to cooperate in the strike and signed separate contracts with the firm. A few months later the company repudiated the agreements, locked out the workers, and declared the firm

an open shop. Disregarding orders from their leaders, members of the IWW agreed to the new setup and went to work as scabs. As a result, the cap company broke the strike and instituted an open shop. Disheartened, some Local 4 members agreed to the new conditions while others left the city in hopes of finding work elsewhere.[33]

Despite the failure of the labor movement, by 1914 Detroit held a number of all-Jewish locals of national unions, including the Ladies Garment Workers Union No. 95, the Carpenter and Joiners Union No. 1191, the Bakers and Confectioners Union No. 78, as well as a local Federated Newsboys Union. The largest and most distinctively Jewish labor organization, however, was the Jewish Peddlers Union, which originated in response to assaults against Jewish peddlers by young ruffians. The ineffectiveness of the police in stopping the attacks led Jewish peddlers in 1900 to establish their own self-defense organization, the Jewish

David W. Simons, real estate developer, banker, civic leader, and member of Detroit's first nine-man city council. (Courtesy of the Archives of Shaarey Zedek.)

Peddlers Protective Union No. 9350. By 1903 the union contained three hundred members engaged in the junk, fruit, vegetable, and dry goods businesses, peddling on foot, with hand carts or with horses.[34]

Like the German Jews before them, a number of Russian immigrants attained economic success and community-wide recognition within their own lifetimes. Whereas the successful Germans concentrated primarily in merchandising and trade, the Russians achieved prominence in a wider variety of fields. David W. Simons was born in Russia in 1856 and came to Detroit in 1870. He began working in his father's junk business, but after the latter's death in 1888, he concentrated on buying and selling real estate and building homes and factories. He became one of Detroit's major developers and contractors and served as president of the Hamtramck State Bank, as commissioner of public lighting, and as a member of Detroit's first nine-man city council.

Abraham Jacobs, also born in Russia in 1856, came with his parents to Detroit from Washington, D.C., in 1868. In 1883 he opened a men's furnishings and clothing manufacturing business. He originated the central heating system used by Detroit and was the only individual in the United States granted a franchise to install public heating and lighting in a city the size of Detroit. Hyman Goldman was born in Russia in 1859 and arrived in Detroit in 1883. He started out as a junk peddler, worked his way into the scrap iron business, and eventually became owner of the Riverside Scrap, Iron and Metal Company and a partner in one of Detroit's largest machinery and marine engine companies.

Mark Mitshkun, born in Vilna in 1855, came to the United States and Detroit in 1871. He began buying and selling rails, locomotives, and cars in 1872 and made a specialty of buying and selling complete logging railroads to lumbermen and loggers in various parts of the United States and Canada. By 1900 he was president of the M. Mitshkun Railway Equipper Company and director of the Detroit Carbuilding and Equipment Company.

Concert singer and teacher Boris Ganapol was born in Russia in 1864 and educated in music at the Imperial Conservatory in Kiev. He arrived in the United States and Detroit in 1891 and after performing as a leading baritone in grand opera, opened the Ganapol School of Musical Art in 1901. Through his school, and as president of the Detroit String Quartette and Hayden String Quartette, he contributed a great deal to the city's cultural life. Isaac Louis Polozker, born in Russia in 1873, came to the United States in 1892 and studied medicine at the Detroit College of Medicine. He received his degree in 1897 and after postgraduate work in Vienna and Berlin assumed a professorship in children's diseases at his alma mater. He was later appointed the physician for Wayne County.[35]

RELIGIOUS LIFE

At first glance, it seemed that the immigrants transplanted their Old World religious institutions and customs to Detroit. Between 1880 and 1914, the community established fifteen Orthodox congregations, all but three of them after 1900. Within the synagogues, the liturgy and ritual replicated Eastern European Orthodoxy. Friday evening services at Congregation B'nai Israel typified those found in all the Orthodox congregations. One non-Jewish visitor reported how some of the worshipers "stood, some sat, some looked one way, some another. Some kept turning about. Some had books in their hands, some had none. Some kept their places, others walked about," and they all "chanted, droned, hummed or toned forth their prayers. It did not sound like reciting the same thing, but rather different parts of the same, each one going as he pleased."[36]

On Saturdays and the major Jewish holidays, the Jewish district appeared quieter than usual; a totally different atmosphere pervaded. The *Detroit News-Tribune* described how, on the two days of Rosh Hashanah in 1896, "all the stores were closed and the streets were filled by small boys in store clothes, chattering gaily on the corner or the steps of the synagogue. Pretty little girls with glistening black

Prominent Eastern European Jews featured in the *Detroit Free Press*, May 31, 1903. (Courtesy of the Burton Historical Collection.)

eyes and hair, tripped airily up and down the street. Mild, patriarchal old gentlemen with their heavy, square prayer books in their hands trudged to and from the synagogue all day. Stout and smiling housewives with their little bonnets sitting neatly on their smoothly combed heads, waddled amiably along the same direction. Sleek and pious gentlemen, with magnificent black side whiskers and high silk hats sitting oddly on the back of their heads, paraded complacently along, conscious of 'froomkeit.' Short, stout

71

Yom Kippur services at Congregation Beth Jacob in 1896. (Courtesy of the Burton Historical Collection.)

men, with bushy black beards, their hairy faces sur-
mounted by little squat hats, trudged along with the
downcast looks of publicans and sinners. Little gentlemen with black beards and neat dark suits came along
in twos and threes. They had the confident air of prosperous businessmen, and they were discussing the
silver question. . . . across the street from the synagogue, . . . a crowd was standing about all day discussing religion."[37]

To non-Jews and German Jews alike, this religious aura and the district's large number of kosher
markets and restaurants indicated that most of
Detroit's Eastern European Jews were Orthodox.
Contrary to outward appearances, indifference and
backsliding among Eastern European Jews grew.
True, the synagogues projected an air of piety and
were filled to capacity during the High Holy Days, but
religious observances declined, as did attendance at
daily and Sabbath services. Especially disconcerting
to the Orthodox was that transgression of the Sabbath, such as violation of the prohibition against
work, became increasingly open and obvious. The
multiplicity of Orthodox synagogues resulted from
ethnic differences and served social and cultural needs
rather than specifically religious requirements. Consequently, Detroit had its "Polisher" (Polish), "Rusish-
er" (Russian), "Ungarisher" (Hungarian), "Ru-
manisher" (Rumanian), "Galitzianer" (Galician), and
"Litvisher" (Lithuanian) synagogues.[38]

In an attempt to stem defections from traditional Judaism, some of the synagogues, such as Nu-
sah Hoari, instituted an elaborate system of fines and
penalties to enforce obedience and punish deviant behavior. These failed to achieve the desired goals, for
errant congregants could always resign from the synagogue and go somewhere else. Congregation Shaarey
Zedek sought to counteract the growing apathy among
its younger members, who had little interest in the
German-language sermons and the religious services
geared to the needs of its older European-bred congregants, by modifying its Orthodox ritual and religious
orientation. William Saulson, the congregation's president, advised hiring an English-speaking rabbi who
would be able "to appeal to the young in their own

Congregation B'nai Israel in 1912. (Courtesy of the Rabbi
Leo M. Franklin Archives of Temple Beth El.)

Congregation Beth Jacob in 1912. (Courtesy of the Rabbi
Leo M. Franklin Archives of Temple Beth El.)

Congregation Beth David in 1912. (Courtesy of the Rabbi Leo M. Franklin Archives of Temple Beth El.)

Ezekiel Aishiskin, rabbi to Congregations Beth David, Nusach Hoary, Beth Moses, Tefereth Israel, and B'nai Joseph, in 1912. (Courtesy of the Rabbi Leo M. Franklin Archives of Temple Beth El.)

Congregation Beth Abraham in 1912. (Courtesy of the Rabbi Leo M. Franklin Archives of Temple Beth El.)

Members of Congregation Mishkan Israel at the dedication of the synagogue in 1912. (Courtesy of the Rabbi Leo M. Franklin Archives of Temple Beth El.)

Congregation Mogen Abraham in 1912. (Courtesy of the Archives of Congregation Shaarey Zedek.)

Congregation Shaarey Zedek in 1903. (Courtesy of the Archives of Congregation Shaarey Zedek.)

William Saulson, president of Congregation Shaarey Zedek, 1903–8. (Courtesy of the Archives of Congregation Shaarey Zedek.)

Rudolph Farber, rabbi of Congregation Shaarey Zedek, 1904–7. He delivered the Congregation's first English sermon. (Courtesy of the Archives of Congregation Shaarey Zedek.)

tongue." Following his advice, Shaarey Zedek hired Austrian-born Rabbi Rudolph Farber, who had been trained in rabbinical schools in Bohemia. On January 22, 1904, Rabbi Farber delivered the congregation's first English sermon, and by October of that year English lectures had become a regular feature of the Friday evening service.[39]

The younger members remained indifferent, and Rabbi Farber resigned in frustration in 1907, to be replaced by Rabbi Abraham M. Hershman (1907–59). A graduate of Columbia University and the Jewish Theological Seminary of America, Hershman served as Shaarey Zedek's rabbi for thirty-nine years. He established a congregational school, reorganized the Sunday school, and formed a Young People's Society. An ardent Zionist, Hershman founded the Kadimah Zionist Society and, later, the Detroit Zionist Organization and wrote numerous pamphlets explain-

Abraham M. Hershman, rabbi of Congregation Shaarey
Zedek (1907–59), and his wife, on their honeymoon in 1909.
A graduate of the Jewish Theological Seminary of America,
he was Detroit's first Conservative rabbi. (Courtesy of the
Archives of Congregation Shaarey Zedek.)

Cornerstone laying ceremony for the Congregation Shaarey
Zedek on November 13, 1913. In the front row (*left to right*)
stand Rabbi Abraham M. Hershman, Rabbi Judah L. Levin,
Congregation president David W. Simons, Louis Granet,
Isaac Shetzer, Isaac Saulson, Louis Smith, and Jacob
Friedberg. (Courtesy of the Archives of Congregation
Shaarey Zedek.)

Congregation Shaarey Zedek on Willis and Brush Streets in 1915. (Courtesy of the Archives of Congregation Shaarey Zedek.)

ing the Zionist movement, as well as collecting funds to support it. He was Detroit's first Conservative rabbi, and under his leadership Shaarey Zedek became one of the founding members of the United Synagogue of America, which was organized under the aegis of Professor Solomon Schechter to advance the cause of Judaism in America and to maintain Jewish tradition while, at the same time, initiating changes compatible with the times. This shift to Conservativism, however, failed to stem dissatisfaction and apathy within Shaarey Zedek.[40]

This movement away from formal Orthodox observance shows the impact of urbanization on people who were basically small-town dwellers. The rapidity with which they abandoned religious practices that proved inconvenient or incompatible with their new environment signifies that the attachment they felt to Judaism was more cultural than religious.

Once their Old World cultural milieu disintegrated so, too, did many of the religious observances associated with it.[41]

THE TALMUD TORAH

Indifference to Orthodoxy affected religious education as well. According to Jewish law, the study of the Jewish tradition, particularly its holy texts, and the maintenance of educational facilities, take precedence over the establishment of synagogues. Large numbers of Detroit's Jewish immigrants, however, neglected to provide religious instruction for their young and sent them only to public schools. Education in America was not merely the acquisition of job skills or social graces, it was also a ladder to wealth and position, a

77

The 1905-6 class of the Bishop School. (Courtesy of the Archives of Congregation Shaarey Zedek.)

means of social ascent. Appreciating this, the immigrants favored the free public school over the Hebrew school as the surest means of guaranteeing their children's future achievement and success.

Hoping to counteract this powerful secular influence, local Orthodox leaders sought to establish a communal religious school in 1892. They failed because of personal rivalries and because the Orthodox congregations, fearing a loss of independence in educational matters, refused to cooperate. The continued decline in observance among the young, coupled with increased Christian missionary activity in the Jewish quarter, soon overrode personal considerations, and in 1895 the community opened an Orthodox Hebrew Free School to teach the children of indigent immigrants. The effort did not last long and due to a lack of support, the school declared bankruptcy and closed its doors.

Undaunted, a number of Shaarey Zedek members and others organized a Talmud Torah Association in 1898 "to establish, maintain and control an institution or institutions for the dissemination of religious knowledge, and especially for the purpose of in-

structing children of the Jewish faith in the history of that religion and its doctrines, in the Hebrew language and for other purposes incident thereto." One year later the Association's school, under the name of Talmud Torah Institute, opened. The school, also known as "The City Talmud Torah," "The Big Talmud Torah," "The Hebrew Free School," and the "Division Street Talmud Torah," held its first sessions in a small rented cottage on Division Street. In 1902 a brick building was erected, the first structure built by Detroit Jews to house exclusively an institution of Jewish learning.[42]

The Talmud Torah's first principal was Dr. Jacob B. Baruch, an ordained rabbi and a physician. Samuel N. Ginsburg, an immigrant from Poland and one of the city's prominent Jews, served as the Talmud Torah Association's first president. Although the school was intended primarily for boys, one room was set aside for girls. Classes convened at 4:00 P.M. daily, Monday through Thursday—no classes were held on Friday and Saturday—and lasted until 7:00 P.M. A coeducational Sunday school operated from 9:30 A.M. to 11:00 A.M. Both schools were communal, and all children, regardless of their parents' circumstances, could attend. Those unable to pay received instruction free of charge. In 1900 the Talmud Torah enrolled 150 pupils in its weekday sessions and the Sunday school enrolled 300.[43]

The Talmud Torah catered to the Orthodox Jews and was supported by them. Because they comprised the least affluent sector of the Jewish commu-

nity and because of the widespread apathy toward religious education on the part of the immigrants, the school experienced constant financial difficulty. Despite a series of fund-raising affairs and periodic appeals to the community for support, the school never really achieved financial independence.[44]

The school exerted a greater influence on the newer immigrants and their children than on the more

The "Division Street Talmud Torah" building, erected in 1902. (Courtesy of the Archives of Congregation Shaarey Zedek.)

Americanized Eastern Europeans, who hesitated sending their children to school with "greenhorns." Concerned about what this lack of religious instruction implied for their own future, Shaarey Zedek, led by Rabbi Hershman, established an afternoon school of its own in 1907. Two years later, however, the Hebrew school of Shaarey Zedek and the Talmud Torah amalgamated, with Rabbi Hershman as the new principal. One of his first innovations was to make the Talmud Torah coeducational. Nevertheless, a sizable portion of the Eastern European immigrants continued indifferent toward religious education and failed to utilize the school.[45]

DISUNITY

Ethnic differences, disagreements over ritual, and personal idiosyncrasies kept the Jewish community fragmented and prevented any lasting unity and cooperation. One of the major problems was that the rabbis had little authoriy to enforce their decisions. In 1892, for example, when Rabbi Aaron Ashinsky, who had come to the city in 1889 as joint rabbi of Shaarey Zedek, B'nai Israel, and Beth Jacob, tried to raise money for a communal Talmud Torah, the presidents of his congregations threatened to withhold his salary unless he stopped.[46]

Eleven years later these same three congregations sought to end the religious confusion and bickering resulting from the lack of a central authority by organizing a Union of Orthodox Congregations and appointing Rabbi Judah Levin to serve as their spokesman. Levin (1862–1926) had been born in Trab, Russia, the son of a rabbi, and educated in his native city and at the yeshiva in Volozhin. After ordination, he served as a rabbi in Russia and held pulpits in Rochester, New York, and New Haven, Connecticut, before being called to Detroit in 1897 by Shaarey Zedek, Beth Jacob, and B'nai Israel to succeed Rabbi Aaron Ashinsky. In Detroit, Levin helped found the United Hebrew Orthodox congregations and the Gemilath Chesed Shel Emeth of that body. He was also

Aaron Ashinsky, rabbi to Congregations Shaarey Zedek, Beth Jacob, and B'nai Israel from 1889 to 1896. (Courtesy of the Archives of Congregation Shaarey Zedek.)

one of the organizers of the Talmud Torah, the Jewish Old Folks Home, and the United Orthodox Rabbis of America and one of the founders of the Mizrachi Zionist Organization of America.[47]

The Union of Orthodox congregations, however, succumbed to the very ills it was created to ameliorate. It failed to bring the unity it desired because it could not speak for the entire Orthodox community and had no means of enforcing its decisions. Beth David's president, Julius Levinson, became incensed that anyone should dare presume to speak for his con-

Rabbi Judah Levin, scholar; religious, communal, and
Zionist leader; educator; and inventor. (Courtesy of the
Archives of Congregation Shaarey Zedek.)

gregation or their rabbi, Jacob Scheinman. "We have
our own rabbi, with whom we are perfectly satisfied,"
he fumed. "We are competent to manage our own affairs, and we do not care for advice from anyone."
Levinson's obduracy with regard to the Union led "an
Orthodox Jew," writing in the *Jewish American,* to
take him to task for his "disgraceful" behavior and
"obnoxious" and "unJewish" acts.[48]

All was not serene within the individual congregations either. The election of a new president at
B'nai Israel in 1894 led to words and then blows between the candidates, with supporters of each rushing
into the fray. Some years later an open meeting held
at Beth Jacob to raise money for cholera victims in
Jerusalem descended into pandemonium when Julius
Levinson claimed there was no epidemic and that the
money was being pocketed by fakers and thieves. After the ruckus died down, one participant remarked
how "Levinson always causes a disturbance."[49]

In 1910 a violent and nasty dispute broke out
between east side Jewish housewives and the kosher
butchers over the price of kosher meat. The women
ambushed the wagons carrying the meat to the shops
and threw the meat onto the street. They then raided
the butcher shops, beat up the butchers, and dumped
the meat onto the ground, all the while yelling "tref"
(unclean). After police were brought in to quell the
fracas, cooler heads in the Orthodox community decided that measures had to be taken to prevent such
incidents from recurring. Under the leadership of
David Simons, Julius Friedenberg, and Rabbi Hershman, these concerned persons began to organize a Detroit *kehilla,* which would be an association of all the
Jewish institutions and congregations in the city.
They hoped the *kehilla* would bring some order to the
existing chaos. By 1913 a viable organization existed,
but it, too, failed to prevent disputes.[50]

COMMUNAL WELFARE

Two factors led the immigrants to create their own
welfare organizations: their long tradition of self-help
and their alienation from Detroit's more Americanized German Jewish community. Centuries of living in
countries where they could expect little assistance
from the civic authorities accustomed the Eastern Europeans to relying on their own resources. Nowhere
was this more manifest than in czarist lands, where
Jews were treated as a separate and distinct group.
This outside pressure combined with and reinforced
religious tenets which declared that all Jews were responsible for each other. This concern was amply
displayed in Detroit, where many Russian Jews, them-

selves recent arrivals and on the verge of destitution, displayed a readiness to assist their brethren. "There is never a household so cramped that newcomers are not welcome," noted the *Detroit Free Press*, "while quarters for more can be found in every home be there one room or half a dozen."[51]

Another factor—not to be minimized—was the antipathy many of the newcomers felt toward the German Jews who controlled the local Jewish charities. The immigrants felt that the German Jews did not understand them and viewed them all as "schnorrers." This spurred the Eastern Europeans to show the Germans that they were not beggars and could care for their own.[52]

Three of the more viable welfare organizations established were the Gemilut Hasadim, the Assembly of David and House of Shelter, and the Anshe Chesed Shel Emeth. The Gemilut Hasadim, or the Hebrew Free Loan Society, was an institution that originated in the Old World. The term "Gemilut Hesed" means "act of kindness," and the highest act of kindness was to aid persons in want by offering them a loan. In this way, the recipient's dignity would be protected. Jewish communities in Eastern Europe organized Gemilut Hesed associations specifically to aid people in a financial emergency by providing them with interest-free loans.

Detroit's Eastern Europeans established its Gemilut Hasadim Society in 1895 with a capitalization of one thousand dollars. The Society granted loans free of interest or service charges to small businessmen, peddlers, and family men in temporary financial straits. It also provided loans for items such as school tuition. The required surety for a loan was the endorsement of two businessmen; but if no endorsers could be found, some valuable could be used as a surety. Repayments were made weekly over a period of eight months, and every effort was taken to protect the self-respect and dignity of the borrower. Names of borrowers were kept confidential, and the transactions were conducted so as not to make it appear that the recipient had received charity. The money used for lending came to the association from subscribers and from charity boxes placed in business establishments.

More than 90 percent of all the money loaned was repaid on time. The Society's report for 1910 stated that it "loaned out several thousand dollars to applicants who were temporarily embarrassed" and "it has not lost one cent of the money it so loaned."[53]

Orthodox Jews founded the Assembly of David and House of Shelter in 1897 to provide food and shelter for transients. The organization initially rented the rooms it needed, but in 1901 it purchased a large house. This building was supported by popular subscription. Recipients usually were given free room and board for three days. Those staying longer paid fifteen cents per meal or forty cents per day. The organization operated independently until 1931, when it became part of the Jewish Welfare Federation of Detroit.[54]

In 1905 a small group of Eastern European Jews joined to form the Hevra Kaddisha Burial Society. Its object was to visit the sick, attend to the needy, and arrange for burials. The organization formally incorporated in May 1907 as the Anshe Chesed Shel Emeth, the name it still retains. A number of other burial societies also existed at this time. The Beth Olam Cemetery Association, made up of the congregations Shaarey Zedek, B'nai Israel, and Beth Jacob, provided cemetery and burial services to its members, while the Torah Kadisha burial society, founded by Eastern European Jews, cared for poor, unaffiliated Jews who died in Detroit.[55]

The same year Anshe Chesed Shel Emeth incorporated, a number of its members decided to establish a Jewish home for the aged. Jacob Levin, an Orthodox Russian Jew, directed this effort. Levin believed that a home was necessary not only for the poor and homeless, but also for the elderly who could no longer maintain their own homes. The home was to be strictly kosher because many elderly people were unwilling to live in the non-kosher homes of their more assimilated children. Levin and others raised ten thousand dollars, with which they purchased the home of Charles Kanter, on Brush and Winder Streets. Income to support the home came from families of residents, membership dues, raffles, annual balls, and Yizkor (memorial) pledges. By 1912 Levin

Adding machine invented and patented by Rabbi Judah Levin. (Courtesy of the Archives of Congregation Shaarey Zedek.)

could report that "eleven people resided at the home and the house and all its furnishings were clear of debt."[56]

In addition to these larger agencies, the Eastern Europeans set up innumerable smaller relief societies to aid the sick and the indigent. Most of these lasted only a short time, due to the community's inability to finance them and the shift in habits of their members. When the immigrants first came to America, they felt a need for the closeness and warmth of small groups and associations. As they became accli-

mated to their new surroundings and felt more secure, they transferred their allegiance to larger and more impersonal forms of organizations. Because of the ongoing influx of immigrants, however, small Eastern European welfare societies continued to spring up. Despite pleas by the more experienced communal leaders to join the well-established groups—so many societies were superfluous and drained the community's limited resources—the practice continued unabated.[57]

SOCIAL AND CULTURAL LIFE

The immigrant Jew's social and cultural life revolved around their homes, synagogues, fraternal orders, mutual aid societies, and *landsmanshaftn*. The celebrations that provided him with the greatest opportunity for socializing were connected with the Jewish festivals and with the joyous occasions in the life of a Jew —birth, brit, bar-mitzvah, and marriage. For Orthodox Jews, the synagogue was the focus for larger celebrations; the home to entertain family and friends on a more modest scale.

Other activities also offered the newcomer some relief from the drudgery of their daily existence. The Yiddish theater was especially popular, and touring companies attracted large and enthusiastic audiences to their performances. Guest lecturers and speakers, who discussed current events and news from the old country and Palestine, were also great favorites. If the speaker was an international pesonality, such as the Zionists Nahum Sokolow and Shmaryahu Levin, large halls had to be reserved to accommodate all those wishing to attend. The social calendar of the Americanized Eastern European also included card parties, dances, and socials.[58]

FRATERNAL ORDERS

Jewish fraternal orders in the United States grew out of the needs of the various groups of the Jewish population that sought friendship, cultural expression, and material benefits in an environment that reflected their respective social and economic backgrounds. While the orders were established primarily for mutual aid and insurance benefits, as well as for the individual social and business interests of the members, most of them also had altruistic purposes of a national and international scope. As soon as they got settled, Eastern Europeans in Detroit, acting no differently than their brethren in other American cities, established local branches of national fraternal orders. A lodge of the Independent Order Sons of Benjamin, Detroit Lodge No. 97, was organized in 1885; a second branch, Aaron Lodge No. 132, came into existence in subsequent years. These lodges had their own cemeteries, and endowment insurance was included in the material benefits for members. The national Independent Order Sons of Benjamin dissolved in 1919.[59]

The Order Brith Abraham, third oldest Jewish fraternal order in the United States (after the B'nai B'rith and the Free Sons of Israel), had a five-fold purpose of aiding members in need, giving medical aid, burying deceased members "in accordance with Jewish law and ritual," providing for families of deceased members, and assisting members to become citizens. Immigrants established two lodges of this order: Michigan Lodge No. 111 in 1888 and Detroit Lodge No. 139, which transferred from Bay City to Detroit in 1907. An offshoot of the Order Brith Abraham, the Independent Order Brith Abraham, arose in New York in 1887. It retained the five-fold purpose of the parent order but added the resolutions to protest discrimination against Jews in other lands, combat attempts to restrict the immigration of Jews to the United States, support American Jewish philanthropy, and aid in the reconstruction of Palestine. This program reflected the influence of the order's primarily Polish and Russian members. The Independent Order Brith Abraham was one of the first in the United States to grant women all the rights the male members enjoyed. Detroit had two lodges of the Independent Order by 1912: Detroit Lodge No. 386 and Independent Detroit Lodge.[60]

Brith Shalom, organized in 1905 to provide financial assistance to families of deceased members and to further worthy Jewish causes, was the first American Jewish fraternal organization to endorse the Basel Program of the Zionist movement and to make substantial financial contributions to the rebuilding of Palestine. The order went so far as to establish a tract of land in Palestine for colonization. Detroit had one lodge, Detroit City Lodge, organized in 1910. Other fraternal lodges in the city before 1914 were the Detroit Lodge 118 (1907) and Michigan Lodge 252 (1911) of the Independent Western Star Order; Michigan Lodge No. 199 (1910) of the Progressive Order of the West; Abraham Lincoln Lodge No. 57 of the Independent Order Free Sons of Judah; and the Home Protection Lodge No. 160 of the Order Knights of Joseph.[61]

One reason for the plethora of fraternal lodges was their members' desire to belong to groups whose constituency was of a similar social standing and cultural background. Likewise, the *landsmanshaft,* a lodge made up of persons from the same town or district in Eastern Europe, reflected the needs of the newcomers to be with old country neighbors and friends—to feel at home among themselves. Whereas the fraternal lodges wrote their constitutions and minutes in English, signifying a more advanced state of acculturation, the *landsmanshaftn* kept their records and conducted their business in Yiddish. The *landsmanshaftn* provided sickness, burial, and death benefits, but most of all they satisfied the immigrants' desire to indulge in nostalgia and cling a bit longer to their past.

This sentimentality tended to be one-sided, with the more pleasant memories eclipsing the bitter ones. Debrushke Kaluzny, who grew up in the small Russian shtetl of Tanisz, remembered picking berries in the warm sunshine, dancing in the fields, and performing the *kazatzka* (a Russian dance). Her husband, Nathan, who hailed from David Horodok, reminded her of the poverty, the dirt, and the pogroms. As in the larger centers of Jewish population, Detroit's Eastern Europeans organized a Turver Unterstitzung [Benevolent] Verein [Association] (1910), David Horodoker Unterstitzung Verein (1910), and a Bereznetzer Unterstitzung Verein (1912). Five years after their founding the Turver Verein and David Horodoker Verein boasted more than two hundred members each.[62]

ZIONISM AND SOCIALISM

The newer immigrants brought with them two ideas which had had a major impact on the environment from which they had come: Zionism and socialism. Both the Zionist movement, which worked to establish a Jewish state in Palestine, and the socialist movement, which sought to bring Jews into the mainstream of revolutionary movements, instilled in the Jewish masses a sense of pride in their destiny. Zionism concentrated on the rights of nations; socialism forecast the victory of industrial workers over the capitalists. As these ideologies became popular among Jews, attempts arose to reconcile or synthesize them. These various philosophies found expression in Detroit and added vibrancy to the immigrant Jew's life.

Jews had yearned for a return to Palestine from the time the First Temple was destroyed in 588 B.C. Psalm 137, written during the exile in Babylon, poignantly expressed this longing: "By the rivers of Babylon, there we sat, sat and wept, as we thought of Zion. . . . If I forget you, O Jerusalem, let my right hand wither, let my tongue stick to my palate if I cease to think of you, if I do not keep Jerusalem in memory even at my happiest hour." Despite a separation of more than two millennia and thousands of miles, pious Jews prayed three times daily for the Restoration, regulated their lives according to the calendar of ancient Israel, and considered themselves a nation in exile. During the 1880s the optimism that characterized earlier decades was shaken by the growth of ideological anti-Semitism in the West and the outbreak of pogroms in the East. As Jewish life in Europe became less secure, Jews took a cue from the German, Italian, and Slavic nationalist movements and aspired to a land of their own, where they could control their own destiny. This hope was accelerated and transformed in 1896 by Theodor Herzl, whose *Der Judenstaat (The Jewish State)* impelled Zionism into the arena of international politics.

Zionism first received attention in Detroit in 1892, when the *Free Press* ran an editorial entitled "Palestine for the Jews," which discussed the steps then being taken to colonize the Holy Land. Five years later, soon after the Federation of American Zionists came into being, the city's first official Zionist organization, the United Zionists of Detroit, appeared. Shortly thereafter, another group of Zionists established the B'nai Zion Gate No. 21 of the Order of the Knights of Zion. By 1914 nine separate Zionist groups existed, four of them women's organizations.[63]

85

The number of Zionist organizations reflected the political, personal, and religious differences fragmenting the movement nationally and locally. The Federation of American Zionists was organized in New York and was led by more Americanized and secular Jews; the Knights of Zion was a Chicago-based organization patterned after fraternal lodges, with a strong appeal to traditional Jews. The Knights called their individual units "Gates," after the words of Psalm 118: "This is the gate of the Lord; the righteous shall enter through it."[64]

A prominent local physician, Dr. Noah E. Aronstam, established the Young Men's Zion Association in 1903 and published a short-lived journal, *The Jewish Advance,* "to champion and promote the advancement of paramount Jewish policies for Jewish destinies." Aronstam, Dr. Albert Bernstein, Sol Fishbone, and Louis Smilansky shared the editorial tasks. The group split up in 1907, with one faction, led by Sol Fishbone, reconstituting as the Young Men's Zion Society, while the other, led by Aronstam and Bernstein, helped Rabbi Hershman found the Kadimah Zionist Society in 1908. Composed of business and professional men, Kadimah aimed "to preserve the purity and maintain the entity of the Jews as a people."[65]

Socialist Zionists believed that the normal social, political, and economic development of Jews could not occur without their having a land of their own—and this land had to be Palestine. They also declared that any Jewish state must be based on socialist principles, with workers owning the land and means of production. The first Zionist socialist group formed in New York in 1903, under the name of National Radical Verein Poale Zion. Two years later a branch of Poale Zion appeared in Detroit and within a year enrolled forty members. By 1910 the chapter felt strong enough to host a national convention. This conference spurred local recruiting efforts, and by 1914 Detroit's Poale Zion listed more than one hundred members.[66]

Few of Detroit's early Zionists ever settled in Palestine. Rather, they sought to provide a sanctuary for their persecuted brethren in Europe and to rebuild Palestine as the major center of Jewish life. Their activities revolved around lectures and educational programs, which dealt with all aspects of the Jewish heritage and which sought to instill a sense of national pride in Jews. In 1903, for example, the United Zionists sponsored a Friday evening lecture series featuring talks on "The Mission of the Jews," "Moses Maimonides and Moses Mendelssohn," "Zionism: Why and Wherefore," "The Russian Jews in the United States," "The Jewish Dietary Laws from a Medical Standpoint," "How to Unite the Orthodox Congregations," and "Palestine versus Uganda," among others.

They also studied Hebrew and Jewish history, collected money for the Jewish National Fund, publicized their movement through concerts, lectures, and the press, and hosted speeches by well-known Zionists like Shmaryahu Levin, Nahum Sokolow, and Louis Brandeis. Zionists and their friends also attended a succession of parties, picnics, and dances, which raised money for their enterprises and provided additional social outlets. Although the actual number of persons enrolled in local Zionist societies remained small, their influence was magnified by the leadership of personalities such as Rabbi Hershman, Rabbi Levin, and Dr. Aronstam. Their constant activity and the reams of publicity they generated spread news of their cause throughout the Jewish community.[67]

The Jewish socialist movement came to Detroit in 1907, when sixteen people established Branch No. 156 of the Workmen's Circle (Arbeiter Ring). Workmen's Circle was a Jewish labor organization created in 1892 for the purpose of bringing together workers of a socialist bent while providing the benefits of a fraternal order. In 1900 the Workmen's Circle became a national organization and from then on stressed its radicalism, opposition to Jewish nationalism, and hostility to religion. The Workmen's Circle provided a setting where workers could meet and exchange small talk and ideas. Through lectures and classes it gave workers, who had no chance of acquiring a formal education, an opportunity to learn. And through afternoon and full-time high schools, the Circle furnished secular Jewish workers with a way of providing their children a secular Jewish education

Rabbis marching down Brush Street in a Zionist parade, circa 1913. They are led by Rabbi Judah Levin, who convened one of the country's first Mizrachi meetings. (Courtesy of the Archives of Congregation Shaarey Zedek.)

and preventing a total break with Jewishness. It also gave its membership the feeling that, despite growing old and less zealous, they still cared about socialism or at least social reform. The Workmen's Circle exerted great appeal in Detroit—by 1916 Branch No. 156 had grown to become the largest branch in the United States and Canada.[68]

Another group of Jewish socialists organized Detroit Branch No. 13 of the Jewish National Worker's Alliance, or "Farband." Because of their strong Zionist sympathies these workers could not join the Workmen's Circle; nor could they join Poale Zion, for they felt that it was not doing enough to reshape the social order and protect the workers' economic interests. From the outset, however, the Alliance cooperated with Poale Zion in cultural and social affairs and in setting up a Jewish folk school. By World War I, Detroit held another branch of the Alliance, Avrunen Branch No. 79.[69]

CIVIC AND POLITICAL LIFE

Before the First World War, the integration of the Eastern European immigrants into the civic life of the city progressed slowly; too many other, more basic concerns occupied their time for them to devote themselves to affairs outside of their community. Also, because of the steady stream of newcomers, the Jewish community encountered a host of internal problems that taxed its energy and militated against the expenditure of much effort on outside concerns. Nevertheless, a few Eastern Europeans did attain the economic security and leisure necessary to achieve some civic prominence. Louis J. Rosenberg became a director of the Society for the Prevention of Cruelty to Children in 1903; William Saulson served as president of the Water Board in 1903; and David W. Simons served on the public lighting commission from 1898 to 1902. Most of the newcomers, however, contented themselves with the exercise of other prerogatives of citizenship—voting and participating in political rallies and campaigns at election time. Like the German Jews earlier, the Eastern Europeans viewed political activity as another means of displaying their good citizenship.[70]

Up to the First World War, the politics of the Eastern Europeans remained mixed; most Eastern European Jews chose candidates for their stands on particular issues rather than following one or another of the major parties. In addition, Detroit's Eastern Europeans rarely voted as an ethnic block, as opposed to the Irish, Poles, and Germans who did. Nevertheless, the Socialist Party attracted many working-class Jews, and in 1899 Julius Bacher, an Austrian-born watchmaker, organized a Jewish branch of the Socialist Labor Party. Mechanics, tailors, shoemakers, capmakers, butchers, grocers, and pushcart peddlers formed the local branch's rank and file. Jewish workers also gave the Democratic Party consistently strong support in the form of numerous Democratic clubs, which sprung up all over the east side before elections. Just how fierce this support could get was demonstrated at one election day rally held by the Hebrew Peddler's Association in 1902. At the meeting, the Association's attorney, Eddie Barnett, made the blunder of proposing that the peddlers endorse "the Republican candidates from congressman down." No sooner had he uttered these words than bedlam broke loose. "Barnett had his watch chain torn to pieces, and the clothing almost torn from his back." Men "were punched in the face," kicked and gouged, while "in the rear of the room was a crowd of maddened men fighting desperately." After the storm subsided, a groggy Barnett admitted "that he had made the mistake of his life." Generally, however, the Eastern Europeans remained splintered politically and were cultivated by candidates of all political persuasions.[71]

A few Eastern European Jews did make their mark politically. David W. Simons was a member of the first nine-man city council. His eldest son, Charles C. Simons, an attorney, was elected state senator in 1902, was a member of the Michigan Constitutional Convention in 1908, and later served as chief judge of the United States Circuit Court of Appeals.[72] Perhaps the most unique of all the Eastern Europeans to appear on Detroit's political scene is Samuel Goldwater.

Born in Konin, Poland, in 1850, Goldwater came to New York with his parents in 1859. After some boyhood adventures as a mule driver on the Morris Canal in New Jersey, Goldwater became a cigar maker, a profession he followed all his life. He moved to Chicago in 1869 and there began his second career as a labor activist, helping to organize the Trades Assembly of Chicago and running for Cook County commissioner on the Socialist Labor ticket. His wife's death left him despondent, and he looked for a change in Detroit. From the moment he arrived in the city in 1886, no important labor activity took place without his having a role in it. At different times, he served as president of the Detroit Council of Trades and the Cigar Makers Local No. 22. Through his activities in the cigar makers union he met Samuel Gompers, and the two men remained warm friends throughout their lives. Goldwater was instrumental in organizing the Michigan Federation of Labor and delivered the keynote address at their first convention in 1889. And during Detroit's streetcar strike of 1890, Goldwater organized the strikers into a union, a feat some called his greatest achievement. His humanity, fairness, and concern for the laborer made Goldwater popular with Detroit's working class, and in 1894 he ran as the "citizen's candidate" for alderman in the Twelfth Ward. He was one of the four aldermen backed by the Democratic Party to win in what was an otherwise Republican landslide.

In 1895 Detroit's Democratic caucus selected him to run for mayor against the popular and Reform-minded incumbent Hazen Pingree. Believing Goldwater to be too "radical," the city's Democratic press and most party members refused him their support. With no money and no help, Goldwater ran a one-man campaign and lost. Though defeated, Goldwater continued to fight for social justice and workers' rights and was reelected to the City Council in 1896. However, the mayoral campaign had taken its toll, and Goldwater never recovered his former health and vigor. In 1898, three years after he campaigned for mayor, he became ill and died. More than five thousand people, from all walks of life, attended his funeral, and the City Council declared an official day of mourning. Upon hearing

Judge Charles C. Simons, Michigan State Senator, 1903–4, and a member of the Michigan Constitutional Convention, 1908. (Courtesy of the Archives of Congregation Shaarey Zedek.)

Samuel Goldwater, labor leader, president of the Detroit Council of Trades, organizer of the Michigan Federation of Labor in 1889, and city alderman in 1894. (Courtesy of the Burton Historical Collection.)

of Goldwater's death, a saddened Samuel Gompers requested the mourners to "drop a flower on Sam's grave for me."[73]

STRANGERS AND NEIGHBORS

The Eastern Europeans elicited a mixed response from the city's general population. Although Detroiters recognized Jews as being of a different faith, the older German Jewish group appeared to be like other Americans in manner and dress. The Eastern Europeans, however, were considered anomalous. Their religious habits and customs were deemed unusual, and their behavior and style of life seemed far different from that of the Jews with whom Detroiters were most familiar. Sensing a good story, Detroit's newspapers featured numerous articles depicting the Jewish district, its inhabitants, and their activities, characteristics, and practices.

Portrayals of the immigrants often combined time-worn stereotypes with descriptions of their admirable traits. Distrusted because of their "peculiar faculty of accumulating and holding on to wealth—of which they scarcely create any—which enables them sooner or later to rule every commercial country in which they are permitted to live in peace," the immigrants were also lauded for their energy, intellectual prowess, and perseverance. They did not "get drunk and disturb the peace on the streets," there "were few criminals of any kind among them," and they were devoted to their families and homes.[74]

The praise notwithstanding, anti-Semitism increased during the 1890s. In this decade of depression, Jewish peddlers began to be assaulted in the city's streets by hooligans. The offenders were youthful members of the Irish and Polish working-class population. The ineffectiveness of the police in stopping the attacks, some of which resulted in the victim's death, led the Jewish peddlers in 1900 to establish their own self-defense organization, the Jewish Peddlers Protective Association.[75]

Hostility toward Jews also became more evident in city politics. Jewish delegates to Democratic and Republican conventions began to hear cries of "no Jew for us," and Jews were increasingly prevented from rising in the parties' hierarchies or receiving patronage posts. This state of affairs caused Ignatz Freund to complain that "the Democrats and Republicans think of us as Jews before they do as Americans. And before election they come to us and call us their Hebrew Friends, and after election day when we want something of them they call us (you know) damn sheenies." Such antagonism in the political sphere led to the convening, in 1894, of an all-Jewish political meeting to discuss these matters. Characterized by the *Detroit News* as "something rare and unique if not wholly out of precedent" for Detroit, the meeting attempted to organize the city's Eastern European Jews to vote for candidates who supported their interests regardless of party affiliation.

The effort failed, however, and did little to alter the negative attitudes toward Jews.[76] When Samuel Goldwater ran for mayor, his Jewishness became an item for discussion. Newspaper articles and cartoons caricatured him as speaking with a Yiddish accent and joked about his willingness to eat pork. And during the presidential campaign of 1896, in which many of Detroit's Jews supported the Democratic candidate William Jennings Bryan, a float drawn through the streets depicted the pawnshop of "Isaac Silberstein," within which "men representing the wandering Jews were auctioning off all kinds of second hand goods." The inscription above the float read, "A Sure Winner if Bryan is Elected."[77]

The major reason for this outburst against the Jews was the economic stress on Detroit's working people caused by the depression of 1893, which lasted until 1897. Private business activity slumped, and the ranks of the unemployed multiplied at an alarming rate. Contemporary and later estimates placed the number of jobless at about 25,000 men, approximately 33 percent of the male labor force in 1894. Those most affected were the foreign-born, who comprised 24,000 out of the 28,000 people on Detroit's Poor Commission rolls. This provoked severe social and class tensions, especially during 1893 and 1894. Many of the

90

unemployed were driven to desperation and clashes with the police became common as Polish, Italian, and Irish workers fought for the same jobs. A poll taken by the Michigan Bureau of Labor between 1893 and 1896 indicated that foreign and native-born workmen alike favored immigration restriction. Despite the fact that Jewish immigrants suffered along with everyone else, the high visibility of the Eastern European immigrants, coupled with the age-old distrust of Jews as exploiters and Shylocks, caused them to be viewed with hostility. This animosity led to violence against Jewish peddlers as they plied their trade in other ethnic working-class neighborhoods and in slurs against Jews in city politics.[78]

What occurred in Detroit was not unique; it formed part of a national pattern. Violence was endemic in this period of economic and social upheaval, and Jewish peddlers were attacked and beaten in New York, Chicago, Milwaukee, and Rochester as well. As early as 1892, Baltimore Jews organized to protect themselves against German and Black gangs that attacked them in the streets.[79]

Beginning in the late nineteenth century, Christian efforts to convert the immigrants became a problem, causing concern among Orthodox and Reform Jewish leaders. Traveling Jewish proselytes delivered lectures in the YMCA and local churches; missionary societies sent a steady stream of representatives to work among the Eastern Europeans; the usually moderate "Church Tramp" column of the *News-Tribune* claimed that salvation came only through a belief in Jesus; and Detroit's Baptist clergy initiated plans to convert the Jews. Rabbi Grossmann of Temple Beth El rebuked the Baptists, saying, "our friends, the Baptist ministers, admit that we are good men, but that we need the gospel. If we are all right without it, it is difficult to see why we need it." His successor, Leo Franklin, also voiced his outrage and opposition to this activity, but there was little he could do to stop it.[80]

The early years of the twentieth century gave rise to other manifestations of anti-Semitism. Jews were subjected to taunts and abuse from other workers in the city's factories, and two of Detroit's automobile

manufacturers, the Chalmers Company and the Studebaker Company, acquired reputations for not hiring Jews. Jewish peddlers continued to be assaulted despite protests by the Jewish community, the presence of the Jewish Peddler's Association, and special pleas reiterating "the right of the Hebrew peddler to live" issued by mayors Maybury and Thompson. The frequency of these attacks and the seeming futility of efforts to curb them led one exasperated municipal judge to exclaim that "I shall stamp out this brutal practice, born of detestable and un-American race hatred, if I have to exhaust the power of this court to do so. The streets of Detroit shall be made as safe for Jew as for Gentile." And the usually conservative *Jewish American* suggested that Jews adopt measures for their own defense, even going so far as to "carry a revolver or other weapon with which to protect themselves."[81]

The Eastern Europeans enjoyed excellent relations with their Italian and Black neighbors. Frequently sharing the same neighborhoods, their children attended the same schools and played together. Major conflicts were few. The same could not be said of the relations between Jews and Poles, as age-old antagonisms persisted in Detroit. Jewish immigrants remembered the Poles as "drunken pogromniks," and clashes between the two groups were common. Meyer Lachman recalled how on one cold, winter day in January 1902, a Polish immigrant came into his father Joseph's jewelry store and dropped off his watch to be repaired. He returned drunk with a companion later that day and tried to take his watch without paying. Joseph locked the door and demanded payment. The customer refused, and a fight ensued. Finally, the Poles jumped through a window, shouting "the Jews are cheating us, kill the Jews." A crowd quickly gathered and began throwing rocks at the store. Joseph and his brother, Sol, quickly turned out the lights and hid in the back till the crowd dispersed.

The next day *Wolne Polskie,* a Detroit Polish newspaper, warned its readers against patronizing Jewish merchants "because they cheat us and laugh at us." Jewish youngsters venturing into Polish neighborhoods risked harassment and beatings, and Poles crossing into the Jewish district took a similar chance. Jewish baseball teams playing teams in the Polish areas needed protective escorts, and when the game ended, they "began to run and kept on running till they reached the Jewish section of town." Alfred Klunover recalled having bodyguards walk with him to the Joseph Campau school and walk him home after class.[82] Relations between the Jewish immigrants and native Detroiters remained strictly formal. City officials and political and religious leaders attended synagogue and religious school dedications but had few other contacts with or interest in the newcomers.[83]

Most of the immigrants desired to adapt to their new American environment as quickly as possible. They went to night school to learn English, adopted American behavioral patterns and norms, such as incorporating American symbols and motifs in

their synagogue and communal programs, and displayed the American flag and their patriotism at every opportunity. On occasion, the need to appear 100 percent American took an incongruous turn as when, at the dedication of the Hebrew Free School in 1902, the orchestra "rendered an elaborate medley of the latest ragtime and coon songs." By 1914 it became increasingly obvious that the cultural patterns of the immigrants had undergone a change: they had become less Russian-Jewish in orientation and more Jewish-American in their style of life.[84] In one area, however, the immigrants did not try to integrate quickly: Russian Jews had the highest ratio of endogamous marriages of all the other immigrant groups in Detroit. At least until World War I, the Jew's drive for ethnic continuity outweighed his desire for assimilation.[85]

NOTES

1. Marc Lee Raphael, *Jews and Judaism in a Midwestern Community: Columbus, Ohio, 1840-1975* (Columbus, Ohio: Ohio Historical Society, 1979), p. 91; *Detroit Evening News,* December 29, 1881, p. 2.

2. Louis Greenberg, *The Jews in Russia,* vol. 2 (New Haven: Yale University Press, 1951), p. 19; Solo W. Baron, *The Russian Jew under Tsars and Soviets* (New York: Macmillan, 1964), pp. 52-56.

3. Baron, *Russian Jew,* 52-62; Greenberg, *Jews in Russia,* p. 50.

4. Greenberg, *Jews in Russia,* p. 50; Baron, *Russian Jew,* pp. 67-70.

5. For Rumania see Joseph Kissman, "Jewish Emigration from Rumania up to World War I" (Yiddish) in *YIVO Bleter* 19, no. 2 (March-April, 1942), pp. 157-91; E. Schwarzfeld, "The Jews of Roumania: From the Earliest Times to the Present Day," pp. 25-62, and "The Situation of the Jews in Roumania Since the Treaty of Berlin (1878)," pp. 63-86, in *American Jewish Year Book* (1901-2); J. Starr, "Jewish Citizenship in Roumania, 1870-1940," *Jewish Social Studies* 3 (1941), pp. 57-80.

6. Raphael Mahler, "Jewish Emigration from Galicia and Its Causes" (Yiddish), in *Geschichte fun der Yiddisher Arbeiter Bavegung in di Fareynikte Shtatn,* Elias Tcherikower, ed., vol. 1 (New York: YIVO, 1943), pp. 113-27; Mark Wischnitzer, *To Dwell in Safety: The Story of Jewish Migrations Since 1800* (Philadelphia: Jewish Publication Society of America, 1948), pp. 44, 83-85, 98.

7. Mary Antin, *The Promised Land* (Boston: Houghton Mifflin Company, 1912), p. 141; Sanford Ragins, "The Image of America in Two East European Hebrew Periodicals," *American Jewish Archives* 17 (November, 1965), pp. 143-61.

8. Sidney Goldstein, "Jews in the United States: Perspectives from Demography," *American Jewish Year Book* 81 (1981), p. 9; Robert A. Rockaway, "The Eastern European Jewish Community of Detroit, 1881-1914," *YIVO Annual of Jewish Social Science* 15 (1974), p. 82.

9. More than 80 percent of the men sent to Detroit by the Industrial Removal Office between 1900 and 1914 were from Russia; see Robert A. Rockaway, "The Industrial Removal Office in Detroit," *Detroit in Perspective* 6 (Spring, 1982), pp. 40-49. The figures cited in the text were acquired from sampling the manuscript schedules of the 1900 population census for Detroit and from the records of the Industrial Removal Office.

10. Melvin G. Holli, ed., *Detroit* (New York: New Viewpoints, 1976), pp. 60, 118-19.

11. Holli, *Detroit,* pp. 119, 281; Olivier Zunz, *The Changing Face of Inequality: Urbanization, Industrial Development, and Immigrants in Detroit, 1880-1920* (Chicago: University of Chicago Press, 1982), pp. 94-104, 286-87, 292. In 1920 Detroit produced 1,905,560 passenger cars and 321,789 trucks (Zunz, *Changing Face,* p. 292).

12. Holli, *Detroit,* p. 118; Zunz, *Changing Face,* pp. 286-87.

Zunz estimates that 88 percent of the Russians in Detroit were Jews (pp. 104-6).

13. Louis Friedman to Industrial Removal Office (Yiddish), April 5, 1907; Louis Polansky to Industrial Removal Office, January 10, 1913, Detroit File, IRO Papers, American Jewish Historical Society, Waltham, Massachusetts; Nathan Kaluzny to author; Robert A. Rockaway, "Ethnic Conflict in an Urban Environment: The German and Russian Jew in Detroit, 1881-1914," *American Jewish Historical Quarterly 60* (December, 1970), pp. 133-34; Jewish Colonization Society, *Amerikanishe Shtedt* (Petrograd, 1911), pp. 16-20.

14. Raymond E. Cole, "The Immigrant in Detroit," May 1915, pp. 5-6, Papers of the Americanization Committee of Detroit, Michigan Historical Collections, Ann Arbor, Michigan.

15. *American Israelite,* September 10, 1891, p. 5, September 29, 1892, p. 2; *Detroit News,* September 1, 1892, p. 1, September 11, 1892, p. 2, September 18, 1892, p. 1, September 21, 1892, p. 2; *Detroit Free Press,* October 3, 1892, p. 3; *Jewish American,* August 10, 1906, p. 4. The *Jewish American* was Detroit's Anglo-Jewish weekly from 1901 to 1911. Throughout this period it was the official organ of Detroit's Reform Jewish community as represented by Temple Beth El. The publisher of the paper was S. M. Goldsmith, a member of the Temple, and Rabbi Leo M. Franklin was editor.

16. Lucy S. Dawidowicz, *On Equal Terms: Jews in America, 1881-1981* (New York: Holt, Rinehart and Winston, 1982), pp. 44-46; J. C. Furnas, *The Americans: A Social History of the United States, 1587-1914* (New York: G. P. Putnam's Sons, 1969), p. 839; John Higham, "Anti-Semitism in the Gilded Age: A Reinterpretation," *Mississippi Valley Historical Review* 43 (1957), p. 573.

17. Dawidowicz, *Equal Terms,* pp. 44-46; Furnas, *The Americans,* pp. 835-42.

18. *Detroit News-Tribune,* September 6, 1896, II, p. 13.

19. *American Israelite,* November 3, 1892, p. 2; *Detroit News-Tribune,* September 6, 1896, II, p. 13; Zunz, *Changing Face,* p. 158; and the *Detroit City Directory of 1910.*

20. Robert W. DeForest and Lawrence Veiller, ed., *The Tenement House Problem,* vol. 1 (New York, 1903; Arno Press, 1970), pp. 146-47; Zunz, *Changing Face,* pp. 158-60, 373-78, 380-93.

21. Whether the lack of city services reflected discrimination imposed on the poorer sections of the city, which might have been seen as poor investments by the public and private agencies involved in equipping the city, or resulted from the inhabitants' resistance to changes imposed upon their "territory" by outsiders, that is, city engineers and businessmen, is uncertain (see Zunz, *Changing Face,* pp. 113-28). See also *Eleventh Census of the United States, 1890: Vital and Social Statistics* 2 (Washington, D.C.: Government Printing Office, 1896), pp. 219-27; *United Jewish Charities of Detroit, Thirteenth Annual Report* (Detroit, 1912), p. 18; *Jewish American,* October 14, 1910, p. 2, October 12, 1906, p. 3; *Detroit Free Press,* April 2, 1911, V, p. 1; Edith Heavenrich to author, January 16, 1969.

22. *Detroit News-Tribune,* September 13, 1896, II, p. 13, September 20, 1896, p. 10; *Detroit News,* August 21, 1904, p. 4, October 29, 1905, p. 3; *Detroit Free Press,* May 9, 1909, pp. 1, 3, April 12, 1911, V, p. 1; *Jewish American,* November 8, 1907, p. 8.

23. *American Israelite,* November 3, 1892, p. 2; *Jewish American,* November 3, 1905, p. 7, October 12, 1906, p. 3, November 8, 1907, p. 8, November 15, 1907, p. 2, January 17, 1908, p. 2, October 14, 1910, p. 2, October 21, 1910, p. 4, November 11, 1910, p. 1, April 28, 1911, p. 8; *Detroit Free Press,* April 2, 1911, V, p. 1; *United Jewish Charities, Twelfth Annual Report* (Detroit, 1911), p. 13; Miriam

Hart to David Bressler, March 13, 1912, and Miriam Hart to David Bressler, August 15, 1912, Detroit File, IRO Papers, American Jewish Historical Society, Waltham, Massachusetts.

24. See the "Annual Reports of the Officers of the Detroit House of Correction," in the *Annual Reports, City of Detroit* for 1884-85, 1896, 1900-01, and 1910; the minutes of the Ladies Society for the Support of Hebrew Widows and Orphans, for December 2, 1895, p. 151, and September 13, 1905, p. 356; General Arrest Register, vol. 27-37 (1900-1910), Detroit Police Department Archives, Burton Historical Collection, Detroit, Michigan. The high arrest and low indictment record resulted from the Irish policeman's predilection for harassing the Jewish immigrant.

25. See the *Detroit City Directory* for 1900, 1905, 1910, and 1914; Miriam Hart to David Bressler, December 5, 1912; Miriam Hart to David Bressler, January 28, 1914, Detroit File, IRO Papers.

26. Zunz, *Changing Face,* pp. 152-53; David Goldberg and Harry Sharp, "Some characteristics of Detroit Area Jewish and Non-Jewish Adults," *The Jews: Social Patterns of an American Group,* ed. Marshall Sklare (New York: The Free Press, 1958), p. 113. Renting remained a characteristic of Russian Jews through World War II. As late as 1950, over 70 percent of Detroit's white ethnics owned their own homes as compared to 52 percent of the Jews (see Goldberg and Sharp, "Characteristics," p. 113). A number of studies suggest that home ownership may have served as a brake to mobility. Stephen Thernstrom in his Newburyport study suggested that Irish immigrants acquired homes at the expense of their children's education; and Daniel Luria, in his study of Boston, showed that home ownership was probably an investment inferior to most others. See Stephen Thernstrom, *Poverty and Progress: Social Mobility in a Nineteenth-Century City* (Cambridge, Mass.: Harvard University Press, 1964), p. 201; and Daniel D. Luria, "Wealth, Capital, and Power: The Social Meaning of Home Ownership," *Journal of Interdisciplinary History* 7 (Autumn 1976), p. 278. See also Zunz, *Changing Face,* p. 153, n. 11.

27. *Detroit Free Press,* May 9, 1909, p. 1, April 2, 1911, p. 15.

28. Zunz, *Changing Face,* p. 221. Out of 2,145 working males listed in the 1907 *Detroit Yiddish Directory,* 334, or 16 percent, peddled.

29. In compiling the Jewish occupational structure, peddlers were classified as "unskilled." If peddlers had been listed as proprietors, the percentage of proprietors, managers, and officials in Table 10 would have risen to 31 percent. Olivier Zunz received permission to sample the still closed 1920 manuscript census schedules for Detroit and found 49 percent of Detroit's Russian Jews working in white collar jobs and as retailers and proprietors versus 34 percent of the Irish, 22 percent of the Germans, 9 percent of the Poles, and 42 percent of the native white Americans (Zunz, *Changing Face,* pp. 340-41).

30. Joseph Fauman, "The Jews in the Waste Industry in Detroit," *Jewish Social Studies* 3 (1941), p. 43.

31. For Jewish economic mobility in other cities, see Thomas Kessner, *The Golden Door: Italian and Jewish Immigrant Mobility in New York City 1880-1915* (New York: Oxford University Press, 1977); Steven Hertzberg, *Strangers within the Gate City: The Jews of Atlanta, 1845-1915* (Philadelphia: Jewish Publication Society of America, 1978); Marc Lee Raphael, *Jews and Judaism in a Midwestern Community: Columbus, Ohio, 1840-1975* (Columbus, Ohio: Ohio Historical Society, 1979); William Toll, *The Making of an Ethnic Middle Class: Portland Jewry Over Four Generations* (Albany:

State University of New York Press, 1982); Mitchell Gelfand, "Progress and Prosperity: Jewish Social Mobility in Los Angeles in the Booming Eighties," *American Jewish History,* 68 (June, 1979), pp. 408-33. For analysis of the Jews' drive to succeed, see Nathan Hurvitz, "Sources of Motivation and Achievement of American Jews," *Jewish Social Studies* 23 (October, 1961), pp. 217-34; Eva Etzioni-Halevy and Zvi Halevy, "The 'Jewish Ethic' and the 'Spirit of Achievement,'" *Jewish Journal of Sociology* 19 (June, 1977), pp. 49-66.

32. Zunz, *Changing Face,* pp. 224, 310; Holli, *Detroit,* p. 124; Sidney Fine, *The Automobile under the Blue Eagle: Labor, Management, and the Automobile Manufacturing Code* (Ann Arbor: University of Michigan Press, 1963), p. 21.

33. J. M. Buidsh, *Geshikhte fun di cloth Hat Cap un Milinery Arbeiter* (New York, 1925), pp. 96-97. This appears to have been part of a larger fight between the IWW and the Jewish women's garment workers unions. The IWW sought to form their own unions within the garment trade, which resulted in "civil war" among the workers. Descriptions of this conflict are found in Hertz Burgin, *Di Geshikhte fun der Idisher Arbeiter Bavegung in Amerika, Rusland un England* (New York, 1913), pp. 599-601, and Melech Epstein, *Jewish Labor in U.S.A.: An Industrial, Political and Cultural History of the Jewish Labor Movement* (New York, 1950; Ktav Publishing House, 1969), pp. 375-83.

34. *American Jewish Year Book* (1907-8), pp. 218-20; *Detroit City Directory,* 1914, p. 128; *Jewish American,* January 9, 1903, p. 6, September 7, 1906, pp. 6-7; *Detroit Free Press,* September 10, 1900, p. 11.

35. Albert Nelson Marquis, ed., *The Book of Detroiters* (Chicago: A. N. Marquis & Co., 1914), pp. 192, 201-2, 264, 395, 442.

36. *Detroit News-Tribune,* June 22, 1902, p. 4. The fifteen congregations were Beth David (1883), B'nai David (1892), Beth Abraham (1892), Beth Moses (1902), Beth Tefilo (1904), Tifereth Israel (later Beth Aaron) (1905), Nusach Hoari (1907), Beth Hamidrash Hagadol Anshe Kovno (1907), Beth Isaac (1908), Mishkan Israel (1911), Mogen Abraham (1911), B'nai Moshe (1911), Beth Joseph (1913), Beth Itschock (1914), and Beth Yehuda (1914).

37. *Detroit News-Tribune,* September 13, 1896, II, p. 13.

38. *Hazefirah,* June 18, 1892, p. 547; *Detroit News-Tribune,* September 6, 1896, II, p. 13, September 20, 1896, p. 10; *Detroit Free Press,* June 16, 1902, p. 3; *Jewish American,* November 1, 1901, p. 4, May 2, 1902, p. 4, January 27, 1905, p. 4, September 15, 1905, p. 4, October 5, 1906, p. 6, February 8, 1907, p. 4, September 20, 1907, p. 4, September 27, 1907, p. 4, October 16, 1908, p. 3, September 9, 1910, p. 3; IRO to Miriam Hart, December 6, 1912, Detroit File, IRO Papers.

39. "Di Konstitushen und Gezein fun di Kongregashin Bet Tefilah Nusach Hoari" (1911); Eli Grad and Bette Roth, *Congregation Shaarey Zedek, 1861-1981* (Southfield, Mich.: Congregation Shaarey Zedek, 1982), p. 40; *Jewish American,* October 7, 1904, p. 6.

40. Grad and Roth, *Shaarey Zedek,* pp. 40, 45; *Jewish American,* October 16, 1905, p. 3, February 8, 1907, p. 4, September 9, 1910, p. 3; *Jewish Standard,* July 26, 1907, p. 4. Abraham Hershman wrote *Rabbi Isaac Ben Sheshet Perfet and His Times* (1943), which dealt with the history of the Jews of Spain in the fourteenth century; *Israel's Fate and Faith* (1952); and *Religion of the Age and of the Ages* (1953). He also translated Book Fourteen of the Code of Maimonides, which was published as *Book of Judges* (1949). For a biog-

raphy of Hershman, see the *Encyclopedia Judaica* (Jerusalem: Keter, 1972), vol. 8, p. 395.

41. The sociologist Charles Liebman maintains that most Eastern European Jews who came to the United States between 1881 and 1915 were not Orthodox in the religious, traditional sense of the word. Defining a religious, traditional Jew as one who sees Jewish law *(halakah)* as a "binding imperative that may be violated only under extraordinary and even then prescribed circumstances," he argues that those immigrants "who grew up in Eastern Europe within a total Jewish culture where life in all its aspects was associated with religion, were unable to distinguish culture from religion." Once the culture that supported these attitudes changed, the "practices which were more deeply rooted in the textual religious tradition were readily abandoned." Thus, most of the ostensibly Orthodox immigrants who came to the United States were not religiously traditional, but rather culturally tied to traditional styles and values. See Charles S. Liebman, "Orthodoxy in American Jewish Life," *American Jewish Year Book,* 66 (1965), pp. 21-98, and "Religion, Class and Culture in American Jewish History," *The Jewish Journal of Sociology* 9 (December, 1967), pp. 227-41. See also David Singer, "David Levinsky's Fall: A Note on the Liebman Thesis," *American Quarterly* 19 (Winter, 1967), pp. 696-706.

42. Irving I. Katz, "Detroit's First Communal Talmud Torah," *Michigan Jewish History* (November, 1960), pp. 15-19; *Hazefirah,* June 18, 1892, p. 547; *American Israelite,* March 21, 1895, p. 3; *Detroit News-Tribune,* September 13, 1896, II, p. 13; *Jewish Gazette,* January 15, 1897, p. 3. The founders of the Talmud Torah were Kate Roth, Samuel Ginsburg, David W. Simons, Abraham Jacobs, William Saulson, Samuel Goldstein, Joseph Rosenzweig, Samuel Rosenthal, Moses Blumrosen, David Blumenthal, Julius Rosenthal, Hyman Buchhalter, Israel Scheinman, Moses Harris, Abe Keidan, Harry Meyers, Philip S. Applebaum, Joseph Levitt, Harris Kaplan, Simon Lewis, Michael Davis, and Aaron Solomon (from the Articles of Association of the Talmud Tora Association of Detroit [1898], Congregation Shaarey Zedek Archives, Detroit, Michigan).

43. Katz, "Talmud Torah," p. 18; *Detroit Free Press,* April 7, 1902, p. 2; *Jewish American,* October 18, 1907, p. 11.

44. *Jewish American,* September 30, 1904, p. 6, December 8, 1905, p. 4, November 11, 1910, p. 4, December 23, 1910, p. 4.

45. *Hazefirah,* June 18, 1892, p. 547; *Jewish Gazette,* February 5, 1897, p. 2; *Detroit Free Press,* June 16, 1902, p. 3; *Jewish American,* October 4, 1907, p. 6.

46. *Hazefirah,* June 18, 1892, p. 547.

47. Judah Levin File, Temple Beth El Archives, Birmingham, Michigan; *Detroit Free Press,* October 29, 1903, p. 1. It was not unusual for a rabbi to serve as spiritual leader of more than one congregation. Rabbi Ezekiel Aishiskin, who came to Detroit in 1901, served as rabbi of the congregations B'nai David, Beth Moses, Nusach Hoari, and Tifereth Israel. Rabbi Joseph Eisenman, who arrived in Detroit in 1910, served Beth Tephilo, Beth Hamidrash Hagadol, and Beth Jacob (see the biography and synagogue files of the Temple Beth El Archives).

48. *Jewish American,* October 21, 1904, p. 4.

49. *Detroit Evening News,* October 23, 1894, p. 1; *Detroit Free Press,* November 17, 1902, p. 2.

50. *Jewish American,* October 7, 1910, p. 5, November 11, 1910, p. 7, February 11, 1911, p. 5; *American Israelite,* May 19, 1910, p. 2; *American Hebrew,* March 28, 1913, p. 6.

51. *Detroit Free Press,* April 2, 1911, V, p. 1.

52. Harry L. Lurie, *General Summary of Survey of Detroit Jewish Community, 1923* (New York: Bureau of Jewish Social Research, 1923), p. 48.

53. *Detroit News-Tribune,* February 19, 1899, p. 21; *Detroit Free Press,* September 27, 1903, p. 1; *Jewish American,* December 9, 1910, p. 7.

54. *American Israelite,* June 6, 1901, p. 2; *Jewish American,* October 18, 1907, p. 11; S. D. Weinberg, *Jewish Social Services of Detroit* [Yiddish] (Detroit: Jewish Welfare Federation, 1940), pp. 130-31.

55. *Jewish American,* November 22, 1907, p. 7, November 18, 1910, p. 5; *American Israelite,* April 3, 1902, p. 2.

56. Sharon Alterman, "A History of the Jewish Home for the Aged" (typescript), 1980, p. 4, Temple Beth El Archives, Birmingham, Michigan.

57. *Jewish American,* October 31, 1902, p. 6, October 9, 1908, p. 6, October 16, 1908, p. 4, November 11, 1910, p. 7, November 25, 1910, p. 5, March 10, 1911, p. 3, March 17, 1911, p. 3.

58. *Jewish American,* December 20, 1901, p. 6, July 4, 1902, p. 6, January 16, 1903, p. 6, March 13, 1903, p. 6, October 9, 1903, p. 2, January 22, 1904, p. 2, January 27, 1905, p. 6, May 4, 1906, p. 5, May 3, 1907, p. 7, May 31, 1907, p. 6, June 7, 1907, p. 4, January 3, 1908, p. 6, May 29, 1908, p. 7, November 11, 1910, p. 3, November 25, 1910, p. 5, December 16, 1910, p. 7; March 24, 1911, p. 9. See also *American Israelite,* November 12, 1908, p. 2, March 5, 1914, p. 3; *American Hebrew,* April 18, 1913, p. 718.

59. Jewish Fraternal Orders File, Temple Beth El Archives.

60. *Ibid.*

61. *Ibid.*

62. Irving Howe, *World of Our Fathers* (New York: Harcourt, Brace, Jovanovich, 1976), pp. 183-89; Debrushke Kaluzny and Nathan Kaluzny to author; Turover Aid Society Papers, Burton Historical Collection, Detroit, Michigan; *The Detroit Jewish Society Book* (Detroit, 1916).

63. *Detroit Free Press,* October 17, 1892, p. 4; *Die Welt,* August 31, 1900, p. 15; *American Hebrew,* March 2, 1900, p. 529; *Jewish Advance,* September 1904, pp. 22-23; "Zionism," Temple Beth El Archives; *Detroit News-Tribune,* November 22, 1901, p. 2; *Detroit Journal,* December 28, 1901, p. 3; *American Israelite,* August 21, 1901, p. 2; *Jewish American,* February 21, 1908, p. 6. The four women's groups were Daughters of Zion, Clara de Hirsch Zion Gate, Roses of Zion Gate, and the Lillies of Zion Gate.

64. Herbert Parzen, "The Federation of American Zionists (1897-1914)," in *Early History of Zionism in America,* ed. Isidore S. Meyer (New York: American Jewish Historical Society and Theodor Herzl Foundation, 1958), p. 251; Melvin I. Urofsky, *American Zionism from Herzl to the Holocaust* (New York: Anchor Books, 1976), p. 83.

65. *Jewish Advance,* September 1904, pp. 12-13, 22-23; *Jewish American,* January 8, 1909, p. 7. Aronstam was born in Latvia in 1872 and came to Detroit in 1892. He received his M.D. from the Michigan College of Medicine in 1898. He perfected a test for latent gonorrhea, published widely on medical subjects, and wrote poetry and a novel. He was an active Zionist throughout his life and organized or headed numerous Zionist groups in Detroit, among which were Kadimah and the Order B'nai Zion (see *Detroit Jewish News,* February 15, 1952, June 30, 1950). Albert Bernstein was born in Po-land in 1882 and came to Windsor, Ontario, in 1883 with his parents. He completed his medical studies in Detroit in 1904 and remained in the city. In addition to helping to organize the Kadimah Society, he was one of the organizers of the Hebrew Hospital Association of Detroit in 1911, which raised funds for the construction of a Jewish hospital.

66. *25 Yahriger Yoyvelium fun der Idishe Sozialistishen Arbeiter Partei Poale Zion Verein, Detroit, Michigan, 1905-1930* (Detroit, 1930), pp. 5-8.

67. *Jewish American,* October 9, 1903, p. 3, December 20, 1901, p. 6, March 13, 1903, p. 6, November 4, 1904, p. 6, May 31, 1907, p. 6, November 22, 1907, p. 6, November 18, 1910, p. 7, December 30, 1910, p. 5, January 27, 1911, p. 7; *Jewish Advance,* September, 1904, p. 21, November, 1904, p. 21; *American Israelite,* November 12, 1908, p. 2, February 23, 1909, p. 3; *Idishe Tagliche Presse* (Cleveland), August 6, 1908, p. 5; *American Hebrew,* May 16, 1913, p. 72, April 18, 1913, p. 718, March 28, 1913, p. 616.

68. Howe, *World,* pp. 357-59; Workmen's Circle File, Temple Beth El Archives.

69. *25 Yahriger Yoyvelium fun . . . Poale Zion,* pp. 18-20; Jewish Fraternal Orders File, Temple Beth El Archives.

70. *Detroit Free Press,* May 31, 1903, V, p. 4; *Detroit News,* March 16, 1912, p. 5; *American Israelite,* July 11, 1901, p. 2; *Jewish American,* July 4, 1902, p. 4, October 31, 1902, p. 4, November 25, 1904, p. 4, November 6, 1908, p. 4, September 2, 1910, p. 4.

71. *Detroit Free Press,* October 28, 1893, p. 2, October 26, 1896, p. 5; *Detroit News-Tribune,* June 4, 1899, p. 19; *Jewish American,* June 17, 1904, p. 4, October 28, 1904, p. 4, November 25, 1904, p. 4, February 8, 1907, p. 4; Lurie, *Detroit Jewish Community,* p. 19; Melvin Holli, *Reform in Detroit* (New York: Oxford University Press, 1969), pp. 10-21; Michael Greene to author, August 5, 1969.

72. Simons File, Temple Beth El Archives.

73. Robert A. Rockaway, "The Laboring Man's Champion: Samuel Goldwater of Detroit," *Detroit Historical Society Bulletin* 27 (November, 1970), pp. 4-9.

74. *Detroit Free Press,* September 27, 1903, p. 3, May 31, 1903, V, p. 4, April 2, 1911, V, p. 1; *Detroit Journal,* December 21, 1889, p. 2.

75. *Detroit Free Press,* December 3, 1892, p. 8; *Jewish American,* November 8, 1904, p. 4.

76. *Detroit Free Press,* October 27, 1893, p. 2, October 29, 1893, p. 4; *Detroit Evening News,* October 24, 1894, p. 1.

77. *Detroit News-Tribune,* October 22, 1895, p. 1; *Detroit Free Press,* November 4, 1895, p. 1, November 1, 1896, p. 4. While anti-Bryan forces in Detroit depicted Jews as the force behind the free silver campaign and the ones most likely to benefit from Bryan's victory, Western Populists explained the hard conditions as the result of a conspiracy between Wall Street and international Jewish bankers to maintain the gold standard.

78. Holli, *Reform in Detroit,* pp. 63-64, 69.

79. Stuart E. Rosenberg, *The Jewish Community in Rochester, 1843-1925* (New York: Columbia University Press, 1954), p. 67; Madison Peters, *The Jews in America* (Philadelphia, 1905), p. 124; John Higham, *Strangers in the Land* (New York: Atheneum, 1971), pp. 92-93; Louis Wirth, *The Ghetto* (Chicago: Phoenix Books, 1966), pp. 180-81; Louis J. Swichkow and Lloyd P. Gartner, *The History of the Jews of Milwaukee* (Philadelphia: Jewish Publication Society of America, 1963), p. 161; Isaac M. Fein, *The Making of an American*

Jewish Community: The History of Baltimore Jewry from 1773-1920 (Philadelphia: Jewish Publication Society of America, 1971), p. 204.

80. *Detroit Free Press,* November 24, 1881, p. 1; *American Israelite,* April 9, 1891, p. 1, March 21, 1895, p. 3; *Jewish American,* October 18, 1901, p. 4, February 9, 1906, p. 4, March 30, 1906, p. 4, November 15, 1907, pp. 1-2, November 22, 1907, pp. 4-5.

81. *Jewish American,* November 8, 1901, p. 4, January 31, 1902, p. 4, March 13, 1903, p. 6, September 7, 1906, pp. 6-7, January 31, 1908, pp. 4, 6, August 28, 1908, p. 4, March 17, 1911, p. 11; David Bressler to Miriam Hart, December 9, 1911; Miriam Hart to David Bressler, December 12, 1911, IRO Papers; Peters, *Jews in America,* p. 124.

82. Zunz, *Changing Face,* p. 392; *Detroit News-Tribune,* September 13, 1896, II, p. 13; *Jewish American,* January 17, 1902, p. 4; interviews with Sadie Hirschman, Meyer Lachman's son Sol Lachman, Michael Greene, Irene Soloway, Nathan Kaluzny, Alfred Klunover, and Edgar Schlussel.

83. *American Hebrew,* February 5, 1886, p. 203, June 29, 1900, p. 186; *American Israelite,* June 21, 1900, p. 2; *Detroit Free Press,* September 10, 1900, p. 1, June 16, 1902, p. 3, March 1, 1903, p. 5, October 17, 1904, p. 3, November 12, 1913, p. 5; *Jewish American,* April 11, 1902, p. 4, March 6, 1903, p. 6, October 28, 1904, p. 6; *Detroit News,* February 18, 1913, p. 15.

84. *Detroit Free Press,* September 10, 1900, p. 1, April 7, 1902, p. 2, June 16, 1902, p. 3; *American Hebrew,* April 11, 1902, pp. 639-40; *Jewish American,* December 5, 1902, p. 4, February 26, 1904, p. 6, March 10, 1911, p. 3; *Detroit Journal,* February 9, 1912, p. 2.

85. Zunz, *Changing Face,* pp. 246-47.

5. A COMMUNITY DIVIDED
Germans and Eastern Europeans

ETROIT'S ACCULTURATED GERMAN JEWS viewed the Eastern Europeans ambivalently. As fellow Jews, the immigrants merited assistance; yet their religious Orthodoxy, Old World mannerisms, and politics perturbed the Germans and heightened their feelings of insecurity regarding their own position in the general community. And their concern about their status as the city's Jewish elite led the Germans to consciously set themselves apart from the newcomers. In a letter to the *American Israelite* in 1882, Magnus Butzel expressed the prevailing view of the city's German Jews toward the immigrants' religious orientation when he wrote that "the liberal interpretation of Jewish doctrines, as accepted and practiced by the majority of American Israelites, finds them further removed from the Chasidim-ridden Russian refugee than from any of the other religious societies that exist in this country."[1] This outlook changed little over the next thirty years, as Detroit's Reform German Jews persisted in seeing Orthodox Judaism as slavish, superstition-filled, and incompatible with American traditions.

Mindful that the city's non-Jews knew little about Jewish religious distinctions, the rabbis and lay-men of Temple Beth El distinguished their practices from those of the Eastern Europeans for the general public's edification. "Our religion is distinctively American," explained Rabbi Franklin, "totally differing from the boneless Orthodoxy of the old world, which cringes before kings and princes." To accentuate the differences, Beth El deliberately avoided close relations with the city's Orthodox congregations and emphasized to the general public "that the ways of these people are not our ways, nor their thoughts our thoughts." This posture caused the pro-Reform *Jewish American* to chastise the Temple for its eagerness to cooperate with Christian churches but not with Orthodox synagogues.[2]

For its part, Detroit's Orthodox community regarded the Reform movement as an attempt to obliterate all specifically Jewish elements from Judaism so as to render Jews indistinguishable from non-Jews. Many Orthodox immigrants considered Reform Jews little better than *goyim* (gentiles) and viewed their participation in American social customs, such as mixed dancing and card playing, as a definite sign of moral decay. The commonness of these activities among the German Jews led one Orthodox newcomer to label Detroit "the modern Sodom." As a result, the city's Orthodoxy displayed little enthusiasm for close contact with the Temple.[3]

The immigrants' political behavior also upset the German community. The Eastern Europeans' political rallies, political clubs, and unabashed bargaining with politicians seeking their votes provoked the Germans because these activities contradicted their stated position against mixing religion with politics. Rabbi Franklin cautioned the immigrants that such pursuits "menaced the patriotism and good name of the Jew in the community." He then assured the general public that Detroit's "respectable Jewish citizenship" advocated the separation of church and state, and Jews "who attempt to unite the two are neither Jews nor Americans." Picking up this theme, the *Jewish American* admonished its readers "that the Jews must not allow anything that appeals to segregated Jewish practices for political purposes" because it would "arouse anti-Semitism."[4]

In the same manner that Eastern European involvement in local politics threatened the Germans, immigrant support for political Zionism aroused the concern and opposition of the entire established community. The Zionist concept of the Jews as a people in exile came under fierce attack during the late nineteenth century. To achieve political equality and demonstrate their loyalty to the countries in which they lived, Jews of the West rejected the concepts of Exile and Return and proclaimed Judaism to be a religion with a universal ethical message. The "mission of the Jews," in their view, was to propagate monotheism and the teachings of the prophets, and the dispersion was a necessary means of achieving this end. In both Central Europe and the United States, Reform rabbis eliminated all liturgical references to an ingathering of the exiles, the restoration of Jewish sovereignty, and the rebuilding of the Temple in Jerusalem. Although Detroit's Reform Jews contributed to emissaries from Jerusalem and to Palestinian charities, they opposed a return to the Holy Land. "America—not Palestine—is the Jew's land of destiny" trumpeted the *Jewish American*, "and Washington—not Jerusalem—is our national capital."[5]

Detroit's German Jews believed that the immigrants had to adopt American customs and ideals and feared that Zionism would endanger their position as loyal Americans. "It is eternally untrue that the Jew is a man without a country. He has found his Canaan in America," asserted the *Jewish American*. "Let dreamers hail the renationalization of Israel as hard as they please—Zionism is a political impossibility; an historical inconsistency and a religious mistake." Rabbi Franklin, who remained intractable on the subject of political Zionism throughout his five decades in the pulpit, insisted that "all talk of Zionism in a national sense by American Jews is nothing short of arch treason to the best government on earth and should be so dealt with." Franklin and other German Jewish leaders stressed to the general community that the lower classes of the Jews organized the city's Zionist societies, while upper-class Jews had nothing to do with them. These attitudes reflected the established community's assimilation, desire for acceptance, and belief that Zionism compromised their hard-won status.[6]

German Jewish concern for their public image led to a careful scrutiny of the immigrants' behavior for anything that deviated from acceptable middle-class norms. The interminable kosher meat wars, synagogue rivalries, and ideological squabbles and the colorful street life of the newcomers prompted scathing condemnation from the German Jews because these topics appeared in print, exposing the entire Jewish community to adverse publicity and ridicule. How could Jews expect their non-Jewish neighbors to treat them as equals, queried the *Jewish American*, so long as they behaved like "ghetto people?"[7]

Economically, a wide gulf separated the two groups (Table 14). However, to further clarify class distinctions, German Jews distanced themselves physically as much as possible from the Eastern Europeans. They lived apart from them (Map 5), refused them entrance into their clubs, and avoided mixing socially. Hoping to breach the mounting social divisiveness, Rabbi Franklin, Bernard Ginsburg, and David Simons founded the Fellowship Club in 1898 to promote social contact between the Germans and Eastern Europeans. The effort failed because neither

Map 5. Residential Distribution of Temple Beth El Members, 1910

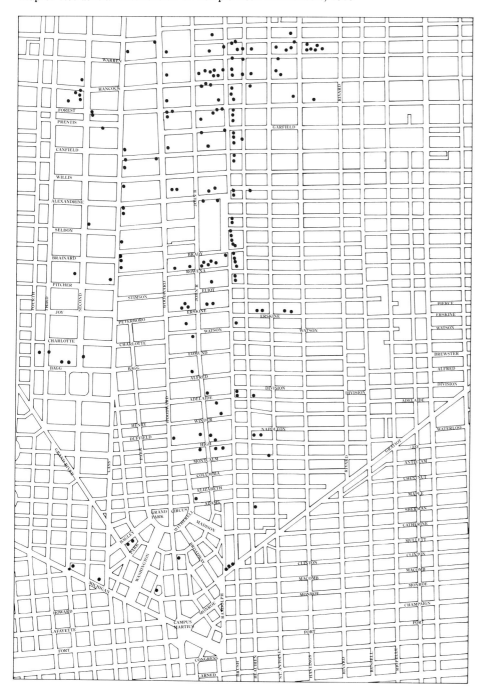

side displayed much interest in a closer relationship. Increasing social apathy among the Germans in regard to the Eastern Europeans eventually led Rabbi Franklin to openly castigate his congregation for its discriminatory behavior, while the *Jewish American* warned against the growth of "anti-Semitic feelings" among Temple members.[8]

Despite the conflicts and cultural differences, a number of the more enlightened German Jewish leaders expressed genuine compassion for the Eastern Europeans and recognized an obligation to assist them. "Forgetting present differences, and remembering only that if the Russian Jew is not all he should be today, it is because oppression has temporarily taken the manhood out of him. Yet he is our brother and as Jews we must regard and receive him as such," admonished Rabbi Franklin. "How dare we expect the world to look with unprejudiced eyes upon us so long as Jew stands against Jew?" Furthermore, "we belong to the minority and the minority is always judged by its lowest representatives. Our great duty, therefore, is to raise our race." This exhortation voiced the attitudes of those motivated to do charitable work on behalf of the immigrants: they toiled out of sympathy, duty, and self-defense.[9]

Sewing lesson from the Self-Help Circle book of Mrs. Leo Franklin and Mrs. Sarah Krolik, 1899. (Courtesy of the Jewish Welfare Federation–United Jewish Charities Archives.)

RELIEF WORK

At the first news of the pogroms in Russia, Temple Beth El collected funds for the relief of the Russian Jews, and when refugees arrived in Detroit, the Beth El Hebrew Relief Society established a committee to help them. This committee found housing and jobs for the newcomers and provided funds and pensions to those who needed them. It quickly became evident, however, that the Relief Society alone could not cope with all the problems of the immigrants. Consequently, nineteen Beth El members, led by Simon Heavenrich and Rabbi Henry Zirndorf, organized the Hebrew Ladies Auxiliary Relief Society in 1882 (its name was changed to Hebrew Ladies' Sewing Society later that year), "for the purpose of alleviating the dis-

tressed conditions of the Russian exiles, both morally and physically." The ladies provided clothing, shoes, and bedding for the destitute; cared for the sick; supplied medical assistance; and paid the rent for those unable to do so. By 1898 the Sewing Society had a membership of 130, cared for 125 families on a regular basis, and disbursed more than $1,100 annually.[10]

With slight variations, Detroit's Jews' initial relief efforts approximated those of Jewish communities in other cities. For example, the first Russian

100

Jews arrived in Cleveland in 1881 and received assistance from individual Cleveland Jews. It was not until 1891, with the establishment of a Russian Refugee Society, that the immigrants actually became the continuous concern of the Jewish community. In Milwaukee a committee to assist the refugees was established in 1881, and Jews and non-Jews cooperated in providing relief. And in Atlanta, the local Reform temple, the Hebrew Benevolent Congregation, quickly raised money and assisted the small number of Russian Jews that came to the city.[11]

In 1889 a group of Beth El choir girls began sewing items for the children of the immigrants. Mrs. Joseph Finsterwald suggested that the girls could benefit the children more if they taught them to sew for themselves. Thus was born the Self-Help Circle which, under the leadership of Sarah Krolik, became a domestic training school. Several years after its founding, the Circle rented a building on the corner of Brush and Montcalm Streets and offered daily and weekly classes in cooking, cleaning, and sewing, and evening and Sunday classes in English and other common school subjects. Attendance at Self-Help classes increased from a few dozen children in the 1890s to two hundred in 1904, when, by then, the Circle had become part of the United Jewish Charities.[12]

Self-help and Americanization became the credo for all future Jewish charitable work with the immigrants. The importance attached to Americanization is evident from the frequency with which the subject appeared in sermons, articles in the Jewish and general press, and even in eulogies. In a tribute to Louis Blitz, a manufacturer, financier, and former president of Beth El, Rabbi Franklin emphasized that the deceased "believed in immigration—but he insisted upon the Americanization of the immigrant."[13]

By the end of the 1880s, the needs of the immigrants overwhelmed the community's limited efforts to assuage them. Recognizing this, Temple Beth El and representatives from the B'nai B'rith, Kesher Shel Barzel, and the Free Sons of Israel and Sons of Benjamin fraternal orders created a Russian Refugee's committee to coordinate and consolidate all relief efforts. Among the officers were Martin Butzel, Sig-

Minutes of the meeting leading to the organization of the United Jewish Charities in 1899. (Courtesy of the Jewish Welfare Federation–United Jewish Charities Archives.)

101

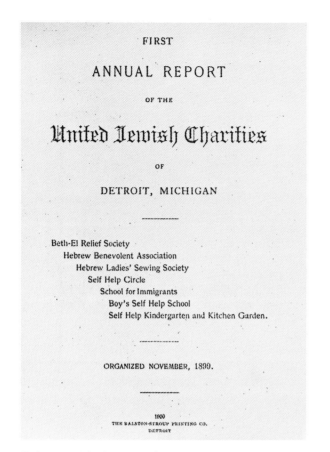

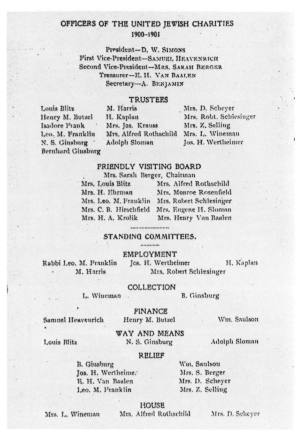

Title page of the first annual report of the United Jewish Charities and a page with the names of the officers and committee members. (Courtesy of the Jewish Welfare Federation-United Jewish Charities Archives.)

mund Simon, David Simons, Simon Heavenrich, and Simon Cohen. In addition to its other work, this organization supported the first Russian Jewish agricultural colony in Michigan, at Bad Axe, through the first decade of its stormy existence.[14]

For many years, Congregation Shaarey Zedek participated in the Beth El Hebrew Relief Society. The Society's existing policies and the negative attitudes toward Orthodox Jews exhibited by some of the German Jewish leaders, however, led members of Shaarey Zedek to withdraw from the charity in 1891 and form their own Jewish Relief Society. Represent-

ing the Orthodox segment of Detroit's Jewish community, this group also assisted the poor, the transient, and the immigrant.[15]

THE UNITED JEWISH CHARITIES

As the immigrants continued coming, the Jewish community established new charities to assist them. Ten separate Jewish charities, some run by the German Jews, others by the Eastern Europeans, existed by

1897. Inevitably, this led to the duplication of efforts, work done at cross-purposes, and a shortage of funds. To end the confusion and waste, the Beth El Hebrew Relief Society, Self-Help Circle, Hebrew Ladies' Sewing Society, and the Jewish Relief Society of Shaarey Zedek, under the chairmanship of Rabbi Franklin, amalgamated to form the United Jewish Charities of Detroit (UJC) in 1899. Four members of Shaarey Zedek and fourteen members of Beth El comprised the organizational committee. Typifying those of the nineteenth-century Charity Organization Movement, which administered most of the relief in America's urban areas, the objects of the UJC were "to make men and women out of our dependent classes . . . to build character . . . to arouse a sense of manhood and womanhood among the poor," to help the poor help themselves, and to centralize fund raising.[16]

From its inception, the UJC functioned through volunteer committees, continuing on a more coordinated level the work of its constituent societies. Initially encompassing committees on relief, employment, education, building, finance, and collection, the UJC later added a medical committee, various subcommittees, and auxiliaries as the need arose. Members of Temple Beth El controlled the UJC, numerically dominating its board of directors and committees, before and after World War I.[17]

For a time, Joseph H. Wertheimer acted as the volunteer superintendent of the organization. It soon became clear that the job required a full-time professional, and in 1901 the UJC hired a Mr. A. A. Epstein to fill the position. He left after only four months, however, and Louis Rosenberg replaced him. He, in turn, supervised UJC affairs until 1903, when Blanche Hart assumed the post. Born in Grand Rapids, Michigan, in 1876 and educated in the Detroit public schools and at the University of Michigan, Hart directed the UJC throughout the period of massive Eastern European immigration and resigned in 1923.[18]

The UJC rented a building at 379 Brush Street as the first location of its offices. However, the building proved crowded and unsanitary, making relocation imperative. Through a gift of $4,000 from Henry Krolik in 1902, the UJC purchased a lot on the north side

Blanche Hart, director of the United Jewish Charities from 1903 to 1923, at Venice Beach in 1912. (Courtesy of the Fresh Air Society Archives.)

of High Street, west of Hastings. One year later, Seligman Schloss donated $5,800 toward the construction of a building as a memorial to his wife, Hannah. Albert Kahn, the architect, offered to make the plans and look after the construction free of charge. After a successful fund-raising campaign, in which anyone contributing $500 or more could name a room in the building, the cornerstone laying took place on April 21, 1903. At the building's dedication, on September 27, 1903, Schloss announced that he would pay for the entire cost of erection, some $12,700.[19]

Known as the Hannah Schloss Memorial, the building was a settlement house containing a medical clinic, day nursery, model kitchen, model dining room, model bedroom, classrooms, library, manual training rooms, auditorium, bathing facilities, the UJC offices, and the loan office of the Hebrew Free Loan Society. A new wing, donated by Bernard Ginsburg in 1908, al-

Seligman Schloss, communal leader who donated the funds to construct the Hannah Schloss Memorial. (Courtesy of the Rabbi Leo M. Franklin Archives of Temple Beth El.)

Hannah Schloss, for whom the Hannah Schloss Memorial is named. (Courtesy of the Rabbi Leo M. Franklin Archives of Temple Beth El.)

The Hannah Schloss Memorial Building. (Courtesy of the Hannah Schloss Old Timers–Jewish Community Center.)

lowed the UJC to add a gymnasium and expand the scope of its operation. The enlarged building, with the original portion designated as a memorial to Hannah Schloss and the new wing to the Ginsburg family, became known as the Jewish Institute.[20]

In its new home, the UJC provided Detroit's immigrant Jews with a wide variety of services that frequently proved crucial to their adjustment. Under the direction of Dr. Louis J. Hirschman, the medical clinic served the public three days a week. The clinic functioned in this way until 1910, when it was reorganized and moved from its original location in the Hannah Schloss building to the basement of the Ginsburg wing of the newly created Jewish Institute. Managed by its medical staff, the new clinic comprised a waiting room and seven examination and treatment rooms. Clinical departments included surgery; medicine; gynecology; obstetrics; eye, ear, and nose; dermatology; and orthopedics. Hospitalization, when necessary, was arranged through several local hospitals, notably Children's, Harper, and Women's. During the early 1900s, the City of Detroit paid for most of the medical costs; in later years the UJC and the patient's family absorbed a portion of the expenses. Dr. Hugo A. Freund and Dr. Max Balin, in that order, succeeded Dr. Hirschman as directors of the clinic.[21]

The child care program of the UJC began early in 1901 with the establishment of a kindergarten. Two years later, a gift from Bernard Ginsburg enabled the UJC to open the Ida E. Ginsburg Day Nursery in the Hannah Schloss Building. For a nominal fee of five cents per day, mothers could leave their children

Bernard Ginsberg, philanthropist, communal and civic leader, and president of the United Jewish Charities, 1904–8. (Courtesy of the Rabbi Leo M. Franklin Archives of Temple Beth El.)

Report of Dr. Louis Hirschman, director of the medical clinic of the Jewish Institute. (Courtesy of the Jewish Welfare Federation–United Jewish Charities Archives.)

Physician's Report.

Detroit, October 26, 1900.

To the Officers of the United Jewish Charities:

Ladies and Gentlemen—I herewith respectfully submit the report of my medical and surgical work among your pensioners for the seven months ending October 31, 1900.

Number of patients treated	23
Number of visits and consultations	359
Number of prescriptions	102
Cost of prescriptions	$35.75
Average cost	35 cents
Cost of surgical supplies	$14.00
Number of surgical dressings	144
Average cost per dressing	9 4-5 cts
Total cost for 23 patients for 7 months	$49.75
Average cost per patient	$ 2.16

(Or approximately one cent per day.)

Number of surgical operations	6
Number of cases receiving hospital care	6
Number of deaths	2
Death rate	4.6 p. c.
Largest number of calls on one patient	94
Smallest number of calls on one patient	1

The following diseases were treated:

Adenoids	1	Haemeroids	1
Appendicitis	2	Intestinal obstruction	1
Blindness	1	Lacerated cervix	2
Bright's Disease	1	LaGrippe	1
Chorea	1	Menopause	1
Chronic Bronchitis	1	Neurasthesia	1
Constipation	2	Necrosis of Tibia	1
Conjunctivitis	1	Ovaritis	2
Epilepsy	1	Paralysis	1
Examination	1	Peritonitis	1
Fractured arm	1	Pulmonary tuberculosis	3
Gall stones	1	Typhoid	1
Goitre	1	Worms	1

I call your special attention to the work of the Visiting Nurses' Association. They made over forty calls on our patients.

Respectfully submitted,
L. J. HIRSCHMAN, M. D.

under the care of a trained nurse from 7:00 A.M. to 6:00 P.M., Monday through Friday. The UJC also operated the Walker Milk Fund Depot in the Hannah Schloss building. Mothers could bring their babies to the Depot for periodic examinations or to pick up milk formula. Older children benefited from the Fresh Air Society, which was formed in 1904 "to take out deserving children for day outings during the hot months" and "to furnish milk and ice or food to the needy sick." Eventually, the Society purchased two houses and three acres of land on the shores of Lake St. Clair for a campsite. Except for the delousing procedure performed at the start of each camping session, the children apparently had a wonderful time.[22]

Beginning in 1906, the UJC arranged for foster care in local private homes for children whose home situations made this step necessary. As the number of children receiving such care increased, the UJC engaged a social worker to visit the homes and supervise their operation. The Detroit Board of Health investigated the suitability of the homes, and the State Board of Charities licensed them. The UJC sent de-

The Fresh Air Society committee, 1912. (Courtesy of the Fresh Air Society Archives.)

Off to Venice Beach on Lake St. Clair, in 1912. (Courtesy of the Fresh Air Society Archives.)

pendent orphans to the Cleveland Orphan Asylum, for which consideration the organization made an annual grant to the orphanage.[23]

The United Jewish Charities' Relief Committee commenced its work in 1899 and furnished immigrants with aid in a variety of emergencies. This help included money for food, rent, and medical expenses; housekeeping services; legal aid; child care; loans; care of transients; matzoth for Passover; transportation costs; adoption help; and prison relief. The Committee met several times each month to review all applications for assistance. Before any formal action was taken, an investigative committee, consisting of one or two people, examined all new or unusual relief requests.

The number of persons applying for help de-

pended to a great extent upon economic conditions in the city. The automobile industry brought to Detroit sharply fluctuating "boom-and-bust" business cycles. The short-range fluctuations resulted from the production rhythms of an industry that shut down yearly for a model changeover that caused temporary mass layoffs. During national economic crises, consumers deferred the purchase of automobiles for a year or two, which had serious repercussions in the salesrooms and on the assembly lines. In 1906, a normal year, 3,317 people applied for assistance in Detroit. In the following year, the panic of 1907 led to widespread unemployment in Detroit, and 5,748 persons received aid. This figure declined to 3,602 by 1909, only to rise again to 5,106 in 1910, when the city suffered another recession. During the economic crisis of 1914–15, a to-

The Adriatic Club in 1912. It was one of the male clubs that met at the Hannah Schloss Memorial Building. (Courtesy of the Hannah Schloss Old Timers–Jewish Community Center.)

tal of 11,491 people—more than one third of Detroit's immigrant Jewish community—applied for relief. By then, disbursements amounted to more than forty thousand dollars per year.[24]

All social, cultural, and Americanizing pro-grams came under the aegis of the UJC's Education and Recreation Department, which offered classes in English, sewing, domestic science, stenography, danc-ing, manual training, and military drill, as well as dances, concerts, and lectures in Yiddish and English

(Table 15). In addition, the department sponsored a wide variety of youth and adult clubs with names like Ace of Clubs, Greener Winkel, Kultur League, Maccabean Sports, Zeirei Zion, Northern Friendship, Hader Zion, Knights of Judea, Mogen Dovid, Roses of Zion, Sholem Aleichem, Washington Progressive, Riptons, Camp Fire Girls, and Trisqaures. Clubs generally organized according to the interests, age, and sex of their members. Thus, there were male and female clubs devoted to Zionism; sports; Yiddish culture, arts, and crafts; scouting; and literary activities. Some clubs, like the Trisquares, under Fred Butzel, com-

The Young Men's Hebrew Association basketball team, which met at the Hannah Schloss Memorial Building, circa 1914. (Courtesy of Fanya Green and the Archives of Congregation Shaarey Zedek.)

bined a number of activities, such as athletic competitions, debates, oratorical contests, and outings. The clubs and the many other doings kept the Hannah Schloss Building and, later, the Jewish Institute humming with activity.[25]

Voluntary subscriptions were the UJC's primary source of income prior to World War I. Following the leads of the Jewish communities of Cincinnati and Boston, the UJC board resolved in 1904 "that all collection made in this city for the benefit of charitable organizations endorsed by the Charities shall be concentrated into one collection to be made by the Charities and to be distributed by them proportionately as agreed." Henceforth, Detroit's Jews had the option of giving once for all. Nevertheless, for many years the number of subscribers as well as the amounts contributed remained low. The annual income from 1900 to 1905 averaged less than $5,000 collected from less than 300 contributors; for the period between 1906 and 1910 less than $15,000 per year was collected from 450 donors (Table 16). The lack of interest and support led the *Jewish American* to make ongoing appeals to the wealthy, reminding them that "there is no more sacred obligation than that devolving upon those who are able, to assist the poor and afflicted. If they will not learn, ostracism should be their heritage." In an attempt to apply social pressure, the newspaper published lists of the givers with the amounts they contributed and threatened to publish the names of those persons who were able to donate to charity and refused to do so. All efforts by communal leaders aimed at remedying the situation met with failure.[26]

As the number of immigrants applying for relief grew into the thousands, the Jewish charities came under increasing pressure. The mounting work load coupled with a barely concealed distaste for the demeanor of the East Europeans affected the opinions and conduct of those managing the funds. Weariness, mistrust, and resentment gradually replaced the spirit of kin-like obligation that had motivated their earlier benevolence. Most officials still failed to understand the immigrants and their traditions and treated them paternalistically—seeing them as wards or children to

be guided, guarded, and protected. Others, however, began seeing their claimants as little more than *schnorrers* (beggars) and reacted harshly to infractions of rules and regulations. In one extreme case, the officers of the Ladies' Society for the Support of Hebrew Widows and Orphans entertained a motion to send a woman pensioner back to Russia for failing to keep her rooms clean and send her children to school. This incident occurred immediately after the pogroms of 1905. Despite her dedication, competence, and professionalism, Blanche Hart's exasperation with the immigrants led her to become increasingly cynical and callous in her dealings with them. In an attempt to counteract the antipathy toward the immigrants, the UJC eliminated all references to the applicant's nationality from its reports.[27]

The response of Detroit's Eastern European Jews toward their benefactors combined both gratitude and resentment. For many, the assistance meant the difference between deprivation and security, but they expressed bitterness at the manner in which the charity was dispensed. Eastern Europeans applied the standards applicable in their native milieu to the Jewish charitable agencies in America. The principle of investigation—superfluous in the shtetl—impressed the Eastern European as unfeeling and unJewish. Years later Michael Greene recalled his own experiences by commenting that "after all, we were Jews, too." Disaffection with the UJC became so prevalent that the *Jewish American* regretfully conceded that most of Detroit's immigrant community felt the charity's officers to be a "hard-hearted lot, without sympathy and without the spirit of true charity in their hearts."[28]

Many members of Detroit's German Jewish community little understood the perspectives and feelings of the Eastern European Jews. Seen as coming from countries and environments considered to be backward, unenlightened, and "oriental" (non-Western), the immigrants were viewed as being a completely different and inferior species of Jew who operated on a lower plane of morality than his more Americanized counterpart. Repulsed by what they regarded as crude and unpolished manners and behav-

Boy Scout Troop 23, sponsored by the Jewish Institute, 1913. (Courtesy of the Hannah Schloss Old Timers–Jewish Community Center.)

ior, some German Jews contemptuously referred to the newcomers as "kikes."[29]

Nevertheless, there were a number of German Jews active in charitable work who recognized that the newcomers' adjustment to American life would prove difficult and sought, wherever possible, to accommodate their special needs. The Orthodox Jews' demand for kosher food was respected, and their desire to work on Sunday rather than on Saturday was defended. In an effort to protect the immigrants' dig-

Fred M. Butzel, philanthropist and communal and civic leader. (Courtesy of the Rabbi Leo M. Franklin Archives of Temple Beth El.)

nity, the UJC inaugurated procedures to prevent persons on relief from assembling at the Jewish Institute, "where one may learn of the disgrace of the other."[30]

The German Jewish philanthropist most revered by the Eastern Europeans for his kindness, compassion, and readiness to assist them was Fred M. Butzel (1877–1948). While his brother Henry ran the family law firm, Fred, also a lawyer, devoted his time to public service. He personally aided hundreds of immigrants with money, jobs, and free legal advice; his office door was always open to anyone with a prob-

lem. When the father of Harry Madison died, leaving the family penniless, Fred Butzel provided a home rent free, financed the children's education, and loaned Harry one thousand dollars to start his own business. So trusted was Butzel that the immigrants went to him to draw up their wills. Called "Detroit's most valuable citizen" by *Detroit Free Press* editor Malcolm Bingay, Butzel officered the United Jewish Charities, Jewish Welfare Federation, Boy Scouts, and Detroit Urban League, among others. The Jewish Welfare Federation of Detroit is today housed in a building that bears his name.[31]

Despite the efforts and goodwill of persons like Fred Butzel, the indignation toward the German Jewish directors of the UJC led the Eastern Europeans to establish their own charities and boycott the UJC. This situation remained basically unchanged till the reorganization of the UJC into the Jewish Welfare Federation of Detroit in 1926.[32]

THE INDUSTRIAL REMOVAL OFFICE

In 1901 a group of influential American Jewish leaders created the Industrial Removal Office (IRO) to draw immigrant Jews out of New York and relocate them in smaller cities where Jews already dwelt and jobs existed. In this way, they hoped to solve the problem of crowding and squalor in New York's ghetto district. From its inception to its liquidation in 1922, the IRO dispatched 79,000 Jews to over 1,700 American cities. Because of its viable Jewish community and the opportunities presented by its burgeoning automobile industry, Detroit became one of the IRO's prime destinations.[33]

Although officially established in 1901, the IRO got its real start the following year at the second National Conference of Jewish Charities held in Detroit. Some of the most notable figures in American Jewish life attended the meeting, among them Dr. Lee K. Frankel, a chemist by profession, who directed the United Hebrew Charities of New York; Judge Julian Mack, then head of the Juvenile Court of Chicago;

Cyrus Sulzberger, businessman and New York civic leader; and Nathan Bijur, a prominent attorney and later a justice of the New York State Supreme Court. The underlying purpose of the Conference was to bring the idea of the IRO before the American Jewish community. Participants were moved to tears as speaker after speaker described the horrors of the immigrant quarters in New York City. Fred Butzel later recalled Cyrus Sulzberger's breaking down in the middle of his speech, overcome by emotion as he pictured the teeming slums of the metropolis.

As a solution to the problem of congestion, the Conference proposed that immigrants arriving in New York be dispersed through a central office to be managed by David M. Bressler. In order to secure the active cooperation of the Jewish charities in as many cities as possible, the IRO subsidized their operation by paying the charities' local agent's salary—from fifty to seventy-five dollars per month—and giving the Jewish community an allowance for every family or individual placed. All of the IRO's activities were subsidized by the Jewish Colonization Association and the Baron de Hirsch Fund.[34]

Detroit's United Jewish Charities—like Jewish organizations in other communities—set up a committee to receive and care for a fixed number of men sent by the IRO each month (only men were sent at first). This arrangement continued until 1904 when, after a personal appeal by Bressler for Detroit to do more, the UJC hired an agent to run the office on a regular basis. Birdie Pick, a young society woman, directed the operation for three years. In 1907 Miriam Hart (no relation to Blanche Hart), a young social worker, succeeded her. From time to time, Blanche Hart, as superintendent of the UJC, and other UJC officers helped out as the need arose. The IRO expected their local agents to find jobs and arrange for lodging, board, transportation, and other necessities of daily living for the immigrants sent. Detroit's office was especially competent in this regard, seeing to most of the arrangements before the immigrants arrived. This businesslike approach led David Bressler to comment on "how well satisfied we have been with the work of our very efficient Detroit agent." During

its short life, the IRO sent over 3,200 men to Detroit (Table 17).[35]

The Detroit agents periodically canvassed the city's economy and job market and reported their findings and recommendations to the IRO. Upon receipt of the information, New York forwarded the resumes of men with pertinent occupations and awaited approval for them to be sent. "Ignatz Binstock," reads one such resume, "wood worker and machine operator. Binstock does not yet speak English, having been in the country but three months, but brings splendid references, showing that he was a good worker in Austria. And if you can find him work in one of the factories of your city, he will undoubtedly make fine progress. He is 25 years old and unmarried."[36]

Frequently, the IRO advertised the skills of worthy candidates without waiting for requests from Detroit: "Morris Wold, tinsmith (special at automobile lamps), is a first class workman and in good health," and "Meyer Burde, machinist (lathe hand), about 12 years at his trade, a very worthy case, and in good health. Have we your permission to send them to Detroit?" Detroit's acceptance or rejection depended on whether an applicant had a trade and could be placed. This reflected the Detroit office's concern that removals not end up on the city's Jewish and non-Jewish charity rolls. Thus, Joe Robinson could be sent "as the Detroit Cap Company will give him steady employment"; but not Max Marks, since "work of the kind he desires is very, very hard to secure." A similar fate befell Yehiel Moshkowitz because "he is a cripple and only able to peddle."[37]

Local companies, learning of the IRO, sent requests for help directly to the New York office. Mr. J. Schwartz of the Progressive Couch Company needed a "first class couch maker, one who thoroughly understands putting leather tufted pads and can make nice side ruffles." Harry B. Clark asked for "a nice yong mens costume tailor." The candidate could "be one who is not able to speack anglish." Both employers promised steady employment to the men hired. In most cases, the IRO referred the employer to the local agent.[38]

The IRO also transmitted to the local offices a

large number of queries dealing with immigrant requests to be sent to relatives or friends; the local agent was expected to investigate and report on the merits of each case. A variety of responses characterized the Detroit office's answers to New York. Sometimes relatives could provide transportation costs: "You may send Annie Trustman to I. Trustman who is sending enclosed five dollars contribution." At other times, the agents rejected the immigrants' requests: "Hyman Marcus does not know anyone by the name of Frieda Shinin or Abe Shinin and family, so of course will not receive them." When a relative could not afford to send money, help might be offered instead: "You may send Jacob Sazzman and daughter to Sara Sazzman who will receive them but cannot contribute toward transportation."[39]

This outward efficiency masked the many headaches encountered by agents in discharging their tasks. The periodic model changeovers and economic recessions in the automobile industry played havoc with the Detroit office's employment quotas, leaving the agents frustrated and helpless. "I have daily from fifty to seventy-five applicants for work and cannot place any," complained Miriam Hart. "Last Tuesday afternoon I personally visited eleven factories on Wednesday twelve on Thursday nine, and was not able to place one man."

Even when times were good, discrimination against Jews in factories sometimes prevented IRO men from being placed. Housing could be a problem: "Again we are confronted by the housing question and are unable to find homes for our families." Although the men sent from New York received a small subsidy from the IRO, many of them arrived in Detroit without funds. This strained the local office's resources and prompted requests for more funds: "On May 29th you sent us Issy Marcus whom you said had in his possession $10.00. The man bought tools with the greater part of his money and what with carfare had not enough left to pay for his weeks board and room. This was paid at our expense. Under these circumstances will you not be responsible?" Some men arrived ill: "Jacob Silverstein was sent to us July 30. Undoubtedly the man had tuberculosis before being

sent here and as his family is in New York and he is unable to work may we send him at your expense, back to your city?"

There were also numerous problems with the removals after they arrived. Some were found to have deserted their families: "Upon investigation have found that Issy Hurstein, sent by your office to this city, Oct. 10th, while posing here as a single man, is deserting his wife in New York." Others refused to work: "No. 14506 Abraham Azilan, he possessed no trade and had worked in lumber yard abroad. He was apparently a strong man. He refused five positions."[40]

Despite generally cordial relations, an undercurrent of tension can be detected in the correspondence between the local agents and the New York IRO office. This mostly concerned their differing perceptions of Detroit's capacity to absorb removals. The Detroit office felt it did more than its share; New York believed Detroit could do more. This dispute was never resolved to either party's satisfaction.[41]

Between 1903 and 1914, Russian immigrants comprised 85 percent of the total number of arrivals, the majority of them having been in the United States less than six months. Sixty percent of all the removals were between ages twenty-one and thirty; 22 percent between thirty-one and forty. And more than half the men sent were married, most with their families still in Europe. Since the Detroit office requested that only industrial workers or men with trades be sent, it is not surprising that 75 percent of the men could be classified as skilled or semiskilled.[42]

The efficiency and goodwill of the IRO and Detroit branch notwithstanding, the adjustment of these men was no easier than that of other Jewish immigrants. The IRO advertised its function in a number of ways, the most successful being notices placed in the New York Yiddish press and in settlement houses. Interested parties made application at the main office; if the applicant qualified, he was placed on the list of prospective removals. The IRO never promised the applicant that it would find him a particular job at a certain salary in the community to which he was being sent. Furnished with a small stipend (usually ten dollars) and sometimes tools, each man was sent to an agent in a specific city who tried to find him work in his trade or something reasonably close to it.[43]

Many of the aspirants misinterpreted or misunderstood IRO policies and procedures, and when expectations remained unfulfilled, complaints and accusations abounded. One man charged the IRO with lying to him by promising to assume all responsibility for having his family admitted to the United States. "You are surely laboring under a misapprehension," came back the reply. "We never made such promise to you, nor have we made it to anyone of our beneficiaries." Another, upset at having to contribute seven dollars toward the cost of his brother's transportation, retorted that the IRO "acted like a robber" in taking the money from him. Angered by what he considered humiliating investigatory procedures, Herman Marcus accused the IRO of degrading him: "The charities was organized for the purpose of bettering conditions of the poor workingman. I am one of those workingmen but I do not like to beg."[44]

Some of the complaints reflected the immigrants' displeasure with the agent's attitude toward them. Although thankful for the assistance, many removals resented the condescension with which the aid was rendered and did not shrink from saying so. The agents, for their part, mistook this sensitivity for ungratefulness. This lack of understanding characterized relations between agents and removals throughout the Detroit office's existence.[45]

Most of the letters from Detroit removals to the IRO contained requests that family or belongings be forwarded to them. "I beseech you to send me my family, as listed with you, as well as my son-in-law and daughter. I also beg you to send my two nephews, Shayeh Chmelzitski and Idshize Weiner, who are struggling in New York and cannot find work," wrote L. Friedman. "We haven't our furniture yet," complained Ike Togel. "So please write us from what depot you send it and what depot it has come to Detroit. Please send us an answer as quick as possible because the children are all sick all ready and we can't wait."[46]

Other letters attested to the trauma and tragedy experienced by some of the removals. Nathan Toplitzky lost four fingers from his right hand in an industrial accident. Upon regaining his strength, he asked the Detroit agent to find him another job. Since no new openings were available, he was sent back to his old employer. Filled with fear at being returned to the same machine where the accident occurred, he refused to work and was fired. He wrote to the IRO and pleaded with them to help him."I now call daily at the office of the committee and beg them to give me another job. However, they do not want to hear me. So sirs and friends, I beg you to have pity on this poor cripple. I am alone in the city without a cent, without a friend, whereas in New York I have many friends who would not allow me to suffer so. I beg of you to write to your committee to find a position for me, for you can not realize how unfortunate I am." David Bressler replied that "I regret very much to learn of your mishap, but trust you will in a very short time have recovered. I have no doubt that our agent in Detroit is doing all she can for you and if you are not employed now, it is not because she is not willing to find employment for you, but because it is impossible to do so. In any event call upon her and I am sure she will give you due consideration." Formal replies of this nature antagonized some of the immigrants, who saw them as proof of IRO insensitivity and lack of compassion.[47]

Not all correspondents held such a dark view of the IRO and its work. Many thanked the agency for its help and evinced satisfaction and optimism with their situation. "I thank you for your noble deed which gave us the opportunity to tear ourselves away from oppressive New York. In Detroit, where you sent us, we can breathe more freely and make a respectable living," wrote L. Friedman. Louis Polansky remarked, "through your courtesy I am now in Detroit, where I am making out pretty good."[48]

Detroit may have been the land of promise for some of the removals. For most, however, it was just one stop in their quest for the American dream. There is strong evidence indicating that a majority of the men sent by the IRO to Detroit left the city within a few years, most of them returning to New York. Loneliness, the fact that they had more relatives and friends in New York, and the lack of work seem to be the chief reasons for their departure. The evidence also suggests that a large number of removals relocated several times before settling down for good.[49]

COOPERATIVE EFFORTS

Despite differences and antagonisms, tentative steps at cooperation between the German Jews and Eastern Europeans did occur. Beginning in the late nineteenth century, Beth El and Shaarey Zedek exchanged pulpits, cooperated in relief work, and a number of their members socialized on a regular basis. This was due primarily to the fact the Shaarey Zedek's membership consisted of acculturated, affluent Jews of Polish descent, lending credence to the notion that class considerations, more than other factors, separated the German from the Russian Jews.

In the twentieth century, the German Jewish and Eastern European Jewish communities cooperation in projects to assist the European Jewish victims of pogroms, to establish a Young Men's Hebrew Association, and to found a Kehillah (an organized Jewish community). Although the Kehillah experiment failed, the other endeavors met with success, partially because religious leaders such as Rabbis Franklin, Hershman, and Levin and laymen like David W. Simons and Bernard Ginsburg enjoyed respect amongst various segments of the two communities and were able to put the communities' welfare above individual differences. This served as a pattern for the future: communal cooperation was achieved to work for overseas relief and to combat local anti-Semitism. Although Detroit had these two distinct communities for many years, cooperation was fostered between specific groups of Germans and specific contingents of Eastern Europeans when they had attained similar levels of affluence and social status.[50]

NOTES

1. *American Israelite*, May 26, 1882, p. 378.

2. *American Israelite*, March 9, 1899, p. 2, March 23, 1899, p. 2; *Detroit Journal*, September 19, 1903; Burton Scrapbook 16:43, Burton Historical Collection, Detroit, Michigan; *Jewish American*, October 23, 1908, p. 4, December 14, 1908, p. 4.

3. *American Israelite*, March 9, 1899, p. 2; *Detroit News-Tribune*, June 22, 1902, p. 4; *Jewish American*, April 11, 1902, p. 4, January 10, 1908, p. 7; *Hayehudi*, March 12, 1908, pp. 2–3.

4. *Jewish American*, July 4, 1902, p. 4, October 31, 1902, p. 4, April 15, 1904, p. 4, July 4, 1904, p. 4, September 20, 1904, p. 4, November 4, 1904, p. 4, September 2, 1910, p. 4; *American Israelite*, November 10, 1892, p. 2.

5. Salo W. Baron and Jeanette M. Baron, "Palestinian Messengers in America, 1849–79: A Record of Four Voyages," *Jewish Social Studies* 5 (July, 1943), p. 258; *Jewish American*, October 25, 1901, p. 4, March 3, 1904, p. 6.

6. *Jewish American*, October 25, 1901, p. 4, April 25, 1902, p. 4, March 9, 1906, p. 4; *American Israelite*, August 29, 1901, p. 2, September 26, 1901, p. 2; *Detroit Journal*, December 28, 1901, p. 3; Leo M. Franklin, "The Jew, His Judaism and His Environment from the Standpoint of Reform" (sermon delivered on Sunday, November 6, 1910), in Leo M. Franklin, *Sermons*, vol. 1, in the Michigan Historical Collections, Ann Arbor, Michigan.

7. *Detroit Journal*, December 21, 1889, p. 2; *American Israelite*, May 19, 1910, p. 2; *Jewish American*, November 19, 1903, p. 3, October 7, 1904, p. 4, June 9, 1905, p. 4, July 6, 1905, p. 2, May 25, 1906, p. 4, December 21, 1906, p. 4, October 23, 1908, p. 4, December 30, 1910, p. 4.

8. *American Israelite*, January 7, 1892, p. 6, May 16, 1912, p. 3; *Jewish American*, September 18, 1903, p. 4, February 3, 1905, p. 4, December 8, 1905, p. 5, March 29, 1907, p. 4, December 4, 1908, p. 4, September 9, 1910, p. 4, December 9, 1910, p. 4; Leo M. Franklin, "Always the Jew" (sermon preached on Yom Kippur eve, 1914), *Sermons*, vol. 1, in the Michigan Historical Collections, Ann Arbor, Michigan.

9. *Jewish American*, November 22, 1901.

10. Congregation Beth El, Executive Board Minutes, 1874–89, Report of President, S. Schloss, September 25, 1881; *Jewish Messenger*, January 6, 1882, p. 2; *American Israelite*, July 21, 1882, p. 22, September 1, 1882, p. 71, December 8, 1882, p. 195, March 2, 1889,

p. 3, October 29, 1891, p. 3; *Detroit Association of Charities, Eleventh Annual Report* (Detroit: J. W. Morrison & Co., Printers, 1890), p. 37; *Detroit News-Tribune*, June 12, 1898, p. 13; Anna W. Chapin, "History of the United Jewish Charities of Detroit, 1899-1949" (typescript) 1949, p. 6, Archives, Jewish Welfare Federation of Detroit, Detroit, Michigan.

11. Lloyd P. Gartner, *History of the Jews of Cleveland* (Cleveland: Western Reserve Historical Society, 1978), p. 108; Louis J. Swichkow and Lloyd P. Gartner, *The History of the Jews of Milwaukee* (Philadelphia: Jewish Publication Society of America, 1963), p. 71; Steven Hertzberg, *Strangers within the Gate City: The Jews of Atlanta, 1845-1915* (Philadelphia: Jewish Publication Society of America, 1978), p. 76.

12. *American Israelite*, December 19, 1889, p. 2; Chapin, "United Jewish Charities," p. 7.

13. *American Israelite*, May 26, 1882, p. 278, August 15, 1901, p. 2; *American Hebrew*, October 5, 1900, p. 599; *Jewish American*, October 12, 1900, p. 4, April 15, 1905, p. 4, December 8, 1905, p. 5, August 21, 1908, p. 4; *Fourteenth Annual Report of the United Jewish Charities of Detroit, Michigan* (Detroit, 1913), p. 11; *Reform Advocate* (Chicago), March 2, 1912, p. 13; Leo M. Franklin, *A Triumphant Life: A Tribute to Louis Blitz* (Detroit: American Press, 1905), p. 17.

14. *American Israelite*, October 15, 1891, p. 5, November 12, 1891, p. 5, March 24, 1892, p. 5, April 7, 1892, p. 5, September 15, 1892, p. 3, September 28, 1892, p. 2, February 3, 1898, p. 2; *American Hebrew*, October 18, 1895, p. 608; Bad Axe Colony Records, American Jewish Historical Society, Waltham, Massachusetts; James A. Rudin, "Bad Axe, Michigan: An Experiment in Jewish Agricultural Settlement," *Michigan History* 56 (1972), pp. 119-30.

15. Chapin, "United Jewish Charities," pp. 7-7a.

16. Minutes, United Jewish Charities, 1899-1908, November 7, 1899, p. 1, April 21, 1904, p. 45, May 5, 1904, p. 46, July 7, 1904, pp. 48-49; *American Israelite*, March 2, 1899, p. 3, November 23, 1899, p. 3; *Detroit Free Press*, September 26, 1903, p. 5. The dominant theory regarding the poor in the United States at the turn of the century pronounced them inferior and attributed their destitution to personal failings such as idleness, intemperance, or ignorance. Middle-class Protestant charity workers, who dominated American charitable work, felt that there were a number of "deserving poor," those who became destitute through no fault of their own, but saw them as exceptions to the mass of undeserving paupers. This harsh view of the poor was espoused by members of the Charity Organization Movement. Almost everybody active in helping the poor in the cities of late nineteenth-century America looked at them from this middle-class Protestant perspective and saw in their roles a chance to offer the poor a model of middle-class life. In turn-of-the-century Detroit, both public and private relief agencies attended to the needs of the poor and shared the same Protestant vision of them. For a fuller description of this, see Olivier Zunz, *The Changing Face of Inequality* (Chicago: University of Chicago Press, 1982), pp. 261-62.

17. See Chapin, "United Jewish Charities," p. 10, and the annual reports of the United Jewish Charities.

18. Chapin, "United Jewish Charities," p. 11; *American Jewish Year Book* 7 (1906), p. 67.

19. Chapin, "United Jewish Charities," pp. 11-12; *Jewish American*, January 9, 1903, p. 4, April 24, 1903, p. 4; *American Israelite*, October 1, 1903, p. 2.

20. *Jewish American*, November 4, 1904, pp. 5-8, November 11, 1904, pp. 7-8, October 27, 1905, p. 6; Detroit Association of Charities, *Twenty-Seventh Annual Report* (Detroit, 1906), pp. 20-21; United Jewish Charities, *Fourteenth Annual Report* (Detroit, 1913), p. 25; *American Hebrew*, May 9, 1913, p. 44.

21. Chapin, "United Jewish Charities," pp. 17-18.

22. Chapin, "United Jewish Charities," p. 19; *American Israelite*, June 23, 1904, p. 2; United Jewish Charities, *Twelfth Annual Report* (Detroit: Langer Printing Co., 1911), pp. 9, 47; private interview with Sadie Hirschman.

23. Chapin, "United Jewish Charities," p. 19.

24. Chapin, "United Jewish Charities," pp. 21-22; Jewish Institute of Detroit, *Twelfth Annual Report* (Detroit: Langer Printing Co., 1911), p. 9; United Jewish Charities, Minutes, 1912-17, p. 62; Melvin Holli, ed., *Detroit* (New York: New Viewpoints, 1976), pp. 124-25.

25. Chapin, "United Jewish Charities," pp. 21-22.

26. Chapin, "United Jewish Charities," pp. 26-27; *Jewish American*, November 2, 1906, p. 4, June 12, 1908, p. 4, February 3, 1911, p. 6; Congregation Beth El, Minutes, 1912-29, November 8, 1914, p. 75. The largest donation in 1900 was $115, made by N. S. Ginsburg; donations of $100 each were made by Bernard Ginsburg, Sigmund Rothschild, David W. Simons, and Seligman Schloss. In 1913, the largest contributions were $1,500 by Leopold Wineman, $1,000 by Seligman Schloss, and $600 by Henry Butzel. Fred Butzel, the "Estate of Henry A. Harmon," Henry Krolik, Oscar Rosenberger, and an anonymus donor contributed $500 each. See the Annual Reports of the United Jewish Charities for listings of contributors and the amounts they gave.

27. Minutes, Ladies' Society for the Support of Hebrew Widows and Orphans, October 5, 1905, p. 257, May 16, 1900, p. 231; J. L. Levin, Rabbi, to B. Ginsburg, April 10, 1904, in the files of the Jewish Welfare Federation of Detroit. See also Miriam Hart to David Bressler, April 12, 1911; David Bressler to Miriam Hart, April 15, 1911; Miriam Hart to David Bressler, January 8, 1912; Miriam Hart to Philip Seman, November 13, 1912; Philip Seman to Miriam Hart, April 7, 1913; and Philip Seman to Miriam Hart, August 21, 1912, all in the Detroit File, Industrial Removal Office Papers, American Jewish Historical Society, Waltham, Massachusetts. *Jewish American*, December 12, 1902, p. 4, February 6, 1903, p. 4; United Jewish Charities, Minutes, 1912-17, p. 66.

28. Michael Greene to author; *Jewish American*, December 12, 1902, p. 4.

29. *American Israelite*, May 26, 1882, p. 378, December 5, 1895, p. 5; *Jewish American*, August 23, 1907, p. 4.

30. Minutes, Ladies' Society for the Support of Hebrew Widows and Orphans, November 15, 1896-December 15, 1898, pp. 168-201; *First Annual Report of the United Jewish Charities of Detroit, Michigan* (Detroit: The Ralston-Stroup Printing Co., 1900), pp. 4-5; *Jewish American*, June 17, 1904, p. 4, October 14, 1904, p. 7, November 11, 1904, p. 8, November 1, 1907, p. 4; *Reform Advocate*, (Chicago), March 2, 1912, p. 13.

31. Manuscript in the Irving I. Katz Archives, Temple Beth El, Birmingham, Michigan; interviews with Harry T. Madison and Irwin R. Shaw.

32. Harry L. Lurie, *General Summary of Survey of Detroit Jewish Community, 1923* (New York: Bureau of Jewish Social Research, 1923), p. 48; *Jewish American*, October 9, 1908, p. 3.

33. This material was previously published in Robert Rockaway, "The Industrial Removal Office in Detroit," *Detroit in Perspective* 6 (Spring, 1982), pp. 40-49. On the IRO, see Samuel Joseph, *History of the Baron de Hirsch Fund* (New York: Jewish Publication Society, 1935), pp. 184-205. For the total number of persons removed by the IRO, see the Annual Reports of the Industrial Removal Office, located in the Industrial Removal Office Papers, American Jewish Historical Society, Waltham, Massachusetts. On similar Jewish agencies, see Joseph, *Hirsch Fund*, and Boris D. Bogen, *Jewish Philanthropy* (New York: Macmillan Company, 1917).

34. Bogen, *Jewish Philanthropy*, p. 114; Joseph, *Baron de Hirsch Fund*, p. 187; Fred M. Butzel, "Autobiography," *Detroit Jewish News*, March 15, 1974, p. 8. David M. Bressler (1879-1942), the general manager of the IRO from 1901 to 1916, spent most of his adult life working with Jewish immigrants. During World War I he joined the American Joint Distribution Committee, in which he played an important role till his death. The Jewish Colonization Association (ICA) and the Baron de Hirsch Fund were both established in 1891 by the German Jewish financier and philanthropist Baron Maurice de Hirsch (1831-96). Hirsch was one of the few nineteenth-century Jewish leaders who believed that the only permanent solution to the plight of the Jews in Russia was emigration. To this end, he founded the ICA to settle Eastern European Jews on farming colonies in North and South America and the Fund to provide a wide variety of aid to Eastern Europe Jewish immigrants in the United States.

35. David M. Bressler to Miriam M. Hart, December 23, 1912, IRO Papers. From 1902 to 1914 there were 4,875 removals to Michigan, ranging from 75 in 1902 to 1,175 in 1913. Over 80 percent of these immigrants were sent to Detroit. See the *Annual Reports of the Industrial Removal Office*, 1902-14.

36. IRO to Miriam Hart, March 31, 1911, IRO papers.

37. IRO to Miriam Hart, January 18, 1912; Blanche Hart to David Bressler, April 19, 1907; Miriam Hart to David Bressler, June 14, 1912; Alice K. Goldsmith to David Bressler, October 6, 1910, IRO Papers. Alice Goldsmith was one of the young volunteers who assisted in the Detroit office when the regular agent was on vacation.

38. J. Schwartz to Removal Office, March 17, 1912; IRO to J. Schwartz, March 19, 1912; Harry B. Clark to Industrial Removal Society, March 13, 1910; IRO to Harry B. Clark, March 17, 1910, IRO Papers.

39. IRO to Miriam Hart, December 26, 1912; Miriam Hart to Philip Seman, September 16, 1913, IRO Papers. Philip Seman (1881-1957) was the assistant manager of the IRO office in New York. After his IRO work, he became director of the Jewish People's Institute of Chicago and was co-founder of Hillel, the international Jewish college student organization.

40. Miriam Hart to David Bressler, January 20, 1914; Miriam Hart to David Bressler, March 13, 1912; Miriam Hart to Philip Seman, June 19, 1913; Miriam Hart to David Bressler, August 9, 1912; Miriam Hart to David Bressler, November 21, 1912; Birdie Pick to IRO, February 28, 1906; David Bressler to Miriam Hart, December 9, 1912; Miriam Hart to David Bressler, December 11, 1912, IRO Papers.

41. Butzel, "Autobiography," p. 8; Blanche Hart to David Bressler, January 25, 1912; David Bressler to Fred Butzel, April 20, 1914; Fred Butzel to David Bressler, April 23, 1914; David Bressler to Miriam Hart, May 13, 1914; David Bressler to Miriam Hart, May 14, 1914; David Bressler to Blanche Hart, January 13, 1913; Miriam Hart to David Bressler, January 24, 1913, IRO Papers.

42. This was deduced from a random sample of 308 men sent to Detroit by the IRO from 1903 to 1914. The sample was taken from the IRO ledger books, located in the IRO collection. The ledgers give the age, nationality, marital status, location of family at time of removal, occupation, and length of time in the United States of the men sent to various cities.

43. See Joseph, *Baron de Hirsch Fund*, pp. 184-205; and Bogen, *Jewish Philanthropy*, pp. 113-22, for an explanation of this process.

44. IRO to Joseph Rader, May 1, 1906; W. Levitt to IRO, April 29, 1906 (my translation from the Yiddish); Herman Marcus to IRO, April 24, 1906, IRO Papers.

45. Miriam Hart to David Bressler, April 12, 1911; David Bressler to Miriam Hart, April 15, 1911; Miriam Hart to David Bressler, January 8, 1912; Miriam Hart to Philip Seman, November 13, 1912; Philip Seman to Miriam Hart, April 7, 1913; Philip Seman to Miriam Hart, August 21, 1912, IRO Papers.

46. L. Friedman to IRO, April 5, 1907 (my translation from the Yiddish); Ike Togel to IRO, April 3, 1907, IRO Papers.

47. Nathan Toplitzky to IRO, March 30, 1908 (my translation from the Yiddish); David Bressler to Nathan Toplitzky, April 2, 1908, IRO Papers.

48. L. Friedman to David Bressler, April 5, 1907 (my translation from the Yiddish); Louis Polansky to IRO, January 9, 1913, IRO Papers.

49. A sampling of 81 men sent to Detroit in 1905 shows that 10 of them left within the year, and 85 percent of those remaining left within three years. And of a sample of 101 men sent in 1907, only 13 could be located in the city in 1909. The 81 names were taken from the Detroit agent's 1905 report to the IRO. The agent noted those men who left the city within the year. The remaining names were checked in both the *Detroit City Directory* and the *Detroit Yiddish Directory* for 1907. The 101 names were taken from the agent's 1907 report to the IRO and were checked in the *City Directory* of 1909. Even granting that many of the men roomed with relatives and friends during these years and hence were not heads of households, it is doubtful that the directory canvass, which attempted to tally all the adults living at an address, would have missed these removals. A similar result was obtained in Columbus, Ohio. See Marc Lee Raphael, *Jews and Judaism in a Midwestern Community: Columbus, Ohio, 1840-1975* (Columbus, Ohio: Ohio Historical Society, 1979), p. 154, note 20. These results cast doubt on the accuracy of IRO claims that 75 percent of the removals found their new surroundings attractive and decided to remain. For IRO claims of success, see the *Annual Reports*, especially the 1912 report, which claimed a 94 percent success rate (*Twelfth Annual Report of the Industrial Removal Office*, 1912, p. 16).

50. *American Israelite*, October 20, 1910, p. 3; *American Hebrew*, February 5, 1886, p. 203; *Detroit Free Press*, October 24, 1910, p. 1; *Reform Advocate* (Chicago), March 2, 1912, pp. 6-7; *Jewish American*, April 11, 1902, p. 4, March 29, 1907, p. 7, April 26, 1907, p. 4; Congregation Beth El Minutes, 1908-12, October 16, 1910, March 12, 1911, November 3, 1912; United Jewish Charities, Minutes, 1899-1908, November 7, 1899, p. 3; Lurie, *Survey*, p. 16. Kehillah is the Hebrew term for the organized local Jewish community. The first effort to organize a Jewish community in the United States occurred in New York, where the experiment lasted from 1908 to 1922. See Arther A. Goren, *New York Jews and the Quest for Community: The Kehilla Experiment, 1908-1922* (New York: Columbia University Press, 1970).

6. FORMATION OF AN ELITE
Attaining Prosperity and Status

B Y MOST CRITERIA, the German Jews and native Jews of German descent comprised the elite of Detroit's Jewish community before World War I. Riding the wave of Detroit's economic boom, the German Jews and their children displayed a steadily increasing prosperity. By 1910 more than 90 percent of Temple Beth El's members could be classified as professionals, proprietors, managers, or white collar workers (Tables 14 and 18). Using the 1877 Temple Beth El roster and examining the occupations of the members and their descendants in U.S. census reports, we find a 23 percent decline in the number of proprietors and managers from 1880 to 1900, a corresponding 27 percent rise in white-collar workers, and a 6 percent increase in professionals. During the same time, none of the original Temple members or their descendants engaged in any skilled or semiskilled occupations (Tables 19, 20, 21).[1]

Instead of following in their parents' footsteps, many of the second generation preferred careers in the professions and white-collar fields, or they opened their own businesses. Magnus Butzel owned a large and successful wholesale clothing firm by 1880, but his sons, Fred and Henry, both graduated from the Uni-

versity of Michigan and practiced law. Samuel Heavenrich manufactured clothing from 1862 to 1904; his son John decided to sell insurance and his other son Walter dealt in auto supplies. Morris Fechheimer owned a wholesale liquor business; one of his sons, Henry, entered the advertising field and in 1914 was president of the Fechheimer Theater Program Company and the Telephone Directory Advertising Company; another son, Moses, became a physician, specializing in genitourinary and venereal diseases.

Isaac Altman sold caps and hats in 1880, moving on to become a furrier by 1890. His son, Louis, clerked for a bank. Louis Lambert owned a wholesale liquor business in 1880; his son, Benjamin, attended business school, managed a wholesale druggist supply firm for nine years, and became a manufacturer of chemicals and pharmaceuticals. Sigmund Rothschild owned a wholesale leaf tobacco business; his son, Louis, assisted him until 1910, when Louis became the sales manager of a power wagon company. Louis Selling sold crockery in 1880 and insurance by 1890. His son, Bernard, graduated from the University of Michigan Law School in 1895 and thereafter practiced and taught law, as well as directing a real estate business.[2]

A few successful second-generation German Jews began their careers under more modest circumstances. The renowned architect Albert Kahn was one such individual. Kahn was born in Westphalia, Germany, in 1869. His father, a rabbi who peddled for a living, emigrated with his family to the United States in 1881. Kahn received his basic education in Germany, but after coming to the United States, he never returned to school. In Detroit, Kahn's father peddled vegetables and fruit, and his mother cooked in a small restaurant near the Michigan Central Railroad station. Kahn worked nights as a busboy in the restaurant and afterward helped his father groom and stable his horse. During the day he worked as an office boy in an architect's office. As in many Detroit homes of that era, the Kahn home did not have indoor bathing facilities. Daily baths were a luxury. Consequently, by the week's end, Kahn reeked of kitchen and stable. One day in 1883 the stench became too much for Kahn's coworkers in the office and he was fired. As he stood crying in the hallway, he was approached by the architect and sculptor Julius Melchers. Sympathizing with the boy, Melchers employed him in his office. In 1890 Kahn won the American Architects scholarship for study in Europe. Upon his return to Detroit in 1895, Kahn opened his own office. By 1914 he had designed Temple Beth El; the Burroughs Adding Machine plant; the Packard, Hudson, Chalmers, Lozier, and Ford automobile plants; and the Detroit Free Press building.[3]

Louis Grossman, rabbi of Temple Beth El, 1884-98. (Courtesy of the Rabbi Leo M. Franklin Archives of Temple Beth El.)

RELIGIOUS LIFE

During the final two decades of the nineteenth century, Beth El instituted further reforms in its liturgy and religious practices. Under Henry Zirndorf's rabbinate (1876-85), the congregation abolished memorial prayers for the deceased except on Yom Kippur and restricted boys making their bar mitzvah to reciting only the blessings before and after the reading from the Torah. Nevertheless, the congregation refused to sever all its links with traditional Judaism.

Magnus Butzel's proposal to dispense with the teaching of Hebrew in the Sabbath school "because it was a dead language and its learning was a waste of valuable time" encountered stiff opposition and lost by a large majority.[4]

Attendance at services, however, remained problematical. "I am sorry to state that the attendance of members with their families for Sabbath service is very slim," reported President Seligman Schloss in 1881. "Something must be done soon," he warned, "if you do not wish that before the expiration of another decade to see our temple closed and our children deprived of their holy heritage. You are re-

120

sponsible to the almighty for yourself and your children to set a better example." Two weeks after Schloss made his assessment, Beth El temporarily canceled its Friday evening services because of low attendance.[5]

In 1884 Zirndorf accepted a position as professor of history and Hebrew literature at Hebrew Union College and was succeeded by Rabbi Louis Grossmann, a graduate of that institution. Viennese-born Grossmann (1863–1926) came to the United States with his parents in 1873. His father and brothers were rabbis, and Grossmann continued the family tradition. He was ordained at Hebrew Union College in 1884 and has the distinction of being the first American-trained rabbi to occupy the pulpit of Temple Beth El. During his fourteen-year stay in Detroit, Grossmann organized the Beth El Alumnal Association, the Woman's Club of Temple Beth El (later the Jewish Woman's Club of Detroit), and the Emerson Circle, a society for the promotion of culture. He was one of the founders of the Self-Help Circle and supported the Palestine Agricultural Colony in Bad Axe, Michigan. Grossmann introduced a free afternoon school for poor Jewish children and the children of parents whose congregations maintained no religious school and opened a Normal School for the training of religious school teachers. He also participated in the organization, in Detroit in 1889, of the Central Conference of American Rabbis.[6]

Under Grossmann's stewardship, the teaching of Hebrew in the Sabbath school ended because, he

Temple Beth El picnic in 1889. (Courtesy of the Rabbi Leo M. Franklin Archives of Temple Beth El.)

claimed, he had no time to teach it. And in 1896 the congregation prohibited men from worshiping with their heads covered, a practice that had been optional until then. Grossmann was far more liberal and Reform-minded than most of his congregation, and he found himself restricted in how far and fast he could progress in making changes. On a number of occasions the Temple's executive board requested that he refrain from further alterations in the ritual because it "caused dissension" and led to a drop in attendance at services. The board also asked Grossmann to "discard all books that were not in accord with Judaism" from the Temple and Sabbath schools and to confine his sermons and lectures "as much as possible to our own authors that helped to write the great literature of Judaism and avoid as much as possible everything outside the pale of Judaism, whereby the limited time spent in devotion may be utilized for the necessary instruction of our religion."[7]

Try as he might, Grossmann could do little to stem the congregation's continuing religious apathy. Julius Freund reported with "regret" in 1896 that "the great majority of our members are suffering from the deep rooted sickness called *indifference*," and that lack of interest caused Friday evening services to be discontinued once again. Parents also appeared unconcerned about their children's religious education. In 1892 Magnus Butzel reflected how "it will be worth more than 100 committee reports if parents *visit the school* and interest themselves in the progress of their children." Three years later Bernard Selling reported that in spite of printed invitations sent to each parent at the beginning of the school year, "asking them to kindly visit school at least once," not one parent responded. "We emulate our Christian neighbors in many things," he noted, "why not in Sunday School life?"[8]

In 1898 Grossmann left Temple Beth El to serve at the Congregation B'nai Jeshurun in Cincinnati as associate rabbi to Isaac Mayer Wise. By the time he departed, Beth El's services resembled those found in Protestant churches. A non-Jewish visitor to Beth El noted how "a strange Christian entering this place of worship as the service was about to commence

would notice very little to distinguish it from an old-fashioned Presbyterian, Baptist or Methodist church. The seating is exactly the same. The people look the same, men and women, boys and girls all sitting together, men and boys bareheaded, women and girls with their ordinary street hats on. The rabbi sitting in a chair to the right of the pulpit, had neither vestment, gown or head covering of any kind—his whole appearance was that of a non-episcopal American Christian minister."[9]

Grossmann's replacement was Rabbi Leo M. Franklin (1870-1948), who served as rabbi of Beth El for forty-two years. Born in Indiana, Franklin grew up in Cincinnati, where he attended the University of

Leo M. Franklin, rabbi of Temple Beth El from 1898 to 1948. (Courtesy of the Rabbi Leo M. Franklin Archives of Temple Beth El.)

Ground-breaking ceremony for Temple Beth El on Woodward Avenue and Eliot Street in 1901. (Courtesy of the Rabbi Leo M. Franklin Archives of Temple Beth El.)

Cincinnati and Hebrew Union College. After his ordination, he served for seven years as the rabbi of Temple Israel in Omaha, Nebraska. Shortly after coming to Beth El, Franklin devoted himself, as he said, to "revitalizing Judaism" in his congregation. To this end, he reintroduced Friday evening services and organized a children's choir, a children's Sabbath morning service, a post-graduation class, and Bible classes for young people and adults.[10]

Under Franklin's prodding, the congregation voted in 1900 to construct a new temple, and on September 10, 1903, the first house of worship built by Temple Beth El was dedicated on Woodward and Eliot. Believing that "if the synagogue was to have any real and telling influence upon the life of the Jew, it had to be central to his life and touch it at every point," Franklin hoped to turn the new building into an "open temple," the center of his congregation's religious, social, cultural, and educational endeavors. In keeping with this goal, Beth El hosted lectures and musical concerts and built a gymnasium in order "to bring the young to the house of God."[11]

Another of Franklin's aims was to bring more of the Temple's traditions into harmony with American conventions. It had long been a practice among European Jews to purchase synagogue seats, with the choice places reserved for the most honored members of the community. This had been one method by which the community could tender respect for and deference to its leaders. Because of the prestige attached to these seats, wealthier members of the community fastened upon them as a means of enhancing their status. Soon, the value of these pews began to be measured in monetary terms, with the more affluent members of the congregation going to great lengths to outbid one another for the privilege of occupying a valued place.

This development frequently led to rivalry and bitterness and interjected an element of sordidness into synagogal affairs. Franklin sought to prevent this when he introduced the free, or unassigned, pew system to Temple Beth El in 1904. He hoped to eliminate "the commercialism that has disgraced the synagogue" by making Temple seats available on a first come, first served basis.[12] Franklin also wanted the Temple to become more democratic. The system of giving wealthier members primacy in a place of worship seemed incompatible with American and Jewish ideals of equality before God. By instituting a free pew system, which put all members of the congregation on "an absolute plane of equality with every other man," the Temple moved closer to what Franklin felt to be the acceptable pattern of behavior for American institutions.[13]

Not everyone agreed with him. The move led to controversy among some of the older members, and seven families, including that of Seligman Schloss, claiming "vested rights," resigned. They all eventually returned, but when the new constitution and bylaws were formulated in 1908, no reference to the ownership of pews appeared in the documents.[14]

The innovation which marked a more radical break with Jewish tradition was the addition of regular Sunday morning services. The Pittsburgh Conference of 1885 expressed the official position of the American Reform movement regarding Sunday services when it noted "that there is a vast number of workingmen and others who, from some cause or other, are not able to attend the services on the sacred day of rest" and concluded "that there is nothing in the spirit of Judaism or its laws to prevent the introduction of Sunday services in localities where the necessity for such services appears or is felt."[15]

Franklin agreed with this position, arguing that the realities of American life necessitated a change in attitude toward the traditional Jewish Sabbath. "I am convinced," he said, "that the time has come when social and economic conditions unite at laying at our feet, not only the expediency, but far more, the duty of providing for our people, a religious service of some kind at such a time as they will and can attend. We must face conditions as they are, and cease fooling ourselves." He did not advocate totally abandoning the traditional Sabbath service, but merely instituting a supplemental morning service on Sunday. The Temple inaugurated Sunday services in January, 1904, and they proved far more popular than the Saturday services.[16]

When Franklin came to Detroit, Beth El numbered 136 members. His leadership and innovations, in addition to the growing number of economically successful Jews who sought to join Detroit's prestige synagogue, boosted the Temple's membership to 310 by 1910. Nevertheless, attendance at Sabbath services remained low. In his 1907 report to the congregation, president Samuel Heavenrich reflected that "while it is true that, in actual point of numbers, there are perhaps more people in attendance than ever heretofore, it must be remembered that our membership is larger than it was, and that, therefore proportionately the attendance no greater. It is not right that a temple which is crowded to its capacity on the high holy days, should on ordinary occasions appear too large for the congregation." Franklin also admitted that the Sabbath services were "not as well attended as they should be" and that the Sunday services, although successful, failed to attract many members "who in all fairness ought to attend."[17]

Similar disinterest appeared in other areas as well. Parents failed to give their full support and cooperation to the Sabbath school and remained "indifferent to their children's attendance." Many Temple members were ignorant of their rich Jewish heritage, their homes and lives devoid of Jewish content. Franklin complained that Temple mothers "set aside Friday evening for going to theater and Sabbath morning for shopping. Parents sent their children to dancing school when they should be attending a religious exercise" and "Jewish festivals were ignored in the home and Christian feasts solemnly celebrated."[18] In this regard, the celebration of Christmas became especially worrisome as more and more Temple members erected Christmas trees, held Christmas parties, and exchanged Christmas gifts. One concerned Temple member fretted that some of the Congregation's most prominent members, "including a former presi-

Temple Beth El on Woodward Avenue and Eliot Street, 1903–22. (Courtesy of the Rabbi Leo M. Franklin Archives of Temple Beth El.)

dent and a number of present office holders, celebrate X-mas in a manner that would do credit to any Episcopalian or Methodist household."[19]

All these trends caused some concerned Temple leaders to conclude that the Reform movement may "have been going too far and too fast" and that "a wild craving to be like other people and the desire to wipe out the marks that distinguish the Jew from his neighbor have created a reckless disregard for the ceremonies that were distinctively Jewish." The Reformers, well meaning though they may have been, had "despiritualized every form . . . rationalized every beautiful tradition . . . depoetized every sublime sentiment," with the result that Reform Jews became indifferent to religion. "In our intellectual bigotry, which we mistook for liberalism," admitted Franklin, "we robbed religion of its spirit and left it a dry hulk, an empty shell, a soulless body." Unless this pattern were reversed, he feared that ultimately there would be "no Jew at all."[20]

To counteract this drift, Franklin and other Temple leaders mounted a campaign to make Reform a "more vibrant and living force," by reintroducing the spiritual side of Judaism and emphasizing the religious aspects of the faith. Just two years after the inauguration of Sunday services, a movement arose within the Temple to revive the traditional Sabbath. "Let us be Jews, live like Jews, worship like Jews," exclaimed one congregant. "Let us be men and prove to the world that we are endowed with sufficient moral courage to face whatever of discredit all non-Jews cast in our way for resuming the old fashioned but *Jewish* Friday evening devotion instead of the convenient Sunday service." Jewish festivals, such as Purim, which had become nothing more than secularized celebrations during the 1870s and 1880s, began to be celebrated as Jewish holidays with Jewish themes. Religious education received greater priority, with increased emphasis placed on adult education. Franklin organized classes in biblical literature, Jewish history, and the Hebrew language. In answer to Temple members who expressed concern about becoming "too Jewish," Franklin reiterated his belief "that the more conscientiously the Jew practices his Judaism the bet-

ter citizen he is bound to be." Despite all these efforts, however, the Jewish religion played a diminishing role in the lives of Detroit's second and third generation German Jews.[21]

The clergy and lay people of Temple Beth El participated in a variety of civic reform movements which aimed at bettering education, housing, health, and labor conditions in Detroit. Their activity stemmed from two impulses: as residents of the city, they were concerned about the quality of its life; and through participation in these causes they could express their sense of civic responsibility and enhance their prestige and the status of their Temple and community.

Rabbis Grossmann and Franklin campaigned for changes in local police procedures and in the treatment of criminals and juvenile offenders, supported improved housing and sanitation for the poor, sought to introduce manual training into the public schools, and pressed for stronger child labor laws. And men and women of the Temple crusaded for stronger health laws, raised funds to eradicate tuberculosis, established scholarships to send needy young men of all denominations to high school and college, and advocated civil service reform.[22]

Beth El allocated funds for needy non-Jews in Detroit and other parts of the United States. This included assisting local charities, such as the Red Cross, the Protestant Orphan Asylum, and the Children's Hospital, and raising money for Ohio Valley flood sufferers and victims of the San Francisco earthquake. The Ladies' Society for the Support of Hebrew Widows and Orphans, while continuing with its primary purpose of assisting local Jewish widows and children, also donated funds to non-Jewish institutions, such as the Visiting Nurses Association. In recognition of their growing activism and importance, the city's political establishment appointed the Temple's Rabbi Franklin, Magnus and Martin Butzel, Samuel and Simon Heavenrich, Sigmund Simon, and others to a number of civic posts and to special citizen's committees representing the City of Detroit and the State of Michigan.[23]

Coincident with this, Temple members became

more involved in local politics. Sigmund Simon, Ignatz Freund, and Martin Butzel worked for the Democrats, while Joseph Weiss and Martin's brother, Magnus, held key positions in the Republican Party. Weiss served as a state senator from 1891 to 1894; Magnus Butzel held the vice-presidency of the Michigan Republican Club in 1895 and the presidency in 1896. By the beginning of the twentieth century most Temple Beth El members identified with the Republican Party, which they saw as more closely representing their economic and class interests and being the more "respectable" of the two major parties.[24]

One of the most brilliant and innovative political figures in Detroit's modern history was David E. Heineman, son of Emil and Fanny (Butzel) Heineman. Born in Detroit in 1865 and educated in the city's public schools and at the University of Michigan, Heineman served as chief assistant city attorney from 1893 to 1896, as a member of the state legislature from 1899 to 1900 (receiving the highest vote of any of the ten legislative candidates on the Wayne County Republican ticket in 1898), as a member and the president of the Detroit City Council from 1902 to 1909, and as city controller from 1910 to 1913. While serving as chief assistant city attorney, he compiled and revised the ordinances of the city and designed the flag of the City of Detroit. He also served as president of both the League of Michigan Municipalities (the largest civic organization in the state at that time) and the League of American Municipalities. His many and varied contributions to the city earned for Heineman the designation as "the most popular Jew in Detroit."[25]

The German Jews remained the elite of the city's Jewish community. Their synagogue, Temple Beth El, was considered to be the leading Jewish institution and one of Detroit's foremost churches. Their club, the Phoenix Social Club, was looked upon as the "leading Jewish social organization in the city" and one of the five most prominent clubs in Detroit. Membership in either of these organizations distinguished upper-class Jews from the rest of the Jewish population, and both institutions remained highly selective in choosing their members.[26]

David E. Heineman, politician and designer of the flag of the City of Detroit. (Courtesy of the Rabbi Leo M. Franklin Archives of Temple Beth El.)

The Phoenix Social Club. (Courtesy of the Rabbi Leo M. Franklin Archives of Temple Beth El.)

127

332

DETROIT BLUE BOOK.

PHOENIX SOCIAL CLUB.

President..LOUIS ROTHSCHILD.
Vice-President..JACOB F. TEICHNER.
Secretary...JACOB D. FREEDMAN.
Treasurer...WALTER S. HEAVENRICH.

DIRECTORS.

LOUIS BLITZ.   ALFRED ROTHSCHILD.
JACOB W. EHRMAN.   CHAS. D. KAICHEN.
BEN. GINSBURG.   HENRY M. FECHHEIMER.

Mr. H. Binswanger.   Mr. B. L. Lambert.
Mr. Robert Berger.   Mr. A. Landsberg.
Mr. Magnus Butzel.   Dr. O. Lowman.
Mr. Martin Butzel.   Mr. Jule Meyer.
Mr. Henry M. Butzel.   Mr. Mark G. Morris.
Mr. Maurice Butzel.   Mr. Harry S. Morris.
Mr. Louis Blitz.   Mr. B. G. Morris.
Mr. H. M. Duffield.   Mr. A. Marymont.
Mr. Jas. N. Dean.   Mr. K. S. Rothschild.
Mr. Harry J. Dean.   Mr. Alfred Rothschild.
Mr. J. W. Ehrman.   Mr. Sig. Rothschild.
Mr. D. J. Eppstein.   Mr. Louis Rothschild.
Mr. Ignatz Freund.   Mr. Harry Rothschild.
Mr. H. M. Fechheimer.   Mr. Julius Rothschild.
Mr. A. Feldheim.   Mr. Sidney Rothschild.
Mr. Rudolph Friedenberg.   Mr. I. Rosenfield.
Mr. J. H Freedman.   Mr. Ad. Robinson.
Mr. Sol. J. Groneman.   Mr. Seligman Schloss.
Dr. L. Grossmann.   Mr. Emanuel Schloss.
Mr. Ben. Ginsburg.   Mr. Albert W. Schloss.
Mr. K. Ginterman.   Mr. Moses Schloss.
Mr. Hugo Hill.   Mr. Moses Schott.
Mr. Eugene H. Hill.   Mr. J. Steinfeld.
Mr. A. M. Hill.   Mr. Sam'l Steinfeld.
Mr. E. S. Heineman.   Mr. J. B. Sinn.
Mr. S. E. Heineman.   Mr. Louis Selling.
Mr. Sam'l Heavenrich.   Mr. Jos. L. Selling.
Mr. Walter S. Heavenrich.   Mr. Zach. Selling.
Mr. John A. Heavenrich.   Mr. S. Simon.
Mr. Emil Heyn.   Mr. Ben. Siegel.
Mr. Moses Hart.   Mr. Jacob Siegel.
Mr. Maurice Higer.   Mr. Louis Strassburger.
Mr. Sig. Hofman.   Mr. Wm. Teichner.
Mr. Herman Kaichen.   Mr. Jacob F. Teichner.
Mr. Chas. H. Kaichen.   Mr. Arthur Victor.
Mr. Herman Krolik.   Mr. Joseph M. Weiss.
Mr. H. A. Krolik.   Mr. Leopold Weineman.

Membership of the Phoenix Social Club, as listed in the *Detroit Blue Book* in 1896. (Courtesy of the Burton Historical Collection.)

Beth El's members enjoyed the highest occupational status in the community, although by 1910 Congregation Shaarey Zedek members came in a close second (Table 22). Socially, Beth El members outdistanced all their rivals. Marquis' 1914 *Book of Detroiters,* "a biographical dictionary of the leading living men of the city of Detroit," listed sixty-nine members of Beth El, as compared to eleven members of Shaarey Zedek. While nineteen members of Beth El appeared in the 1912 edition of *Dau's Blue Book,* a compilation of Detroit's "most prominent householders" and "fashionable addresses," only one member from Congregation Shaarey Zedek was listed. This single Shaarey Zedek member was Bernard Ginsberg, who also maintained a membership in Temple Beth El.[27]

A breakdown of the Beth El members appearing in the *Book of Detroiters* shows that 57 percent were native born, 26 percent were German born, and 14 percent were born in Eastern Europe. All of the European-born members had been in the United States for more than twenty years. In regard to their educational backgrounds, 26 percent had some college, 6 percent had finished high school, while 36 percent had attended American public schools only. Occupationally, 19 percent were professionals; the rest were owners and proprietors. Of those listing political affiliations, 80 percent were Republican and only 1 percent was Democrat. Twenty-three percent of those who were married had three children, 30 percent had two children, and 16 percent had one child. Sixteen percent had five or more children. Almost all of those who had two children and less were native born. The most popular leisure activities listed by this group included outdoor sports, automobiling, and fishing.

By contrast, only three of the eleven Shaarey Zedek members appearing in the *Book of Detroiters* were native born; seven had been born in Russia and one in Poland. As with Beth El, all of the foreign-born members had been in the United States for more than twenty years. Two of the Shaarey Zedek men had attended business college, one had finished high school, and four had attended public school. All eleven owned their own businesses. All were married, five with two children, five with six or more children, and one childless. All of those who listed political affiliations identified themselves as Republicans. Four listed automobiling and two recorded reading as their favorite recreations.

Restricting its membership to the most wealthy and prominent German Jews, practically all of whom were members of Temple Beth El, the Phoenix Social Club was the hub of the elite German Jew's social life. The Phoenix maintained its own building, which housed wine cellars, a bar, bowling alleys, billiard rooms, card rooms, dining rooms, and a ballroom. Most of the entertaining done by the club took place in this building, using these facilities. Reflecting the wealth and status of its membership, in 1914 the Phoenix opened a country club on the outskirts of the city and held a golf tournament to celebrate the occasion.[28]

The women of Temple Beth El established their own exclusive club, the Jewish Woman's Club of Detroit, in 1891, "to discuss Jewish subjects" and promote "fellowship." At the end of its first year, the club's membership numbered 250; by 1913 it stood at 550 women. Activities encompassed civic and charitable work, and the club loaned money to help "needy and deserving Jewish girls get a high school or busi-

ness education." The club's official colors were pink and white and its flower was the carnation. From the outset, Detroit's social registries included the Jewish Woman's Club in their lists of exclusive clubs.[29]

In addition to their clubs, the Jewish elite socialized at an endless series of concerts, theater performances, dances, parties, and balls. They vacationed in cottages along the shores of Lake Michigan or on one of the inland lakes and traveled around the United States. By the first decade of the twentieth century, the wealthiest among them spent their vacations in Europe. Card playing became an especially popular pastime, and upper middle-class Jewish women organized clubs with names such as "The Bon Ton Pedro

Two Phoenix Social Club evening programs from 1898. (Courtesy of the Rabbi Leo M. Franklin Archives of Temple Beth El.)

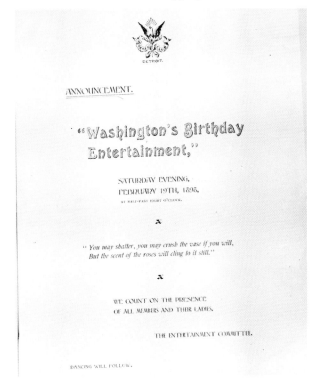

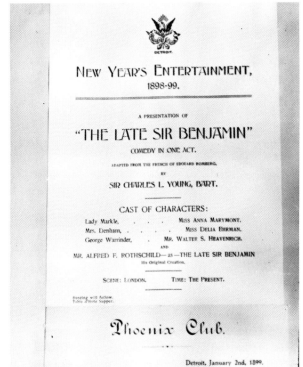

Canoe day at Belle Isle, summer 1906. (Courtesy of the Detroit Historical Museum.)

Club," "The Jolly Twelve Pedro Club," "The Night Owl Progressive Prize Euchre Club," and the "Four Leaf Clover Whist Club."[30]

Social functions continued to be an accepted means of raising money for philanthropy, although some observers complained that little remained for charity once the expenses incurred in staging the affairs were paid. Due to the strenuous efforts of the United Jewish Charities to eliminate "wasteful and unscientific" means of fundraising, large benefit balls became less prevalent in the twentieth century than they had been in the nineteenth. However, smaller, less formal types of fundraising affairs, such as socials, persisted. The professionalization of social work in the twentieth century led to a marked decline in charitable activity among Detroit's affluent Jewish women, and concerned communal leaders seized upon card parties as a convenient way of reviving their flagging interest. Frequently, however, more interest was shown in the card party than in the philanthropy it promoted. But, as one realistic observer of the Jewish social scene noted, unless something had a social purpose connected with it, few Jewish women would bother to join.[31]

CITIZENS AND NEIGHBORS

The greatest cooperation between native and German Jews and non-Jews in Detroit in the years between 1881 and 1914 occurred in the areas of interdenominational activities and civic life. Temple Beth El's rabbis actively promoted better relations between their congregation and the city's Protestant denominations, and it was in this sphere that the most cordial associations existed. Motivated by their desire that Jews be accepted as equals and as an integral part of American life, the rabbis initiated pulpit exchanges between Beth El and Detroit's Congregationalist, Methodist, Episcopalian, and Unitarian churches. Rabbi Franklin believed the pulpit exchanges were in-

valuable in fostering a better understanding between Jew and non-Jew because "Jews are not infrequently looked upon by good Christians as being creatures entirely different and apart from the rest of humanity." He thought that "a single sermon preached by an intelligent Jew from a Christian pulpit will serve to correct the mistake. And the reverse is equally true. There are many things that we could learn from and about our Christian neighbors—for often we in our ignorance misjudge them as harshly as they do us."[32]

Through these formal exchanges Rabbis Grossmann and Franklin became well-known and frequent speakers at church programs, delivering talks on topics such as "The Church and Social Service," "The Modern Jew and His Belief," "The Jews of Today,"

Strolling on Central Avenue on Belle Isle in 1902. (Courtesy of the *Detroit News* Archives.)

"The Rights of Minorities," and "Is Unbelief Liberalism?" In 1902 Franklin and other liberal clergymen and laymen organized the Citizen's Interdenominational Thanksgiving Service, one of the first in the country to unite Protestants, Catholics, and Jews in offering prayers on Thanksgiving. The service received national attention and editorial comment in the *Times* of London, England.[33]

Because of these activities, the rabbis of Beth El were considered to be among the "moral leaders" of Detroit. In the late nineteenth century, Rabbi Grossmann won much admiration and respect, and the city's press regularly featured his sermons in their Sunday editions. Upon his departure from Beth El in 1898, Mayor Maybury held a public farewell reception in his honor. Grossmann's successor, Rabbi Franklin, became so highly respected for his interfaith activities that he was invited to represent Detroit's Jewish community at every important civic and social engagement. Acutely conscious of his role in the general community, Franklin felt that "standing at the head of the largest Jewish congregation in this part of the country," he "must assume the responsibility of acting as a representative of the Jewish life of the city when called upon to do so." In recognition of his outstanding public service, Henry Ford presented him with an automobile in 1913. Ford continued this practice annually until 1920, when Franklin refused the gift in protest of Ford's burgeoning anti-Semitic activities.[34]

Although German and native Jews may have been acceptable in the civic arena and in interdenominational activities, in the social sphere their exclusion was virtually complete. Detroit's most exclusive metropolitan clubs until World War I were the Yondotega Club, the Detroit Club, and the Detroit Athletic Club. Despite their recognized economic and civic prominence, no Jews appeared on the Yondotega's or Detroit Club's membership rosters from 1900 to 1950.

The Detroit Athletic Club experienced two phases in its history. During the first, beginning with the club's founding in 1887, its purpose was to field amateur athletic teams. In 1913 the club was reorganized to cater more generally to the city's business executives. The Detroit Athletic Club of the earlier

phase listed eight Jews on its 1893 roster out of a total membership of 767. Among these Jews were the Butzels, Heavenriches, and Heinemans. With the club's reorganization in 1913, only one Jew, David E. Heineman, remained among the membership. Seven years later no Jew appeared on the club's roster, despite the fact that the membership of the club had increased almost fourfold since 1893. While a select group of German and native Jewish professional and commercial notables had achieved sufficient status to be listed in *Dau's Blue Book* and Marquis' *Book of Detroiters*, their club memberships reveal an inability to penetrate the more exclusive social enclaves of the city. To all intents and purposes, the social elite in Detroit remained Gentile.[35]

The first explicit and widely publicized act of social discrimination against a Jew in Detroit occurred in March, 1893, when the Detroit Athletic Club rejected Herman Freund, a prominent German Jewish businessman, for membership. The incident became a cause célèbre and brought the whole question of anti-Semitism to public attention. Although his son, Jacob, was a member, Freund had been forewarned by friends that he would be blackballed because of prejudice existing within the club. After his rejection, Freund asked the president of the club whether his religion had been the reason. The president, F. K. Stearns, replied evasively that "it may, or it may not. I do not feel at liberty to express an opinion. I regret being drawn into this controversy, as I have no fault to find with you personally." An investigation by some of Detroit's German Jewish leaders led them to conclude that religious prejudice had indeed been the reason for the exclusion. A number of the club's directors admitted as much to the investigators, and former board members told Freund that "several members of the board had an aversion to having Israelites accepted as members."[36]

In the wake of these disclosures, the *The Detroit Evening News* ran an editorial entitled, "Why Is the Jew Hated?" The *News* hoped that the discussion would be "a calm one, as becomes scientists, not heated and vindictive after the manner of Christian controversy," and requested that Rabbi Grossmann "address himself to the task." Grossmann replied that he knew of no city where the various religious denominations "are more friendly disposed" to one another than in Detroit. And in his eight years in the city there had not been one intersectarian conflict and "surely none which has involved the Jewish faith." He further felt that "the alleged prejudice against the Jews is much exaggerated" and that "prejudice is the inevitable companion of the crude and the rude." He concluded by requesting that "in the interest of good will which ought to prevail, do not propose a discussion of the Jews."[37]

Not to be dissuaded, the *News* accused the rabbi of wanting to "drop the whole subject." The paper argued that "if the world would only drop it, nothing would be more agreeable." The problem was that "the World will not drop it" and "the Jews themselves will not drop it." It was therefore impossible to suppress discussion of such "a universal phenomenon." The *News* concluded by again asking, "what is the nature of the anti-Semitic bacillus?"[38]

The next respondent was a Protestant clergyman, the Reverend Mr. Plantz. Prefacing his remarks by disclosing that he personally had no sympathy with religious prejudice, he launched into an attack on the Jews, accusing them of bigotry and blaming them for the anti-Semitism. "The prejudice against the Jew is certainly equaled by the Jews' prejudice against the Gentile," he said. Indeed, the literature of the Jews was "full of words of intolerance." If the Jew would associate more with non-Jews, "forget that he is a Jew in the national sense," and forego that "exclusiveness" which often borders on "race bigotry, much of the prejudice that exists against him would soon pass away." Then, contradicting himself, he claimed that it was the Jew's "craftiness," his "success as a schemer," his thirst "to get the best of the bargain," and his "unscrupulousness" in financial transactions which had created anti-Semitic feeling in the United States and Europe.[39]

The *News* concurred with part of Plantz's analysis by also fixing the blame for anti-Semitism on the Jews. "There is absolutely no prejudice against the Hebrew in this or any other country which they themselves have not invited but made mandatory on the rest of the world," it editorialized. The Jews' refusal to mix with other peoples carried an "imputation against all Gentile blood which Gentiles must meet in some way." Grossmann expressed dismay at these assertions and asked sadly what had happened to Detroit, "our good old staid town of peaceable people?" What had happened in Detroit during the 1890s was that "the Jew in this city was to a great extent an ostracized person. He was looked upon with suspicion and there was anything but brotherly feeling for him."[40]

Despite their exposure, the openly discriminatory policies of the Detroit Athletic Club continued into the twentieth century. In 1907, Jacob Mazer, a Jewish member of the club (supposedly a member because of his basketball playing ability), resigned from the club because it rejected an applicant solely because he was Jewish. Fred Butzel declined an invitation to dine with President Woodrow Wilson at the Detroit Athletic Club "because the luncheon was given on the premises of a club that does not accept Jews as members." And Albert Kahn, who designed and constructed the club's building, refused to attend the luncheon honoring its completion because of the club's discriminatory policy against Jews.[41]

Discrimination against Jews in Detroit was not only practiced by the Detroit Athletic Club. On the basis of his experience with the directors of the local YMCA, Rabbi Franklin became convinced that "Jews are tolerated, not welcomed" in the club. "Their money is needed, but they are not wanted." And it was common knowledge in the German Jewish community that there were certain "exclusive" neighborhoods that were closed to Jews. These realities prompted the *Jewish American* to concede that while "Jews have earned the respect and goodwill of their Christian neighbors in the commercial world, in the social circle they are still outcasts, much the same as centuries ago."[42]

After forty years of supposedly good relations with their neighbors, Detroit's German Jews hoped for complete acceptance. These expectations resulted from the fact that, in their minds at least, their faith (Reform Judaism), manners, behavior, and appearance were all distinctively American. In addition, they exchanged pulpits with local churches, sponsored interdenominational services, cooperated in civic and charitable work, and mingled on a formal and informal basis with public officials, business leaders, clergymen, and civic groups. The growth and persistence of anti-Semitism bluntly reminded them that they were Jews and still unacceptable, which created anxiety and disillusionment among them. Since they had little experience in combating anti-Semitism and lacked any local organization or institution to help them, the community's leaders faced the dilemma of how to respond. Nevertheless, they utilized the resources available to defend themselves.[43]

Rabbi Franklin composed articles and lectured widely on Jewish history and traditions in an effort to educate the general public. Newspapers and stage productions were monitored and taken to task for references or depictions offensive to Jews. The community thus showed special sensitivity to the study of Shakespeare's *Merchant of Venice* in the schools. "Surely there are other works of Avon's bard, that portray his style, his strength and his genius quite as clearly as this one, the study of which, especially in the hands of teachers who are not entirely free from prejudice, and not always as fully equipped as they might be, causes many a heart-ache to the Jewish pupil, and oftentimes suffuses his cheek with the flush of mingled humiliation and indignation," commented the *Jewish American.* "As a rule Shylock is portrayed as the typical Jew, which all well-informed readers know is the very reverse of the truth. There is not a single characteristic of the famous miser and usurer that is essentially Jewish, except his love for his daughter." And contrary to their stated opposition to mixing religion and politics, German Jews warned local politicians about the consequences of using anti-Semitism to win votes.[44]

The Jewish community increased its efforts at keeping Bible readings, prayers, and the celebration of Christmas out of the public schools, and the invoking of Jesus' name at public functions was also criticized. The *Jewish American* protested that "ministers of ordinary tact and intelligence should persist in praying

in the name of Jesus at gatherings of a public character, where they must know that such prayers will offend the religious sensibilities of some in the audience." If a prayer must be said, the paper continued, "let it be one which is not offensive to any, and into which all may enter with equal fervor."[45]

At the same time, communal leaders hoped to lessen anti-Semitism by projecting a favorable image, by ingratiating themselves with the non-Jewish world, and by accommodating to Gentile desires. This meant the Jew had to be above reproach and behave in a manner that would reflect only credit upon himself and his people. "One way of preventing verbal attacks and the caricaturing of Jews was to give the lie to this by living on a high moral plane," advised the *Jewish American.* "It will not stop aspersion, but will do more than speeches." In keeping with this, the loyalty of Detroit Jewry had to be above reproach, which meant the avoidance of everything that set them apart from their neighbors and made them appear different, foreign, or alien. Association with "international" Jewish causes threatened this goal. Magnus Butzel, writing to the well-known New York attorney and communal leader, Meyer Samuel Isaacs, explained that Detroit's German Jews desired the "denationalization of the Jew," hence "there is an aversion to belong to an 'Alliance Israelite *Universelle*,' using the word in its liberal sense," because this appelation has "given cause for Rishus" (malice) against Jews.[46]

The German Jewish establishment never ceased reminding the Gentile community of the strength of Jewish patriotism, the rarity of Jews appearing on the public dole, and the low number of Jewish criminals. Thus, references in the press to a criminal's Jewishness elicited sharp protest from the *Jewish American* because it contradicted the image of moral probity which the community sought to project. "We do not know whether it is because they cannot learn it, or because they simply do not wish to, that some of our newspapers insist, despite correction and rebuke and threat, to point out the religion of every Jew who happens to get into trouble," complained the *Jewish American* in one such editorial. "Any sheet that will go out of its way to point out the religion of a

The front and editorial pages of the *Jewish American* (1901-11), edited by Rabbi Leo Franklin. (Courtesy of the Rabbi Leo M. Franklin Archives of Temple Beth El.)

police court offender, is nasty and unworthy of support." Alluding to a more sinister motive, the newspaper concluded "that had these people been Catholics, or Presbyterians, or Methodists, or Unitarians, or Episcopalians, or ethical culturists, or Christian Scientists, or heathens, or anything but Jews, their religion would not have been referred to."[47]

No matter what the German Jews did, however, anti-Semitism endured. This realization, together with a sense of injured pride and honor, caused some of them to become adamant in their Jewishness. They continued to encourage interfaith cooperation but placed greater emphasis on strengthening Jewish consciousness and Jewish identity. The *Jewish American* became an instrument to strengthen Jewish awareness. The stated object of the paper was to be a Jewish journal in spirit and content, "to be in sympa-

thetic touch with every movement that concerns the welfare of our people; awake to every danger that threatens because we are Jews and alive to the duties of Jews as well as to his rights." At the same time, the paper promised to be "tireless in its effort to arouse to duty those born within our fold and bearing our name, who through empty or unworthy lives have lost their religious birthright." To achieve its stated goals, the paper featured only subjects of Jewish content and interest, kept the community aware of Jewish causes and holidays, and fostered a spirit of self-esteem by militantly admonishing Jews that the time for postures of "modesty and retirement" and placing faith in the goodness of "christian charity" was over. Henceforth, Detroit's Jews should stand up for their beliefs, assert their rights, and, above all, never forget to be "proud that you are a Jew."[48]

NOTES

1. These occupational groupings are similar to those of the Eastern European Jewish immigrants, but within the groups, especially that of proprietor, the differences are great (compare the list of Beth El members' occupations with that of the 1907 community as a whole). In terms of capital and employees, native Jews owned and managed much larger concerns.

2. Congregation Beth El membership rosters, 1877, 1880, 1900, and 1910; *Detroit City Directory*, 1880, 1900, and 1910; Albert N. Marquis, *The Book of Detroiters* (Chicago: A. N. Marquis and Company, 1914), pp. 90, 173, 232, 234, 295, 339, 418, 428, 435.

3. Robert Conot, *American Odyssey* (Detroit: Wayne State University Press, 1986), pp. 168-69; Marquis, *Book of Detroiters*, p. 273.

4. Congregation Beth El Executive Board Minutes, 1874-89, February 6, 1881, p. 162, July 7, 1884, p. 229; Irving I. Katz, *The Beth El Story* (Detroit: Wayne State University Press, 1955), pp. 88-89.

5. Congregation Beth El Executive Board Minutes, September 25, 1881, p. 175, November 6, 1881, p. 176.

6. *The Reform Advocate* (Chicago), March 2, 1912, p. 4; Grossman File, Temple Beth El Archives.

7. Congregation Beth El Executive Board Minutes, September 4, 1887, p. 303, March 4, 1888, p. 311, November 2, 1890, p. 185, September 13, 1896, p. 157. See also Katz, *Beth El*, p. 94.

8. Temple Beth El Annual Reports, 1874-1950, reports of Magnus Butzel, September 25, 1892; Bernard Selling, September, 1895; Julius Freund, September 13, 1896.

9. *Detroit News-Tribune*, June 22, 1902, p. 4. At Wise's death, in 1900, Grossmann succeeded him as rabbi. He also received appointment as professor at Hebrew Union College, teaching theology, ethics, and pedagogy. As professor of pedagogy, he pioneeered in applying educational methodology to Jewish education and wrote a number of teacher guidance pamphlets on the subject. He wrote *Judaism and the Science of Religion; Hymns, Prayers and Responses; The Real Life* and *Glimpses into Life.* He also published two volumes of collected sermons, *The Jewish Pulpit,* and collaborated with David Philipson in the publication of the *Selected Writings of Isaac M. Wise.* He retired as professor emeritus of Hebrew Union College and rabbi emeritus of B'nai Jeshurun in 1922.

10. The information about Franklin is taken from a biography written by Irving I. Katz and deposited in the archives of Temple Beth El.

11. Leo M. Franklin, *History of Congregation Beth El, 1900-1910* (Detroit, 1910), pp. 30-32; Beth El Executive Board Minutes, 1899-1908, August 3, 1904, p. 160, August 8, 1904, p. 164; Temple Beth El Annual Reports, 1874-1950, report of Leo M. Franklin, October 31, 1904, Temple Beth El Archives, Burton Historical Collections, Detroit, Michigan.

12. Temple Beth El Annual Reports, 1874-1950, report of Leo M. Franklin, October 31, 1904.

13. *Jewish American*, May 6, 1904, p. 4, November 25, 1904, p. 4; *American Israelite*, May 5, 1904, p. 2; Franklin File, Temple Beth El Archives.

14. Beth El Executive Board Minutes, 1889-1904, September 27, 1903-April 27, 1904, pp. 125-52, November 8, 1904, pp. 174-75; Franklin File, Temple Beth El Archives.

15. David Philipson, *The Reform Movement in Judaism* (New York: Macmillan Co., 1931), p. 376. Earlier attempts at holding Sunday services occurred in Baltimore (1854) and Chicago (1874). The Baltimore experiment lasted six months; the Chicago effort, initiated by Temple Sinai, continued and eventually displaced the Temple's Saturday services, which were discontinued in 1887.

16. Temple Beth El Annual Reports, 1874-1950, report of Leo M. Franklin, October 14, 1902; *Jewish American*, November 4, 1904, p. 2; *Detroit News*, January 18, 1904, p. 10; Congregation Beth El Minutes, 1908-12, report of President Henry Butzel, October 19, 1909; *American Israelite*, October 30, 1913, p. 3, January 15, 1914, p. 2.

17. Franklin File, Temple Beth El Archives; Temple Beth El roster, 1910; Beth El Annual Reports, 1874-1950, report of Samuel Heavenrich, October 29, 1907, and report of Leo M. Franklin, October 30, 1905.

18. Beth El Annual Reports, 1874-1950, report of Leo M. Franklin, October 30, 1905. *Jewish American*, January 10, 1902, p. 4; February 8, 1907, p. 4; September 27, 1907, p. 4; April 24, 1908, p. 4; October 23, 1908, p. 4; September 9, 1910, p. 4; September 16, 1910, p. 2; January 27, 1911, p. 4.

19. *Jewish American*, December 20, 1901, p. 4, December 19, 1902, p. 2, December 28, 1906, p. 7, December 13, 1907, p. 8; *American Israelite*, January 6, 1916, p. 4.

20. *Jewish American*, January 31, 1902, p. 4; April 25, 1902, p. 4; June 28, 1907, p. 4; April 17, 1908, p. 4.

21. *Jewish American*, April 11, 1904, p. 4; March 17, 1905, p. 6; June 15, 1906, p. 4; February 22, 1907, p. 6; September 20, 1907, p. 6; March 10, 1911, p. 3. *American Israelite*, January 5, 1913, p. 3; November 13, 1913, p. 4; October 8, 1914, p. 3.

22. *American Israelite*, December 22, 1892, p. 8, January 12, 1893, p. 2, June 10, 1909, p. 2, December 25, 1913, p. 3, March 5, 1914, p. 3; *Jewish American*, February 9, 1906, pp. 1-3; *American Hebrew*, January 20, 1893, p. 403; *Detroit Free Press*, October 26, 1896, pp. 1-2; *Detroit News-Tribune*, January 22, 1905, p. 1, October 22, 1906, p. 1; *Detroit Journal*, November 24, 1906, p. 1; Phyllis Lederer, "A Study of Jewish Influences in Detroit" (M.A. thesis, Wayne University, 1947), p. 88; *Yearbook, Jewish Woman's Club, 1909-1910* (Detroit, Michigan, 1910), p. 5. These efforts formed a part of the Progressive era in American history, which was a broad-based movement among civic-minded middle-class Americans who sought to correct certain basic wrongs in the nation's political and economic life.

23. *American Israelite*, March 7, 1884, p. 7, October 1, 1886, p. 1, November 14, 1895, p. 3, May 3, 1906, p. 2; *Detroit Free Press*, October 14, 1892, p. 2, January 2, 1896, p. 3; Congregation Beth El, Ladies Auxiliary Minutes, November 18, 1914; Congregation Beth El Minutes, 1912-29, April 4, 1913; Ladies' Society for the Support of Hebrew Widows and Orphans, Minute Books, 1888-1907. Magnus Butzel served on the Board of Education in 1881 and the Library

Commission in 1885; Edward Kanter served on the Board of Poor Commissioners from 1882 to 1884, when Simon Heavenrich replaced him. Sigmund Simon was president of the Board of Poor Commissioners in 1890 and again in 1905; Magnus Butzel served as vice-president of the Board of Directors of the Detroit Public Library in 1891 and as president in 1893; Louis Blitz served on the Board of Appeals of the Chamber of Commerce in 1893, while Martin Butzel served on the Lighting Commission. Bernard Ginsburg served on the Public Lighting Commission in 1904 and as president of the Detroit Public Library Board in 1914; Ignatz Freund was a member of the Board of Poor Commissioners from 1905 to 1909 and its president in 1909; Henry M. Fechheimer served on the City Plan and Improvement Commission in 1908, and Albert Kahn served on the Art Commission from 1904 to 1907. See the *Annual Reports of the City of Detroit* for the years from 1883 to 1910; *American Hebrew*, July 29, 1891, p. 128; *American Israelite*, February 28, 1891, p. 2, January 15, 1893, p. 2, April 20, 1893, p. 2, January 15, 1914, p. 3; *Jewish American*, September 9, 1904, p. 6, September 29, 1905, p. 6, April 20, 1906, p. 6, November 9, 1906, p. 6.

24. *American Israelite*, March 5, 1891, p. 1, November 3, 1892, p. 2, March 1, 1894, p. 2, December 27, 1894, p. 2, February 28, 1895, p. 2, January 24, 1896, p. 7; *Detroit Free Press*, October 29, 1892, p. 2, October 25, 1894, p. 5.

25. *Michigan Tradesman* (Grand Rapids), February 28, 1906, p. 1; John C. Lodge, *I Remember Detroit* (Detroit: Wayne University Press, 1949), pp. 94-95; Lederer, "Jewish Influences," pp. 86-87; *Reform Advocate*, March 2, 1912, pp. 22-23; Marquis, *Book of Detroiters*, p. 234.

26. *Jewish American*, February 2, 1902, p. 4, May 20, 1904, p. 4; Temple Beth El Annual Reports, 1874-1950, report of Leo M. Franklin, October 31, 1904; Congregation Beth El Minutes, 1899-1908, March 4, 1900, p. 20, January 5, 1902, p. 83; Congregation Beth El Minutes, 1912-29, report of the hospitality committee, October 20, 1914; *Constitution of the Phoenix Social Club* (Detroit: Wm. Graham Printer, 1884); Martin Marger, "The Force of Ethnicity: A Study of Urban Elites," *Journal of University Studies* 10 (Winter, 1974), p. 88.

27. See Marquis, *Book of Detroiters*, and *Dau's Blue Book for Detroit* (Detroit: Dau Publishing Co., 1912).

28. *American Israelite*, September 13, 1872, p. 6, October 4, 1872, p. 10, January 20, 1888, p. 8, May 14, 1914, p. 3, September 17, 1914, p. 3; Phoenix Social Club Scrapbook, 1896-1905, Temple Beth El Archives, Burton Historical Collections; *Jewish American*, March 16, 1906, p. 6.

29. *American Israelite*, April 19, 1891, p. 1; *Year Book, Jewish Woman's Club, 1909-1910*, pp. 7, 21; *American Hebrew*, May 16, 1913, p. 72; *Reform Advocate*, March 2, 1912, p. 16; *The American Jewess* (Chicago), September, 1896, p. 655; *Dau's Blue Book*, p. 17; *Blue Book: A Social Directory of Detroit* (Detroit: Blue Book Publishing Co., 1896), p. 312.

30. Minutes, Ladies' Society for the Support of Hebrew Widows and Orphans, 1888-1907, July 30-August 26, 1890, p. 51; *American Israelite*, July 17, 1890, p. 5, January 20, 1910, p. 3; *Jewish American*, February 6, 1903, p. 6, April 15, 1904, p. 6, December 21, 1906, p. 6; April 5, 1907, p. 6, July 26, 1907, p. 4, November 15, 1907, p. 5, April 28, 1911, p. 5.

31. *American Israelite*, February 10, 1888, p. 10, November 10, 1892, p. 2, November 12, 1914, p. 3; *Jewish American*, April 10,

1903, p. 6, December 30, 1904, p. 6, November 19, 1907, p. 5, November 22, 1907, p. 6, December 16, 1910, p. 5.

32. *Jewish American*, March 14, 1902, p. 4.

33. *Jewish Messenger*, July 7, 1882, p. 2; *American Israelite*, December 4, 1890, p. 5, March 5, 1891, p. 1, May 21, 1891, p. 5, February 16, 1893, p. 2, August 3, 1899, p. 2, April 21, 1910, p. 3, October 30, 1913, p. 3; *American Hebrew*, December 16, 1887, p. 107, February 10, 1899, pp. 538-39; *Jewish American*, January 24, 1902, p. 6, February 28, 1902, p. 6, November 14, 1902, p. 4, April 15, 1904, p. 6, May 13, 1904, p. 6, September 16, 1904, p. 6, November 4, 1904, p. 2, January 20, 1911, p. 6; *Detroit Free Press*, November 22, 1902, p. 4; Congregation Beth El Minutes, 1912-1929, January 2, 1913.

34. *Detroit Free Press*, May 15, 1892, p. 28; *Detroit Sunday News-Tribune*, September 27, 1896, p. 20; *American Israelite*, June 9, 1892, p. 2, October 6, 1898, p. 2, November 3, 1898, p. 2, May 1, 1913, p. 2; Congregation Beth El Minutes, 1912-29, report of the rabbi, October 20, 1914; Franklin File, Temple Beth El Archives.

35. Marger, "Force of Ethnicity," pp. 82-90.

36. *Detroit Evening News*, March 23, 1893, p. 1; March 25, 1893, p. 4. Much of this material was published previously in Robert Rockaway, "Anti-Semitism in an American City: Detroit, 1850-1914," *American Jewish Historical Quarterly* 64 (September, 1974), pp. 42-54.

37. *Detroit Evening News*, April 3, 1893, p. 4; April 5, 1893, p. 4.

38. *Detroit Evening News*, April 7, 1893, p. 4.

39. *Ibid.* The Reverend Plantz's attitude was not an uncommon one. See Egal Feldman, "The Social Gospel and the Jews," *American Jewish Historical Quarterly* 58 (March, 1969), pp. 308-22.

40. *Detroit Evening News*, April 20, 1893, p. 4, April 27, 1893, p. 1; *Detroit Courier*, May 19, 1906, clipping in Beth El Scrapbook, 1901-1911, in the Temple Beth El Archives. The *News* conveniently forgot that the whole episode began when a Jew (Freund) sought to "mix" with Gentiles by joining the Detroit Athletic Club.

41. *Jewish American*, October 4, 1907, p. 4; *Jewish Independent* (Cleveland), July 28, 1916, clipping in the Fred M. Butzel File, American Jewish Archives, Cincinnati, Ohio; interview with Sadie Hirschman.

42. *Modern View*, February 17, 1905, p. 12; *Jewish American*, April 14, 1905, p. 4; interview with Sadie Hirschman.

43. The American Jewish Committee was established in 1906 to combat anti-Semitism and to protect the civil and religious rights of Jews all over the world. The Anti-Defamation League of the B'nai B'rith was created in 1913 to protect the status and rights of Jews in the United States.

44. *Jewish American*, October 24, 1901, p. 4; October 25, 1901, p. 4; November 8, 1901, p. 4; January 31, 1902, p. 4; September 26, 1902, p. 4; March 13, 1903, p. 6; June 22, 1904, p. 4; July 25, 1904, p. 4; March 17, 1905, p. 4; April 7, 1905, p. 6; August 11, 1905, p. 4; December 4, 1906, p. 4; August 10, 1907, p. 4; September 13, 1907, p. 6; January 17, 1908, p. 4; March 13, 1908, p. 4; August 7, 1908, p. 4; August 13, 1908, p. 4; August 28, 1908, p. 4; October 10, 1908; July 27, 1911, p. 6. Also see *Detroit News*, November 1, 1896, p. 10; *Detroit Free Press*, October 20, 1914, p. 4; *American Israelite*, June 2, 1910, p. 2, July, 1913, p. 1.

45. *American Israelite*, December 3, 1896, p. 3; *Jewish American*, March 31, 1905, p. 4; December 14, 1906, p. 4, June 23, 1909, p. 4.

46. *Jewish American*, May 1, 1908, p. 4; Magnus Butzel to M. S. Isaacs, April 27, 1885, Meyer Samuel Isaacs Papers, American Jewish Historical Society, Waltham, Massachusetts. The Alliance Israelite Universelle, founded in France in 1860, was the first modern international Jewish organization created to help Jews, wherever they lived, combat anti-Semitism.

47. *Jewish American*, May 30, 1902, p. 4.

48. *Jewish American*, October 17, 1902, p. 4; October 6, 1905, p. 5; January 6, 1906, p. 4; June 15, 1906, p. 4; July 24, 1908, p. 4; September 22, 1905, p. 4.

CONCLUSION

IN THIS STUDY, I have described the development of the Detroit Jewish community's major religious, educational, social, and philanthropic institutions and its principal leaders, from the community's beginnings to the outset of World War I. At the same time, I tried not to neglect telling the story of the community's lower, but far from inarticulate, classes. And wherever possible, I compared Jewish economic and social strata with that of other Detroit ethnic groups and other American Jewish communities.

Economic mobility is a central theme in American and American Jewish history, and so it is in this study as well. I have shown that by 1880 Detroit's German Jews had a higher proportion of white-collar workers than did the city's British, Irish, German, Polish, and native white American groups. Instead of following in their parents' footsteps, most of Detroit's second generation German Jews preferred careers in the professions or opened their own businesses. While the economic rise of the Eastern European Jews did not match that of the earlier German Jews, by 1900 the Eastern Europeans had a higher proportion of white collar workers than all the other Detroit ethnic groups except for native white Americans. These statistics approximate those of the Jews in other cities around the United States. I also found that three times as many Jewish working women engaged in white collar occupations than did Detroit's non-Jewish women.

Notwithstanding the classic stereotype of the Jew as peddler and the fact that by 1890 Jews dominated Detroit's waste industry, less than 20 percent of the city's Eastern European Jews peddled for a living. Contrary to the Jewish experience in New York and other large urban centers, few of Detroit's working-class Jews enrolled in the labor movement. This reflected local conditions, as Detroit remained a non-union town until the 1930s.

Both German and Eastern European Jews exhibited an extraordinary degree of geographic mobility, with few individuals or families remaining at the same address for more than a few years. Despite Industrial Removal Office claims that 75 percent of the men they sent to a community chose to remain, over 80 percent of the removals sent to Detroit left the city within three years.

Jewish religious practices underwent a change in Detroit during the period from 1850 to 1880, as they did in other American Jewish communities. Temple Beth El engaged a series of educated and enlightened rabbis who, with the support and encouragement of influential laymen, instituted a series of reforms in the liturgy and the observance of holidays. Despite all their efforts at "modernizing" the rituals and service to make them more palatable to Americanized and native members, religious apathy and non-attendance remained problematic. By the twentieth century, however, Beth El began to backtrack on some of its earlier reforms. Feeling that Reform may have gone too far, congregational leaders sought to reintroduce more of the traditional aspects of Judaism. Nevertheless, religion played a diminishing role in the lives of Detroit's second and third generation German Jews.

Backsliding and indifference affected the Eastern European Jews as well. Religious observances declined and violations of the Sabbath became increasingly open and obvious. One congregation, Shaarey Zedek, sought to counteract the apathy of its Americanized members by modifying its Orthodoxy and joining the Conservative movement in Judaism. These measures, however, failed to stem disinterest within the congregation.

Disunity was the rule rather than the exception within Detroit's Jewish community. Class, cultural, and religious differences separated the Germans from the Eastern Europeans; and ethnic differences, disagreements about rituals, and personal idiosyncracies kept the Eastern European Jewish community fragmented. In spite of these distinctions, however, the groups cooperated for overseas relief and to combat local anti-Semitism.

Relations between Jews and non-Jews remained amicable in the formal and interdenominational sectors of city life. This was characterized by pulpit exchanges and Jewish participation in Detroit civic and political affairs. Nonetheless, an undercurrent of anti-Semitism persisted throughout the period encompassed by this study. Its most obvious manifestation occurred in the social sphere, where Jews suffered almost total exclusion.

Detroit remained an Anglo-Saxon Protestant stronghold, with Jewish penetration of the social elite kept to a minimum until well after World War II. At times, anti-Jewish antagonism turned ugly, with Eastern European immigrants being harassed and physically attacked by Irish and Polish ruffians. These incidents led the Jewish community to take defensive measures to protect itself and had the additional effect of reinforcing many Jews' sense of identification. Ironically, anti-Semitism accomplished for the community what religious reforms and communal efforts failed to do: it caused Detroit's Jews to more strongly identify as Jews. Finally, there is another, more subtle, theme which permeates this study: the ongoing tension between the Jews' desire to become full-fledged, fully participating Americans and their desire to maintain a Jewish identity and some semblance of Jewishness. This tension was never satisfactorily resolved during the period under discussion, nor in the decades that followed.

APPENDIX A

TABLE 1	TABLE 2
Detroit Jewish Males:	Detroit Male Workers:
Occupational Distribution, 1880	Occupational Distribution, 1880

OCCUPATIONAL GROUP	NO.	%
Professional and semiprofessional	5	3
Proprietor, manager, official	95	56
Clerical and sales	16	9
Skilled	14	8
Semiskilled and service	12	7
Unskilled and menial	27	16

Source: Manuscript Census Schedules, Detroit, 1880.

OCCUPATIONAL GROUP	NO.	%
Professional and semiprofessional	1,813	8
Proprietor, manager, official	351	2
Clerical and sales	3,594	15
Skilled	7,881	34
Semiskilled and service	4,573	19
Unskilled and menial	5,175	22

Source: Tenth Census of the United States, 1880: Population 1 (Washington, D.C.: Government Printing Office, 1887), p. 876.

TABLE 3
Detroit Male Jews and Detroit Males: Occupational Status, 1880

OCCUPATIONAL GROUP	JEWS NO.	%	DETROITERS NO.	%
White-collar	116	69	5,758	25
Skilled	14	8	7,881	34
Semiskilled and unskilled	39	23	9,748	41

TABLE 4
Ethnicity and Occupational Status, Detroit, 1880

ETHNIC GROUP	WHITE-COLLAR %	SKILLED %	SEMISKILLED OR UNSKILLED %
Native white American	54.2	23.9	21.9
British	27.7	42.1	30.2
Irish	17.6	23.5	59.0
German	13.8	43.9	42.4
Polish	31.8	17.6	50.6

Source: Olivier Zunz, *The Changing Face of Inequality: Urbanization, Industrial Development, and Immigrants in Detroit, 1880-1920* (Chicago: University of Chicago Press, 1982), p. 39.

TABLE 5
Employed Male Jews and Employed Male Detroiters by Industrial Group, 1880

INDUSTRIAL GROUP	JEWS NO.	%	DETROITERS NO.	%
Agriculture	0	0	378	1
Clerical	16	10	262	1
Domestic and personal service	1	1	5,207	17
Manufacturing and mechanical arts	25	17	13,905	46
Professional service	5	3	942	3
Public service	0	0	871	3
Trade	118	71	6,140	20
Transportation	0	0	2,524	8

Source: Tenth Census of the United States, 1880: Population 1, p. 876.

TABLE 6
Occupational Status by Congregation, 1878

TEMPLE BETH EL	NO.	%
Total members	95	—
Total occupations	80	—
Professional and semiprofessional	2	3
Proprietor, manager, official	61	76
Clerical and sales	9	11
Skilled	2	3
Semiskilled and service	6	7
Unskilled	0	0

SHAAREY ZEDEK	NO.	%
Total members	82	—
Total occupations	57	—
Professional and semiprofessional	1	2
Proprietor, manager, official	27	47
Clerical and sales	6	10
Skilled	4	7
Semiskilled and service	6	11
Unskilled	13	23

BNAI ISRAEL, BNAI JACOB, BETH JACOB	NO.	%
Total members	33	—
Total occupations	28	—
Professional and semiprofessional	0	0
Proprietor, manager, official	6	21
Clerical and sales	1	4
Skilled	3	10
Semiskilled and service	6	21
Unskilled	12	43

TABLE 7
Occupational Status of
Orthodox Congregations: Totals, 1878

ORTHODOX CONGREGATIONS	NO.	%
Total members	115	—
Total occupations	85	—
Professional and semiprofessional	1	1
Proprietor, manager, official	33	39
Clerical and sales	7	8
Skilled	7	8
Semiskilled and service	12	14
Unskilled	25	29

TABLE 8
Winder Street between St. Antoine and Hastings

	1910		1914		1910		1914
227	Gannon, Joseph	227	Williamson, Mrs. Della	245	Jackson, Daniel	245	Solomon, Mollie
		227	Clark, Arthur	245	Scott, Alfred		
228	Millman, Joseph	228	Cohen, Hyman	245	James, John		
228	Goldstein, Louis	228	Sulzman, Max			246	Moscowitz, Jacob
229	Gipperich, Clara	229	Tipperich, Clara			247-51	Michigan State Tel. Co.
230	Johnson, Mary	231-35	Congregation	248	Jacob, Abraham	248	Friedman, Joseph
			Beth Abraham	253	Weingarden, Julia	253	Wade, William
230	Levin, Solomon			254	Mulden, Sarah	254	Dixon, James
232	Friedman, Abraham	232	Itzkowitz, Oscar	255	Wilkes, Emanuel	255	Throgmartin, Thomas
232	Miller, Meyer	232	Nachman, Eli	256	Griffen, Albert	256	Jackson, Anderson
232	Winkorsky, Samuel	232	Katz, Nathan	257	Warrensky, Ike	257	Robinson, Isaac B.
		232	Cohen, Louis	258	Fineberg, Henry	258	Fineberg, Henry
234	Dorb, Louis	234	Eichner, Herman			258	Jenkins, Mrs. Ella
234	Boschwitz, Louis	234	Klein, Harry	259	Vacant	259	Bloomfield, Louis,
236	Lepowetzky, Naum	236	Potaschnik, Louis	259	Cohen and Gilbert		Alksmith
236	Lowes, Louis	236	Deutsch, Aaron	260	Butler, Sarah	260	Zupnitzke, Meyer (meats)
236	Kekst, Louis	236	Bernath, Samuel			260	Ratkovski, Louis
236	Velenski, David	236	Spayer, Ignace	261	Simkins, Andrew	261	Miller, Samuel
236	Hill, Arthur			262	Heidner, Edward	262	Wermuth, Isidor
237	Goos, Jacob	237	Urinovitch, Jacob	262	Hirsch, Sigmund	262	Harris, Mrs. Bertha
		241	Friedman, Louis			262	Gordon, H & Sons
		241	Gedrich, Max				(creamery)
		241	Berger, William	263	Cohen, Samuel	263	Vacant
		241	Dvorkin, Nathan	264	Gordon, Harry (creamery)		
		243	Resnick, Harry			265	Gordon, Harris
		243	Leifman, Morris	267	Yivatski, Samuel	267	Harris, Roy
		243	Frank, Max	268	Gutmann, Christian	268	Gutmann, Christian
		243	Labin, Benjamin		(baker)		
244	Jacobson, Herman	244	Jacobson, Herman	270	Hinderstein, Moses	270	Withers, Joseph
		244	Ware, Mrs. Martha				

TABLE 9
Detroit Jewish Community: Occupations, 1907

OCCUPATION	NO.	OCCUPATION	NO.	OCCUPATION	NO.	OCCUPATION	NO.
Agent	65	Delicatessen	1	Manufacturer's agent	14	Salon keeper	21
Apprentice	4	Dentist	3	Machinist	47	Sailor	1
Architect	1	Detective	1	Machine operator	6	Secondhand clothing	3
Art goods	1	Deputy sheriff	2	Manager	33	Secondhand goods	12
Artist	4	Detroit Electric Company	1	Manufacturer	8	Salesman	20
Auctioneer	2	Draftsman	1	Merchandise	3	Saleswoman	4
Automobiles	2	Dressmaker	17	Messenger	4	Secretary	2
		Driver	16	Milk dealer	3	Shirtmaker	2
Barber	21	Druggist	12	Milk store	2	Shoemaker	43
Bag manufacturer	1	Dry goods	44	Milkman	1	Shoe dealer	4
Baker	11			Motorman	2	*Shohet* (ritual slaughterer)	5
Bargain store	1	Electrician	1	Musician	8	Skirt manufacturer	1
Bartender	8	Elevator operator	1	Millinery	18	Stationery	1
Barrel maker	3	Engineer	2	Music dealer	3	Stenographer	38
Bench worker	3	Expressman	3			Stock keeper	2
Billiards	1			Notions	8	Superintendent	3
Blacksmith	7	Farmer	1			Skilled worker	6
Bicycles	1	Fireman	1	Operator	4	Seamstress	9
Bookkeeper	35	Fish and chicken	1	Optician	15		
Bottles	4	Fish dealer	5	Overalls	1	Tabac (snuff)	3
Broker	1	Foreman	13			Table supply	1
Broom maker	1	Fruit store	2	Painter	24	Tailor	116
Butcher	26	Furniture	8	Pants maker	1	Teacher	44
Butler	1	Furrier	9	Paper cutter	1	Teamster	7
				Paper stock	1	Ticket agent	2
Cashier	4	Glass cutter	1	Peddler	276	Ticket office	2
Cap maker	55	Glove maker	1	Picture frames	4	Towel supply	1
Candy store	3	Grocer	71	Plumber	8	Travel agent	65
Carpenter	49			Photographer	3	Trunks	1
Carpets	3	Hay and feed	1	Polisher	4	Trimmer	2
City agent	4	*Hazzan*	1	Porter	1		
Chemist	1	Hardware	3	Policeman	4	Upholsterer	2
Clocks	2	Helper	2	Pocketbook	1		
Charity superintendent	4	Hotel keeper	1	Presser	10	Vegetable peddler	4
Clothing	96			Printer	23	Vice-president	1
Clerk	392	Importer	2	Physician	25		
Cigar maker	27	Inspector	1	Pawnbroker	2	Waiter	1
Cigar factory	9	Insurance	2			Watchman	1
Coat supply	1	Insurance agent	4	Rabbi	4	Watchmaker	1
Collector	5	Investments	1	Railroad broker	1	Window trimmer	1
Compositor	1			Real estate agent	19	Window cleaner	1
Conductor	1	Jewelry	20	Reporter	1	Wines	1
Confectioner	8	Junk peddler	54	Restaurant	2	Wrapper	1
Costumer	1	Journalist	1	Roofer	1		
Coppersmith	1						
Corset manufacturer	3	Laborer	98				
Cutter	16	Laundryman	1				
Crockery	5	Lawyer	25				
Coal company	3	Leather goods	3				
		Liquors	4				
		Locksmith	1				

Source: *Di Detroit Iddishe Direktory, 1907* (Detroit: L. Knoppow & Sons, 1907). (Exact translation. Although many of the occupations listed are not technically "occupations," they appear here as they were given in the *Yiddish Directory*.)

TABLE 10
Occupational Status for
Selected Detroit Ethnic Groups, 1900

ETHNIC GROUP	HIGH WHITE-COLLAR %	LOW WHITE-COLLAR %	SKILLED %	SEMI-SKILLED AND UN-SKILLED %
Russian Jews	4	25	31.9	38.9
Native white Americans	10.5	45.4	29.7	14.5
Irish	2.6	17.9	23.7	55.8
German	1.2	15.5	42.8	40.5
Polish	0	5.7	32.5	61.8

Source: Zunz, *Changing Face,* p. 221.

TABLE 11
Eastern European Jewish Males:
Occupational Status, 1907

OCCUPATIONAL GROUP	NO.	%
Professional and semiprofessional	72	3.6
Proprietor, manager, official	354	17.5
White-collar	518	25.6
Skilled	631	31.2
Semiskilled and unskilled	445	22.0

Source: Di Detroit Iddishe Direktory, 1907.

TABLE 12
Eastern European Jewish Males and
Detroit Males: Occupational Status, 1910

OCCUPATIONAL GROUP	NO.	DETROIT MALES %	JEWISH MALES %
Professional and semiprofessional	2,885	3	3.6
Proprietor, manager, official	9,363	8	17.5
White-collar	14,848	13	25.6
Skilled	45,198	40	31.2
Semiskilled and unskilled	41,243	36	22.0

Source: Thirteenth Census of the United States, 1910: Population (Washington, D.C.: Government Printing Office, 1913), p. 554.

TABLE 13
Jewish Females and Detroit Females:
Occupational Status, 1910

OCCUPATIONAL GROUP	DETROIT FEMALES NO.	%	JEWISH FEMALES NO.	%
Professional and semiprofessional	3,332	8	32	11
Proprietor, manager, official	0	0	5	1
White-collar	11,327	28	207	74
Skilled	9,067	22	36	13
Semiskilled and unskilled	16,812	41	0	0

Sources: Di Detroit Iddishe Direktory, 1907; Thirteenth Census of the United States, 1910.

TABLE 14
Eastern Europeans and Beth El Members:
Occupational Distribution, 1910

OCCUPATIONAL GROUP	EASTERN EUROPEANS NO.	%	TEMPLE BETH EL MEMBERS NO.	%
Professional and semiprofessional	73	4	40	13
Proprietor, manager, official	354	17	177	57
White-collar	518	26	85	27
Skilled	631	31	8	2.5
Semiskilled and unskilled	445	22	0	0

Sources: Di Detroit Iddishe Direktory, 1907; Temple Beth El membership roster, 1910.

TABLE 15
Hannah Schloss Memorial
239-41 High Street
Educational and Entertainment
Department Schedule,
1904-5

Ida E. Ginsburg Day Nursery (Daily except Saturday and Sunday), 7 A.M. to 6 P.M.
Advanced Sewing Class for Girls (Daily except Saturday), 4 P.M., Sunday, 9 A.M.
Sewing Class (Sample Work)—Monday, 4 P.M.
Sewing Class (Sample Work)—Tuesday, 4 P.M.
Kitchen, Garden (Bedroom Work, Dining-room Work, Kitchen Work, General Cleaning, Bathroom Work)—Tuesday, 4 P.M.
Millinery—Tuesday, 4 P.M.
Dancing—(Girls 11-14 years)—Wednesday, 4 P.M.
Daily Sewing Class—Thursday, 4 P.M.
Daily Sewing Class—Friday, 4 P.M.
Library Hours for Children—Saturday Afternoon
Elementary English—Sunday, 9 A.M.
Advanced Sewing Class—Sunday, 9 A.M.
Cooking Class—Sunday, 10 A.M.
Boys' Manual Training (Every evening except Friday and Sunday)— 8 P.M.
Dancing, Stenography, English, History, Cooking, Literature, Millinery, Military Drill—Evening classes in these subjects will be formed for men and women over 16 years of age. Applicants must register for these classes on Monday, October 10, 8 P.M.; Tuesday, October 11, 8 P.M.; Wednesday, October 12, 8 P.M.

N.B.—A small fee is charged for these classes.

MONTHLY CALENDAR
October-April

Public Dance .... 1st Wednesday, 8 P.M.
Concert .... 2nd Wednesday, 8 P.M.
Lecture (Yiddish or English) .... 3rd Wednesday, 8 P.M.

Public Holiday Celebrations
Thanksgiving Day   Lincoln's Birthday
Washington's Birthday   Decoration Day
Dates to be announced later

Jewish Holiday Celebration
Hanukkah Festival   Purim Festival
Dates to be announced later

Mother's Club—Meetings Saturday afternoons
Admittance to the evening entertainments, etc., by card only. Cards furnished free upon application at Superintendent's office daily (except Saturday and Sunday), 10:30-12:00; October 1, 11, 12, 8 P.M., Sunday afternoon in October, 2:00-3:00 P.M.

TABLE 16
United Jewish Charities Contributions,
1900-1915

YEAR	AMOUNT RAISED	NO. OF CONTRIBUTORS
1900	$ 3,674	247
1901	3,826	265
1902	3,704	245
1903	4,270	258
1904	4,687	306
1905	7,297	315
1906	9,094	360
1907	10,258	368
1908	12,593	447
1909	13,870	453
1910	14,942	433
1911	18,188	431
1912	21,966	489
1913	24,497	534
1914	29,107	608
1915	34,333	660

Source: Annual Reports, United Jewish Charities of Detroit, 1900-1915.

TABLE 17
Jews Sent to Michigan and Detroit
by the IRO, 1901–14

YEAR	MICHIGAN	DETROIT	% SENT TO DETROIT
1901	104		
1902	75		
1903	162		
1904	187		
1905	239	160	66
1906	290		
1907	450	402	89
1908	180	121	67
1909	191		
1910	443	412	93
1911	394	319	80
1912	804	705	87
1913	1,175	1,118	95
1914	285		

Source: Annual Reports of the Industrial Removal Office, 1901–15 (located in the American Jewish Historical Society, Waltham, Massachusetts). The figures for Detroit are incomplete.

TABLE 18
Temple Beth El Members: Occupations, 1910

OCCUPATION	NO.	OCCUPATION	NO.	OCCUPATION	NO.	OCCUPATION	NO.
Advertising agent	3	Electric company	2	Machine company	1	Sales manager	3
Agent	2	Engineer	1	Market	4	Salesman	5
Architect	1			Manager	17	Saloon owner	1
Auto supplies	2	Fish market	1	Manufacturer	4	Secretary	2
		Furnace company	2	Manufacturer's agent	9	Shoes	1
Baker	1	Furniture store	1	Men's furnishings	8	Shirt manufacturer	1
Bank teller	2	Furrier	5	Milliner	2	Solicitor	1
Barber	1			Music school director	1	Steel company	1
Bookkeeper	1	Glass company	1			Storage company	1
Broker	4			Neckware company	2		
Buyer	1	Hides	2	Novelty company	2	Tailor	6
		Home furnishings	1			Teacher	1
Caterer	1			Optician	3	Ticket agent	2
Cattle dealer	1	Insurance agent	10			Tobacco company	2
Cartoonist				Paint company	1	Travel agent	22
(for the *Detroit News*)	1	Jewelry store	3	Painter	1		
Chemical company	2	Junk dealer	2	Paper company	6	Wagon company	1
Cigar manufacturer	10			Pawnbroker	4	Wholesale clothing	3
Clothing company	20	Knitting mill	3	Pharmacist	2	Wholesale woclens	1
Cleaners	2			Physician	2	Wines	1
Clerk	7	Lawyer	10	Printing company	2	Woodenware company	1
Corset manufacturer	3	Leaf tobacco company	3	Produce company	3		
Coal company	5	Leather goods	2	Proprietor	3		
		Liquor dealer	1	Poultry company	1		
Dentist	1	Lumber company	1				
Department store	1			Rabbi	1		
Distiller	1			Real estate	5		
Dry goods	3						
Drugs	3						

Source: Detroit City Directory, 1910.

TABLE 19
Occupational Distribution of 1877 Temple Beth El Members in 1880

OCCUPATIONAL GROUP	NO.	%
Professional and semiprofessional	3	4
Proprietor, manager, official	54	74
White-collar	9	12
Skilled and semiskilled	7	10

Sources: Temple Beth El membership roster, 1877; Temple Beth El membership roster, 1880; *Detroit City Directory, 1880.*

TABLE 20
Occupational Distribution of 1877 Beth El Members and Their Descendants in 1900

OCCUPATIONAL GROUP	NO.	%
Professional and semiprofessional	9	10
Proprietor, manager, official	48	51
White-collar	36	39
Skilled and semiskilled	0	0

Sources: Temple Beth El membership roster, 1877; Temple Beth El membership roster, 1900; *Detroit City Directory, 1900.*

TABLE 21
Occupational Distribution of 1877 Beth El Members and Their Descendants in 1910

OCCUPATIONAL GROUP	NO.	%
Professional and semiprofessional	12	13
Proprietor, manager, official	48	53
White-collar	30	33
Skilled and semiskilled	0	0

Sources: Temple Beth El membership roster, 1877; Temple Beth El membership roster, 1910; *Detroit City Directory, 1910.*

TABLE 22
Occupational Distribution of Temple Beth El and Congregation Shaarey Zedek Members, 1910

OCCUPATIONAL GROUP	NO.	SHAAREY ZEDEK %	BETH EL %
Professional and semiprofessional	6	6	13
Proprietor, manager, official	59	63	57
White-collar	19	20	27
Skilled and semiskilled	7	7	2.5
Unskilled	3	3	0

Sources: Temple Beth El membership roster, 1910; Congregation Shaarey Zedek membership roster, 1908; *Detroit City Directory, 1910.*

APPENDIX B

ISIDORE KALISCH (1816–86), a native of Krotoschin, in Prussian Poland, had pursued his Jewish studies at yeshivot and secular studies at the universities of Berlin, Breslau, and Prague. In the 1840s he wrote a German patriotic poem, "Schlacht Gesang der Deutscher," which was set to music and widely sung, and became a journalist, expressing ideas that were considered seditious for the Germany of that day. He participated in the Revolution of 1848 and eventually had to leave Germany. In America, he turned to the rabbinate, filling pulpits in Cleveland, Cincinnati, and Milwaukee. He actively participated in the first conference of American rabbis in the United States, held in Cleveland in 1855, and edited, with Rabbis Wise and Rothenheim, the *Minhag America.* In Cleveland and Milwaukee he introduced reforms, wrote theological tracts and essays on religious subjects, polemicized in the English-Jewish press with both Orthodox and Reform critics, and wrote poems for German periodicals. Leaving Milwaukee for New York in 1860, Kalisch later joined a group of New York's Jewish leaders in urging the government to appoint Jewish chaplains for Jewish soldiers serving in the Union army. As a result of their efforts, President Lincoln appointed Jew-ish chaplains for the first time in American history. From 1862 to 1864, Kalisch served as spiritual leader of the Indianapolis, Indiana, Hebrew Congregation. During his two-year sojourn at Temple Beth El (1864-66), Kalisch introduced no major new reforms but he was the first rabbi to deliver sermons in English, he dedicated Shaarey Zedek's first synagogue in 1864, conducted a memorial service for Abraham Lincoln in the Rivard Street synagogue, and published a volume of his German poems entitled *Toene des Morgens-Landes* (Sounds of the Orient). Ever restless, Kalisch accepted a call from the Hebrew Congregation in Leavenworth, Kansas. He left Kansas in 1868 and conducted a day and boarding school in New York City. After a year, he entered the lecturing field. From 1870 to 1872, he served as rabbi in Newark, New Jersey; from 1872 to 1879 as rabbi in Nashville, Tennessee. He returned in 1875 to Newark, where he devoted the remainder of his life to literary work, writing Hebrew poems, tales, and fables and translating German and English poets into Hebrew.

Kalisch's successor at Temple Beth El, Rabbi Elias Eppstein (1832-1906), was born in Saarwelling, Alsace-Lorraine, the son of a rabbi, and received his formal secular education at Bonn and his rabbinical ordination from Rabbi Moshe Mertzig. He came to the United States in 1849 and became a teacher in New York. In 1864 he accepted a call from Congregation Beth Israel in Jackson, Michigan, serving as preacher, teacher, and cantor. Coming to Detroit in 1866, he received an annual salary of fifteen hundred dollars plus use of the parsonage, rent free. Eppstein wrote a *Confirmant's Guide to the Mosaic Religion,* the first Jewish children's textbook published in Michigan. Eppstein may have been unhappy with the Congregation or they with him, for in August, 1868, Beth El advertised in the *Israelite* for "a gentleman who is qualified to act as Reader and Minister. Candidates must produce testimonials as to their qualifications. None but a thorough theological scholar need apply." Eppstein's opportunity to leave came in January, 1869, when Congregation B'ne Jeshurun of Milwaukee advertised for a rabbi and offered an annual salary of three thousand dollars. Eppstein went to Milwaukee, delivered a trial sermon in German as well as a lecture in English, and got the job. He served B'ne Jeshurun for ten years.

Upon the commendation of Rabbis Max Lilienthal and Bernard Felsenthal, two of America's most distinguished Reform theologians, Beth El invited Dr. Kaufmann Kohler to become its next rabbi. Martin Butzel, Marcus Cohen, and Herman Trueman, the committee set up to contact Kohler, assured him "that the majority of the congregation will gladly give their support for a free and humane development of Judaism under the scholarly leadership of a man who will know how to furnish scientific and theological bases for still further progress in the field of the improvement of Jewish conditions. At any rate a majority of those members who bear the *burdens* of the congregation are animated by such sentiments." Kohler accepted, becoming Beth El's rabbi in 1869.

No one within the ranks of American Reform Judaism enjoyed a more distinguished reputation than Kaufmann Kohler (1843-1923). Born in Furth, Bavaria, Kohler grew up in an Orthodox family, and, for a time, studied under Samson Raphael Hirsch, the leading figure of mid-nineteenth-century German Or-

thodoxy. Ultimately, however, Kohler came under the influence of the Reform scholar and spokesman Abraham Geiger. Kohler received his doctorate in 1867 and his rabbinical ordination from the notable Reformer Dr. Joseph Aub two years later. Kohler remained in Detroit only two years; during this time, however, he married Johanna Einhorn, daughter of Rabbi David Einhorn. In 1871 Kohler accepted the pulpit of Sinai Congregation in Chicago, and in 1879 he succeeded his father-in-law at Temple Beth El in New York. He convened the Pittsburgh Conference in 1885, and his draft became the basis for its famous platform. The Hebrew Union College appointed Kohler its president in 1903, a position he held till his retirement in 1921. A combination of rationalist and believer, he held that the task of the Jew was to lead the world to a universal religion and that the Messianic era was approaching in his own day. Through his presidency of the College and his prodigious scholarship—he published more than two thousand items—Kohler made a major impact on American Reform Judaism of his day.

Rabbi Emanuel Gerechter (1842-1927), Kohler's successor, was born in Borek, Prussia, and educated by his father, a teacher, as well as at the Talmudical College and Gymnasium of Lissa and at Breslau. He came to the United States in 1866, serving as rabbi of New York's Congregation B'nai Maaminim (Sons of the Believers) till called to Detroit. The novelist Edna Ferber remembered him as "a definitely engaging little man possessing charm and personality. . . . He walked with a slight scholarly stoop . . . , a high-bridged nose, very keen brown eyes between two pairs of glasses, one white, one blue lensed. . . . His sermons delivered in English on Friday nights and on Saturdays in German, were exemplars of dullness." When Leopold Wintner became Beth El's rabbi in 1873, Gerechter continued on as cantor, reader, and teacher. One year later Gerechter accepted a position as spiritual leader of Temple Emanuel in Grand Rapids, Michigan, also serving as professor of German at the Central High School and Ladies' Beacon Seminary. From 1880 to 1892 he officiated as rabbi of Congregation B'ne Jeshurun in Milwaukee, and from 1892 to 1920 as rabbi of Temple

Zion in Appleton, Wisconsin, and professor of Hebrew and German literature at Lawrence University. The biographical material on these men was compiled from Lloyd P. Gartner, *History of the Jews of Cleveland* (Cleveland: Western Reserve Historical Society, 1978), pp. 33-36; Louis J. Swichkow and Lloyd P. Gartner, *The History of the Jews of Milwaukee* (Philadelphia: Jewish Publication Society of America, 1963), pp. 42-46, 178, 370 notes 69, 70, 411 note 48; the Kalisch, Eppstein, and Gerechter Files, Temple Beth El Archives, Birmingham, Michigan; Irving I. Katz, *The Beth El Story* (Detroit: Wayne State University Press, 1955), pp. 79, 186; *Israelite,* August 21, 1868, p. 21; "A Call to Detroit—1869," *American Jewish Archives* (April, 1967), p. 39; Irving I. Katz, "Rabbi Kaufmann Kohler Began His Detroit Ministry in 1869," *Michigan Jewish History* (January, 1979), pp. 11-15.

SELECTED BIBLIOGRAPHY

Note: The following bibliography is confined to cited materials about Detroit and Detroit Jewry. Other sources consulted are listed in the notes.

PRIMARY SOURCES

MANUSCRIPTS

Public Documents

General Arrest Register. Volumes 27-37, 1900-1910. Detroit Police Department Archives. Burton Historical Collection, Detroit, Michigan.

United States Census Schedules, 1850-90. Wayne County, City of Detroit, Michigan. Population. (microfilm)

Institutional Records

Congregation Beth El. Annual Reports of the Presidents, 1874-1950. Temple Beth El Archives. Temple Beth El, Birmingham, Michigan.

———. Executive Board. Minutes (includes reports of the rabbi, president, and Sabbath school board president). Book 1, 1874-89. Book 2, 1889-99. Book 3, 1899-1908. Book 4, 1908-12. Book 5, 1912-29. Temple Beth El Archives.

———. Hebrew Ladies Sewing Society. Minutes, 1882-87. Temple Beth El Archives.

———. Jewish Widows Aid Society. Minutes, 1907-13. Temple Beth El Archives.

———. Ladies Auxiliary Association. Minutes, 1912-16. Temple Beth El Archives.

———. Ladies Society for the Support of Hebrew Widows and Orphans. Minute Book, 1888-1907. Temple Beth El Archives.

———. School Board. Minute Book, 1871-98. Temple Beth El Archives.

———. Schwestern Bund. Minutes, 1891-1910. Temple Beth El Archives.

———. Schwestern Bund. Minutes, 1910-22. Temple Beth El Archives.

———. Sisterhood Club. Minutes, 1901-9. Temple Beth El Archives.

———. Woodmere Cemetery Internment Record Book, 1871-88. Burton Historical Collection, Detroit, Michigan.

———. Woodmere Cemetery Records of Burials, 1871-1913. Burton Historical Collection, Detroit, Michigan.

Industrial Removal Office. Papers. American Jewish Historical Society, Waltham, Massachusetts.

Turover Aid Society. Papers. Burton Historical Collection, Detroit, Michigan.

United Jewish Charities of Detroit. Minutes, 1899-1908. Jewish Welfare Federation, Detroit, Michigan.

Family and Personal Papers, Memoirs, Correspondence,
and Scrapbooks

Burton, Clarence M. Scrapbooks. Burton Historical Collection, Detroit, Michigan.

Butzel, Fred M. Papers. American Jewish Archives, Cincinnati, Ohio.

Butzel, Henry M. Autobiography. American Jewish Archives, Cincinnati, Ohio.

Congregation Beth El. Scrapbook, 1901-11. American Jewish Archives, Cincinnati, Ohio.

―――. Scrapbook, 1900-1950. Burton Historical Collection, Detroit, Michigan.

Franklin, Leo Morris. Sermons. Michigan Historical Collections, Ann Arbor, Michigan.

Freedman, Joseph. Letter to the Reverend Isaac Leeser, June 7, 1853. Leeser Collection. Dropsie University, Philadelphia, Pennsylvania.

Heavenrich, Samuel. Memoir. Temple Beth El Archives.

Heineman, David Emil. Scrapbooks. Michigan Historical Collections, Ann Arbor, Michigan.

Palmer, Friend. Scrapbooks. Burton Historical Collection, Detroit, Michigan.

Phoenix Social Club. Scrapbook. Temple Beth El Archives.

Wechsler, J. Letter to the *American Israelite*, May 11, 1864. Temple Beth El Archives.

Zirndorf, Heinrich. Papers. American Jewish Archives, Cincinnati, Ohio.

PUBLISHED SOURCES

Newspapers and Journals

American Hebrew. New York. 1880-1914.
American Israelite. Cincinnati. 1854-1916.
Detroit Free Press. 1850-1915.
Detroit Journal. 1906.
Detroit News. 1850-1915.
Die Deborah. Cincinnati. 1855-65.
Di Iddishe Tagliche Presse. Cleveland. 1908.
Jewish Advance. Detroit. 1904.
Jewish American. Detroit. 1901-11.
Jewish Gazette. New York. 1892-1900.
Jewish Messenger. New York. 1880-1902.
Jewish News. Detroit. 1942-55.
Occident. Philadelphia. 1850-69.
Reform Advocate. Chicago. 1912.

Public Documents

United States, Census Office. *Seventh Census of the United States: 1850.* Washington, D.C.: Robert Armstrong, Public Printer, 1853.

―――. *Eighth Census of the United States: 1860. Population.* Washington, D.C.: Government Printing Office, 1866.

―――. *Ninth Census of the United States: 1870. Population and Social Statistics.* Volume 1. Washington, D.C.: Government Printing Office, 1872.

―――. *Tenth Census of the United States: 1880. Population, Compendium and Social Statistics of Cities.* Volume 2. Washington, D.C.: Government Printing Office, 1887.

―――. *Eleventh Census of the United States: 1890. Population and Compendium.* Washington, D.C.: Government Printing Office, 1896.

―――. *Twelfth Census of the United States: 1900. Population.* 2 volumes. Washington, D.C.: Government Printing Office, 1901.

―――. *Thirteenth Census of the United States: 1910. Population.* Volume 1. Washington, D.C.: Government Printing Office, 1913.

Annual Reports, Constitutions, and Proceedings

Americanization Committee of Detroit. "The Immigrant in Detroit, 1915." Michigan Historical Collections, Ann Arbor, Michigan.

Congregation Beinei Israel. *Constitution.* Detroit, 1874.

Congregation Beth El. *Bulletin, 1901-1922.*

―――. *Constitution and By-Laws.* Detroit: Schober and Co., Printers and Binders, 1876.

―――. *Constitution and By-Laws of the Beth El Hebrew Relief Society of Detroit, Michigan.* Detroit: Detroit Printing Company, 1878.

―――. *Year Book*, 1911, 1912, 1913, 1914.

Congregation Bet Tefilah Nusach Hoari. *Di Konstitushen und Gezein.* Detroit, 1911.

Congregation Shaarey Zedek. *Constitution and By-Laws.* Detroit, 1908.

Detroit. *Annual Reports*, 1871-81, 1883-1910.

Detroit. *Thirty-Fifth Annual Report of the Board of Education, 1877.* Detroit: Post and Tribune Book and Job Printing Establishment, 1878.

Detroit Association of Charities. *Annual Reports*, 1880/81-1913.

Industrial Removal Office. *Annual Report*, 1901-15.

Jewish Woman's Club. *Yearbook*, 1907-8, 1909-10, 1913-14.

Phoenix Social Club. *Constitution and By-Laws.* Detroit: Wm. Graham, Printer, 1884.

25 Yahriger Yoyvelium fun der Idishe Socialistishen Arbeiter Partei Poale Zion Verein, Detroit, Michigan, 1905-1930. Detroit, 1930.

United Jewish Charities. *Annual Report*, 1900-1916.

Young Men's Hebrew Association of the City of Detroit. *Constitution and By-Laws.* Detroit, 1891.

Directories and Social Registers

Blue Book: A Social Directory of Detroit. Detroit: Blue Book Publishing Co., 1896.

The Book of Detroiters. Chicago: A. N. Marquis and Co., 1914.

Dau's Blue Book for Detroit. Detroit: Dau Publishing Co., 1912.

Dau's Blue Book for Detroit. New York: Dau Publishing Co., 1914.

Detroit Blue Book. Detroit: Detroit Blue Book Co., 1881.

Detroit City Directory, 1848-1916.

Detroit Jewish Society Book. Detroit: Arthur A. Polachek, 1916.

Di Iddishe Direktory fur dem Yahr, 1907. Detroit: L. Knoppow and Sons, 1907.

Other Sources

Benjamin, I. J. *Three Years in America, 1859-1862.* Vol. 2. Philadelphia: Jewish Publication Society of America, 1956.

Burgin, Hertz. *Di Geshikhte fun der Idisher Arbeiter Bavegung in Amerika, Rusland un England.* New York, 1913.

De Forest, Robert W., and Veiller, Lawrence, eds., *The Tenement House Problem.* Vol. 1. New York, 1903. Reprint. New York: Arno Press, 1970.

Farmer, Silas. *A History of Detroit and Wayne County.* Detroit: S. Farmer and Co., 1890; Reprint. Detroit: Gale Research Co., 1969.

Leake, Paul. *History of Detroit.* Chicago: Lewis Publishing Co., 1912.

Wise, Isaac M. *Reminiscences.* Cincinnati: Leo Wise and Company, 1901.

INTERVIEWS

Michael Greene. August, 1969.
Sadie Hirschman. August, 1969.
Nathan Kaluzny. August, 1964.
Debrushke Kaluzny. August, 1964.
Alfred Klunower. August, 1969.
Sol Lachman. August, 1982.
Edgar Schlussel. August, 1969.
Irwin Shaw. August, 1969.
Irene Soloway. August, 1983.

SECONDARY SOURCES

PUBLISHED SOURCES

"A Call to Detroit." *American Jewish Archives* 19 (April, 1967): 34–40.

Budish, J. M. *Geshikte fun di Cloth Hat Cap un Milinery Arbeiter.* New York, 1925.

Edgar, Irving I. "The Early Sites and Beginnings of Congregation Beth El." *Michigan Jewish History* (November, 1970): 5–11.

Fauman, S. Joseph. "Jews in the Waste Industry in Detroit." *Jewish Social Studies* 3 (January, 1941): 41–56.

_____. "Occupational Selection among Detroit Jews." *Jewish Social Studies* 14 (January, 1952): 17–50.

Franklin, Leo M. *History of Congregation Beth El, 1900–1910.* Detroit, 1910.

Grad, Eli, and Roth, Bette. *Congregation Shaarey Zedek.* Detroit: Congregation Shaarey Zedek, 1982.

Goldberg, David, and Sharp, Harry. "Some Characteristics of Detroit Area Jewish and Non-Jewish Adults." In *The Jews: Social Patterns of an American Group,* edited by Marshall Sklare. New York: Free Press, 1958.

Heineman, David E. "Jewish Beginnings in Michigan Before 1850." *Publications of the American Jewish Historical Society* (1905): 47–70.

Holli, Melvin G., ed. *Detroit.* New York: New Viewpoints, 1976.

Katz, Irving I. *The Beth El Story.* Detroit: Wayne State University Press, 1955.

_____. "Detroit's First Communal Talmud Torah." *Michigan Jewish History* (November, 1960): 15–19.

_____. "Jewish Education at Temple Beth El, 1850–1871." *Michigan Jewish History* (June, 1968): 24–29.

_____. *The Jewish Soldier from Michigan in the Civil War.* Detroit: Wayne State University Press, 1962.

_____. "Rabbi Kaufmann Kohler Began His Detroit Ministry in 1869." *Michigan Jewish History* (January, 1979): 11–15.

_____. "Sisterly Love Society Existed in Detroit in 1859." *Michigan Jewish History* (January, 1972): 16–18.

Lodge, John C. *I Remember Detroit.* Detroit: Wayne University Press, 1949.

Lurie, Harry L. *General Summary of Survey of Detroit Jewish Community, 1923.* New York: Bureau of Jewish Social Research, 1923.

Marger, Martin. "The Force of Ethnicity: A Study of Urban Elites." *Journal of University Studies.* Ethnic Monograph Series 10 (Winter, 1974).

Meyer, Henry J. "The Economic Structure of the Jewish Community in Detroit." *Jewish Social Studies* 2 (April, 1940): 127–48.

Rockaway, Robert A. "Anti-Semitism in an American City: Detroit, 1850–1914." *American Jewish Historical Quarterly* 64 (September, 1974): 42–54.

_____. "The Eastern European Jewish Community of Detroit, 1881–1914." *YIVO Annual of Jewish Social Science* 15 (1974): 133–50.

_____. "Ethnic Conflict in an Urban Environment: The German and Russian Jew in Detroit, 1881–1914." *American Jewish Historical Quarterly* 60 (December, 1970): 133–50.

_____. "The Industrial Removal Office in Detroit." *Detroit in Perspective* 6 (Spring, 1982): 40–49.

_____. "The Laboring Man's Champion: Samuel Goldwater of Detroit." *Detroit Historical Society Bulletin* 27 (November, 1970): 4–9.

Russell, John Andrew. *The Germanic Influence in the Making of Michigan.* Detroit: University of Detroit, 1927.

Warsen, Allen A. *Addenda to Autobiographical Episodes.* Oak Park, Michigan, 1974.

_____. "An Important Discovery." *Michigan Jewish History* (January, 1970): 4–7.

_____. "Analysis of a Discovery." *Michigan Jewish History* (June, 1970): 14–16.

Weinberg, Samuel D. *Idishe Instituzies un Anstalten in Detroit.* Detroit: Jewish Welfare Federation, 1940.

Zunz, Olivier. *The Changing Face of Inequality: Urbanization, Industrial Development, and Immigrants in Detroit, 1880–1920.* Chicago: University of Chicago Press, 1982.

UNPUBLISHED MONOGRAPHS

Chapin, Anna W. "History of the United Jewish Charities of Detroit, 1899–1949." Typescript. Jewish Welfare Federation of Detroit.

Grad, Eli. "Congregation Shaarey Zedek Detroit, Michigan: A Centennial History, 1861–1961." Typescript. Temple Beth El Archives.

Lederer, Phyllis. "A Study of Jewish Influences in Detroit." M.A. thesis. Wayne University, 1947.

INDEX

Abraham, Chapman, 3
Adams, Henry, 58
Adler, Liebman, 23-24, 31-32, 33-34, 35
Adler, Samuel, 39
Aged, Jewish home for, 82-83
Agricultural colony, Bad Axe (Mich.), 102, 121
Ahabas Achjuous (Sisterly Love), 33
Aishiskin, Ezekiel, 74, 94 n. 47
Alliance Israelite Universelle, 46, 138 n. 46
Altman, Isaac, 119
Altman, Louis, 119
American Fur Company, 9
Americanization, 46, 48, 92, 101
American Jewish Committee, 138 n. 43
American National Bank, 9
Anshe Chesed Shel Emeth, 82
Anti-Semitism: and attacks on peddlers, 90, 91; in automobile industry, 91; combating, 133-36; conversion attempts, 91; during Civil War, 26; during economic depression, 90-91; and Eastern European immigration, 58; of German-Americans, 24-26; Jewish, 98, 100; and Jewish identity, 140; Jews blamed for, 133; in politics, 90; and social discrimination, 27-28, 132-33; in Yom Kippur Day riot, 26-27
Arbeiter Ring (Workmen's Circle), 86, 88
Aronstam, Noah E., 86, 95 n. 65
Ashinsky, Aaron, 80
Askin, John, 5

Assembly of David and House of Shelter, 82
Atlanta (Ga.), 101
Automobile industry, 54-55, 69, 91, 107

Bacher, Julius, 88
Bad Axe (Mich.), agricultural colony in, 102, 121
Balin, Max, 104
Baltimore (Md.), anti-Semitism in, 25, 91
Barnett, Eddie, 88
Baruch, Jacob B., 78
Bendit, Solomon, 7
Benet, Stephen Vincent, 3
Benjamin, I. J., 36
Bennett, William James, 7
Bernstein, Albert, 86, 95 n. 65
Beth Abraham Synagogue, 74
Beth David Synagogue, 74, 80-81
Beth El, Temple: Americanization in, 46, 48; charter members of, 48 n. 1; in civic reform, 126; cooperative efforts by, 116; day school of, 38; founding of, 31, 32; free pew system in, 124; interfaith activities of, 37, 131-32; moral leadership of, 132; Orthodox secession from, 33-35; philanthropy of, 43-46, 126; rabbis of, 33, 36-37, 120, 121, 122-23, 132, 151-53; reform of liturgy and ritual, 120, 122, 140; refugee relief work of, 100-102 (see also United Jewish Charities of Detroit); religious apathy in, 38, 120-21, 122, 124-25; religious education in, 38-39,

121-22, 123, 126; residential patterns of membership, 45, 99; revival of Jewish tradition in, 123-24, 126; sites of, 26, 34, 35, 37, 123; status of membership, 42, 127-29; Sunday services in, 124; transition to Reform, 32, 33, 36-37; women's club of, 129
Beth Jacob Synagogue, 41, 42, 72, 73, 80, 81
Beth Olam cemetery, 40
Beth Olam Cemetery Association, 82
Biblical History (Adler), 39
Bijur, Nathan, 113
Bikkur Cholim society, 31, 43, 46
Bingay, Malcolm, 112
Blitz, Louis, 101, 137 n. 23
Bloom, Adam E., 27
B'nai B'rith lodges, 48
B'nai Israel Synagogue, 41, 42, 46, 47, 70, 73, 80, 81
B'nai Jacob Synagogue, 42, 47
Board of Poor Commissioners, 27, 29 n. 25
Book of Detroiters, 128, 132
Brandeis, Louis, 86
Bresler, Charles, 8, 10, 31
Bressler, David M., 113, 115
Brith Abraham fraternal order, 84
Brith Shalom fraternal order, 84
Bryan, William Jennings, 90, 95 n. 77
Burial societies, 82
Burnstine, Jacob, 20
Butzel, Fred M., 109, 112, 113, 119, 133
Butzel, Henry, 112, 119

Robert A. Rockaway teaches Jewish history at Tel Aviv University in Israel. He has taught at the University of Michigan and the University of Texas, El Paso. Dr. Rockaway received his M.A. and Ph.D. from the University of Michigan, and earned his B.A. at Wayne State University. He is the author of many articles.

The manuscript was edited by Anne M. G. Adamus. The book was designed by Mary Primeau. The typeface for the text and the display is Century Old Style.